CLEM HASKINS
Breaking Barriers

**Clem Haskins
with Marc Ryan**

SPORTS PUBLISHING INC
a division of Sagamore Publishing
Champaign, IL

Editor, book layout: Susan M. McKinney
Book, cover design: Michelle R. Dressen
Cover photos: Wendell Vandersluis

ISBN: 1-57167-143-9

Printed in the United States

SPORTS PUBLISHING INC
a division of
Sagamore Publishing
Champaign IL 61820
http//www.sagamorepub.com

This book is dedicated to my parents for their guidance and the faith they instilled in me, my wife and children for their undying love and support, as well as my family and many friends for giving me the strength to endure.

—C.H.

To my family—Dad, Mom, Mike, Tom, Bob, Dan and Jon—for their love and support.

To Dianne, my best friend and the love of my life.

— M.R.

"No true success is ever enjoyed without sacrifice and effort. If he who enjoys success did not pay for it, someone else did."

—*Author unknown*

CONTENTS

ACKNOWLEDGMENTS

I would like to especially thank the following people for the ways in which they have touched my life:

- The personal friends of my family who have helped to make the transitions smooth
- The players I played with and the players I coached
- The parents who trusted me to coach and continue to guide their sons
- Coaches who have coached me as well as those who have coached with me
- Opposing coaches, officials and colleagues whom I have come to know personally after the buzzer has sounded
- College presidents and athletics directors who had enough faith in me to entrust their programs to me
- All athletics boosters who supported and continue to support my efforts in molding productive citizens
- My office administrative staff at Western Kentucky University and the University of Minnesota, as well as the athletics department extended staffs at the respective schools
- The athletic trainers who worked with me at Western Kentucky University and the University of Minnesota
- My fellow coaches at Western Kentucky University and the University of Minnesota for their ability to empathize
- Educators who encouraged me and helped me to realize the importance of an education
- NBA teams that gave me the opportunity to follow my dream
- My fraternity brothers of Sigma Pi Phi-Omicron Boulé
- The doctors who have made it possible for me to play and coach the game I love
- My pastors and fellow church members, whose prayers have helped sustain and guide me through my Christian journey

Clem Haskins

I can't even begin to thank everyone who helped make this book possible. Because of that, let me apologize up front for anyone who I forget to mention.

I knew heading into the project that it was one that would involve a tremendous amount of time—interviewing, transcribing hours upon hours of tapes, researching, writing, editing, checking and rechecking facts and dates—but I never imagined that it would consume my life and nearly every minute of my spare time like it did.

Clem and Yevette Haskins have an incredibly special relationship and it was a real honor to be able to tell his life's story. They rolled out the red carpet and made me feel right at home from the start. I would call Yevette a co-MVP throughout the project. She is a tremendous person and was a great help.

The other co-MVP was my wife Dianne. She provided so much support to me every step of the way. She helped me out in so many ways and it really became a "team" effort in every sense of the word in the Ryan household.

I'd also like to say thanks to Lenny Wilkens, Steve Wieberg, Gene Keady, Jerry Sloan and Bobby Jackson. Real class acts, each and every one of them.

Paul Just at Western Kentucky deserves a big thank you as well. Never too busy to take time out of his schedule, he provided a wealth of information and insight to this effort.

Ed Givens at Middle Tennessee State, Brooks Downing at Kentucky, Doug Hauschild at Dayton, Louis Stout at the Kentucky High School Athletic Association, Kay Haverland, Becky Taylor with the Campbellsville-Taylor County Chamber of Commerce, Craig Miller at USA Basketball, Dave Coskey and Jodi Silverman with the Philadelphia 76ers, Heather McNeill of the Phoenix Suns, Arthur Trische of the Atlanta Hawks, Mark Kelly of the Utah Jazz, Kent Wipf and Jim LaBumbard of the Minnesota Timberwolves and Mark Adams at Purdue, along with the media relations offices at the Washington Bullets and Chicago Bulls, also deserve a big thank you.

I am really blessed to work with such great people at the University of Minnesota, starting with our director of athletics, Dr. Mark Dienhart.

From the full-timers to our volunteer helpers, I am surrounded on the media relations staff by some extremely talented and hard-working folks at the U of M: Bill Crumley, Brad Ruiter, Greg Capell, Wendell Vandersluis, Bob Marcus, Karen Zwach, Jerry Lee, Erich Bacher, Rhonda Lundin, Mark Olson, Mike Vidnovic, Damon Gunn, Randy Kaufman and Megan Bouche.

I would be remiss if I didn't thank my mentors in the sports information/media relations profession—Larry Scott, Craig Miller and Bob Peterson. I also had so many wonderful teachers and coaches during my years as a student-athlete at both Rosemount High School and Moorhead State University. Many thanks to them all.

Last, but not least, I want to thank all the fine people at Sagamore Publishing who helped make this book become reality, especially Peter Bannon, Michelle Dressen, Susan McKinney and David Kasel.

I would like to say a special thanks to Sagamore's Mike Pearson, a friend who was always there to listen to me and give me encouragement along the way. His professionalism and attention to detail kept me going when I couldn't see the light at the end of the tunnel.

Marc Ryan

FOREWORD

L ife is a challenge, accept it. All any of us want is the opportunity to succeed. Life is not fair and nothing is promised. There are many roadblocks and pitfalls for all of us in life, enough to make you want to give up at times. Clem Haskins has met those challenges head on, and the challenges were twice as hard for him as an African-American.

Breaking Barriers takes you on a journey from Campbellsville, Kentucky, to the top of the sports world. The 1967-68 season was Clem's rookie year in the NBA with the Chicago Bulls. There were only 12 teams in the league at that time and the competition for jobs was fierce. Making an NBA team was not an easy task back then. The characteristics that helped Clem survive in the NBA—knowledge of the game, tough-mindedness, commitment, accountability and a true love of the game—have also served him well in becoming a great coach.

Back in those days we were fierce competitors on the court, but very supportive of one another off the court. During those times in the NBA we were still fighting for decent salaries, medical benefits, a pension plan and so forth. The players were closer back then because we took a number of vacations together as part of the NBA Players Association. I got to know Clem and his lovely wife, Yevette, on those trips and always enjoyed their company.

When Clem became head coach at Western Kentucky in 1980, I began to watch his career. I knew all along that if he ever got the opportunity to be a head coach at a Division I school he would do well. Our relationship remained friendly through the years. I continued to watch and root for Clem when he became head coach at the University of Minnesota.

In April of 1995, I was selected head coach of the 1996 "Dream Team" to represent the USA in the 1996 Olympic Games in Atlanta. There wasn't a doubt in my mind who I was going to select as my number-one assistant: Clem Haskins.

I knew that Clem was a no-nonsense guy; he would be organized and he would not be in awe of the professional players. Clem also had international coaching experience and would be a perfect fit for me. Needless to say, we "brought home the gold." Clem then went on to lead his 1996-97 University of Minnesota team to a fantastic run for the NCAA Championship.

The Olympic experience allowed me to view Clem Haskins, the man, up close. I must tell you the Olympic Games were one of my greatest experiences because it gave me the opportunity to work with Clem. It was a rich experience and he reconfirmed to me the type of person he is. A man of honesty, pride, integrity, intense commitment, and above all, a man with family values.

The Golden Gopher men's basketball program and the University of Minnesota, along with the entire state of Minnesota, are much better off because of the contributions of Clem Haskins.

Lenny Wilkens
Head Coach, Atlanta Hawks

TOP OF THE MOUNTAIN

Everything really started to sink in as the clock ticked down in the 1997 NCAA Midwest Regional championship game on March 22 at the Alamodome in San Antonio, Texas. A first-ever appearance in the Final Four was just around the corner for me and the University of Minnesota basketball program.

It had been a long, hard road to get to that point in my career. I wanted to savor every second, to soak it all in. My life has had its share of peaks and valleys. For every fastball, there have been just as many, if not more, curveballs thrown in my direction.

It was time to celebrate when the final buzzer sounded and we were on our way to Indianapolis after an 80-72 victory over UCLA. First and foremost, it was incredibly special to be able to enjoy the moment with my family; my wife, Yevette, our daughters Clemette and Lori, and our son Brent. They have been with me every step of the way, through thick and thin. It was also a treat to enjoy the moment with our extended family; our present players and staff, as well as our former players and staff. Once you're a member of our "family," you're always a member.

I've long said that the Minnesota fans are the very best in all of college basketball. Thousands of Golden Gopher fans followed us on the NCAA Tournament trail to give us the homecourt advantage. They were a big part of the celebration as well.

I remember during my pro career in the National Basketball Association (NBA) when I was working in my yard in Phoenix one day and I had a vision that I would be coaching at a college someday. I didn't know where, but I was going to be a coach and I was going to take a team to the Final Four. I know it sounds crazy, but it's true.

It took me 25 years to get there. But I had a vision. God is leading me. He's given me an opportunity to be in a profession where I can make a difference with people. I really believe that. From high school, to college, to the NBA, to Western Kentucky and now Minnesota, I have made a difference in the community. God has led me in that direction. I feel like I have helped mold the state of Kentucky. That yes, a black man can do the job. I have made a difference in the state of Minnesota. I think that's how God has used me through sports to help mold young men and help build communities.

It's not how many games or championships I've won. It's the lives that I've touched along the way. Along the way, of course, you need to win enough games in order to earn the respect of people.

Respect. If there's one thing that I've always strived for in my life it's that I want to earn people's respect. In order to respect me, however, you must understand me. I've been fighting all my life for what's right. I try to be honest and fair at all times, and do the very best job that I can in whatever I'm doing.

The Final Four capped off an incredible year in the Haskins' household. It all started in the summer of 1996 when I served as an assistant coach on the U.S. Olympic Team that won the gold medal in Atlanta.

It seemed like I went straight from the gold medal game to the first day of practice at Minnesota. In February we clinched the school's first Big Ten title since 1982 with a victory at Michigan. Then we started our phenomenal run to the Final Four in Indianapolis.

I feel like I have finally reached the top of the mountain. I've earned the respect I've fought so long for in the coaching fraternity. It's incredible when I think of all the great coaches who have never had the opportunity to coach in the Final Four.

In a lot of ways it's unfair that to so many people getting to the Final Four puts a stamp of approval on a coach's career. That's what people don't understand; there are so many outstanding coaches around the country who will never get their just due as a result.

Until we made our run to the Final Four, very few people around the country knew that I had won 300 games during my career. That was one of the best-kept secrets in college basketball.

Due to the success we had during the 1996-97 season, I was fortunate enough to win most of the national coach of the year awards. It's funny, because I still think my best job of coaching took place my first two years at Minnesota when I took over a program that was about as low as a Division I program could be.

We were 19-37 in those first two seasons, and lost 21 straight Big Ten games at one point, but we were putting down a solid foundation for the future—step by step, brick by brick. There's too much emphasis today on wins and losses in college basketball.

Even though it was our first trip to the Final Four in 1997, people forget that I've coached in a lot of big games during my career. We've been to both the "Sweet 16" and the "Elite Eight" before.

Long before all of the coach of the year awards came my way, I knew in my heart that I could coach with the very best in the business. It took a trip to the Final Four, however, for people to realize that on a national level. When we made it to Indianapolis, it was like "hey, this guy must know what he's doing."

I take a lot of satisfaction in knowing that my teams are always well prepared every time we step out on the basketball court. I used to get upset when people didn't tell me that I had done a good job. Win or lose, I don't worry about what people think anymore. I'm more at peace with myself now.

Don't get me wrong. I'm still not completely satisfied. I'm driven to win a national title at the University of Minnesota. I've accomplished so much in my career, but winning the national title would be the icing on the cake. That's all that's left for me to do.

It's been a difficult climb to the top of the mountain. To fully appreciate the view at the top, however, you must first look at the difficult journey on the way up.

THE EARLY YEARS

CHAPTER TWO

I was born on August 11, 1943, and grew up a "farmboy" just outside Campbellsville, Kentucky. Campbellsville is the county seat of Taylor County, located about 85 miles from Louisville, Lexington, Frankfort and Bowling Green.

A lot of people call Taylor County the "heart of Kentucky." That's because it's shaped like a heart and it's basically smack dab in the middle of the state. It's nearly 300 square miles in all, and is bordered by Marion and LaRue counties to the north, Casey to the east, Adair to the south and Green to the west.

It was a small town when I was growing up. In fact, I think there were only one or two traffic lights in town. When I was a kid there were no malls, just a Main Street in downtown Campbellsville. The economic growth of the city and the entire county has been amazing. By 1990, Taylor County had a population that surpassed 21,000, with about 95 percent of it white.

Much of that growth can be traced back to the arrival of the Union Underwear Company in Campbellsville in 1948. The plant, which manufactures Fruit of the Loom products, is the world's largest producer of men's and boys' underwear and is the second largest textile plant in the country. It employs about 3,000 people and has been, and still is, a big part of the Haskins family.

My Dad's name was Charles Columbus Haskins, but most people just called him Columbus. Dad was just shy of six feet tall and weighed about 168 pounds. He stayed that weight pretty much his whole life. It was amazing. He'd get on a scale and he would always weigh somewhere between 165 and 168 pounds. My Mother's full name is Lucy Edna Haskins, but she's known as Miss

Lucy. A slender, but strong lady her whole life, my Mother is about five-foot-five.

At six-foot-four, a lot of people wonder where I got my size from, since neither of my parents were tall people. I think it came from uncles on both sides of my family. One of my uncles, Jim Penick, was about six-foot-five, six-foot-six. Another uncle of mine, Belknap Smith, was probably six-four, six-five. My great uncle, Dude Penick, was about six-five. My great grandfather, John Ike Smith, was a big man too. He was about six-foot-four or five.

My Mother and Dad both lived on farms in Green and Adair counties growing up. They lived anywhere from 10 to 20 miles outside of Campbellsville. My Mother was the youngest in a family of 14 children. My dad was the oldest of seven children.

My Dad's mother and my grandmother was Lottie Haskins. My Dad's father was Shed Haskins. My great grandmother was Willie Haskins. They owned a little farm, had a lot of cattle and were sharecroppers all their lives. I did not know my grandfather or grandmother on my Mother's side; Grandpa John Ike and Grandma Liza. Both passed away when I was just a kid so I don't remember them.

My Mother and Dad started dating at an early age and were married in June of 1934. I don't know all the details on how they met, but back in those days they had big social gatherings at the church on Sundays and that's where they first met. We're Southern Baptists and church has always played an important role in our family.

Education was not important in the South at that time. As a result, my parents only had third or fourth grade educations. Years ago in the South, the oldest child in the family always worked to help support the younger children. When you were between 10 and 12 years of age, you started working to provide money for the family and to help put food on the table. So that's what happened to my Mother and Dad. They had to quit school to work and make money. This was before television, radio, telephone, running water and all those modern conveniences.

Most of the blacks back then were sharecroppers and they worked for other people and for minimum wages. At that time the minimum wage was anywhere from a dime to twenty-five cents an hour. That was big money back in those days. I remember when I first started working in the mid-to-late '50s, the minimum wage was 50 cents an hour. So I can imagine my Dad worked many days for 10 cents an hour.

My grandfather, Shed Haskins, was a sharecropper, so he lived on a farm. My Dad quit school after the third grade to go work in the fields; he cut hay, cut or stripped tobacco, and also worked in the corn and bean fields. Most people worked with their hands back in those days.

My Mother always worked for other people at that time. She began washing clothes and cleaning houses for people when she was just a young girl, 12 or 13 years of age. My Mother also became a midwife; she used to go help deliver a baby and then stay with that family for a week or a month or six months, whatever was needed. She was just a kid herself, about 13 or 14 years of age when she started doing that.

This was all well before integration. The school that my parents went to was just a one-room schoolhouse for blacks only. Kids had to walk to and from school anywhere from a mile up to 10 miles each day. The teachers were all black and very few were college educated. In fact, most probably had no more than an eighth-grade or ninth-grade education. They taught the kids to read and write, maybe add a little bit, and that was the extent of the education.

The blacks in the rural areas could go through only the fifth or sixth grade. There were no black high schools in Green or Adair counties. After that you had to go into town to the all-black Campbellsville Durham High School. So there were no black public high schools for my Dad and Mom to go to in a 10-to-20 mile radius from where they lived. You have to remember that there weren't nicely paved roads like today. You're talking a team of horses and a wagon too. It would have taken them close to a full day to get into Campbellsville.

There were several schools around the state where blacks would go to boarding schools to get a high school education. The biggest barrier was the cost. Plain and simple, my grandparents didn't have the money to send Mother and Dad away to boarding school. So many blacks never got an education because of a lack of money, and my Mother and Dad fell into the same category.

My Dad was never a slave, but he worked for slave wages. Blacks were free, but the mentality was still that blacks worked for the white man, and they worked for minimum wages. They had no say over anything. For the most part, they didn't own anything. They could own some land, but then they had to go to the bank to get some money from the white man to buy the fertilizer or to buy food at the stores that were owned by the whites. So basically, they were still living under slavery rules to a degree.

I was the fifth of 11 children in our family. My brother Willie was the oldest, followed by Charles, Lummie, Eliza Mable, me, Sara, Paul Samuel, Betty Lou, Nora, Merion and Joyce. There's a difference of 20 years between Willie, the oldest who was born in 1936, down to Joyce, who is the youngest.

The most people we ever had living in the house together at one time was eight. Willie and Charles were married and had moved out of the house before Merion and Joyce were even born. My Mother and Dad have a total of 18 grandchildren, and my father actually saw his fifth generation before he died; his son Willie, granddaughter Wanda Goodin, great granddaughter Shakara Goodin and great-great granddaughter Shakila Goodin.

My Mother and Dad were sharecroppers when they first got married. They lived with a black couple and worked their land for them. The guy they lived with for several years was an invalid, so my mother took care of him. My Dad worked his farm for a couple of years, and when the man died, he willed my parents some of his land and the right to live there. That's how my father got his start.

Later my Dad traded several farms and we moved several times to different farms in the area. Each farm was a little bit bigger and better than the previous one; the first one was in Taylor County. Then we moved to a farm back in Green County for a few years; I must've been four or five years old then. Then we moved from Green County back to Taylor County in 1948 or 1949 and moved again from Taylor County to Springfield, Kentucky in Washington County around 1950, before moving back to Taylor County again in 1952. Dad bought a small farm and we lived out on Greensburg Road until about 1955.

We sold that farm in 1955 and moved to the farm out on Roberts Road. Dad actually bought it in about 1951, but we didn't move there until four years later. My Mother has lived in that same house since 1955. Of course, we've renovated the house several times since then, but she still lives there. I not only own the land now where I grew up, but I also have a house just down from Mother's where Yevette and I stay whenever we go back to Campbellsville. I've also purchased a lot of land around our farm as well; it adds up to about 500 acres in all.

Our farm wasn't that far from town, about three miles away, and we'd go to town once or twice a month. We didn't have a television, a telephone, or any luxuries like that when I was a kid, but we were a happy family. There was a lot of love, a lot of caring and a lot of understanding in our family. My parents' deep-rooted religious beliefs were passed along to all of us kids.

Our house had three bedrooms, two of which were upstairs. So the boys slept together in one room upstairs and the girls slept together in the other. We didn't have any running water, so there was no bathroom. We got our water from the spring on our farm and then we'd carry it to the house. The spring was probably about 200 feet from the house.

We used an old-time washing machine to wash our clothes. My Mother made our soap. It was hard times, but it taught us how to work. I learned to iron when I was only four or five years old. We used an old heating iron that you put on top of the stove. My Mother taught both the boys and girls in our family how to iron, wash dishes, and all sorts of everyday household chores at a very early age. We didn't think anything of it, that's just the way it was.

We were really happy kids. We didn't have any store-bought toys, any material things to bicker over. We made our own games, our own fun. We made mud pies, hay houses out in the barn, those kinds of things; we created our own fun. It seems like most kids today need a VCR or some computer games in order to have fun. We didn't have much, but we were happy with what we did have.

The first family car that I remember we had was a Ford. It was a Model "A" or Model "T," I don't remember which. It was certainly interesting when we went to Pleasant Run Baptist Church every Sunday. We'd pile on top of each other in the car and then make our way to the church in Greensburg. There were four families that basically filled the church up; the Haskins family, the Young family, the Maddox family and the Curry family. There were about 40 kids total between our four families alone.

There were always special times throughout the year when our entire family got together; Christmas, Easter, Thanksgiving, Mother's Day and Father's Day. Those were special times for us to drop whatever we were doing in our own lives and to come together as a family.

We all had our own place to sit at the kitchen table, and it's still that way. When I go home to Kentucky now, I still have a special place at the table where I sit. The same goes for all my brothers

and sisters. From day one, my Mother told us where we were supposed to sit and it didn't change after that. No one sat in my seat
and I didn't sit in Sara's, Paul's, Betty's or anyone else's. That's just
the way it's always been.

Dad sat at the head of the table and Mother was at the foot, or
nowadays they'd call it the end of the table. Times have changed,
but back then the men ate first before the women. That's the way I
was brought up, that was the mentality. It wasn't a matter of right
or wrong, that's just the way it was at that time. No one ate anything until Dad blessed the table. We gave thanks to the Lord before we ate a thing.

Unlike most families today, we all ate together. You could not
leave the table until you ate everything; we didn't have a refrigerator to store leftovers. My Dad said that we could take all the food
we wanted, but we could not leave anything on our plates. My
Mother prepared three hot meals for us every day and we ate together as a family. She didn't have to ring a bell and yell for us to
come and eat. We ate at 6 a.m., noon, and 6 p.m. every day. It was
like clockwork for us.

Good cooking is something that runs in our family I guess.
Grandma Lottie made the best water cornbread you'd ever put your
lips around. She could not make enough of that stuff. We went to
their house usually every other Sunday and I couldn't wait to eat
her water cornbread. Let me set the record straight on this one. My
mother's a great cook, but she could never make water cornbread
like Grandma Lottie's. And my great grandmother, Willie, her water
cornbread was even better than Grandma Lottie's. I can vaguely
remember her. I have fond memories of my great grandmother and
my grandmother. Everything they cooked tasted so good and they
never used a recipe. They used their hands to measure so much
salt, so much sugar, so much of this and that, and when it came out,
it was magnificent. As a kid, I couldn't wait for those meals.

But you have to understand that as a kid back in those days,
when we had guests we didn't eat with the grownups. Kids ate
second and we got seconds. We got whatever was left. We didn't
get a good piece of chicken. I didn't get a good piece of chicken
until I became a teenager. All we got was the chicken neck, or the
chicken feet. That sounds crazy, but back in those days, they ate
necks, they ate backs, and they ate chicken feet. Now you talk about
that today, and most kids probably don't know what chicken feet
are.

The grownups ate all the drumsticks, all the wings, and all the breasts. The kids just got what was left over. That's why I was envious of preachers for a long time, because the preachers would come over to the house on Sundays, and they would eat up all the good meat; that's the truth. In the south, you see, every Sunday after church everyone would have a big family meal.

One week it would be at the Haskins' house, the next week at one of my aunt's or uncle's and so on. And we didn't get chicken every Sunday. We didn't want to kill all the chickens because they laid eggs. Eating chicken for dinner back then would be like going to a restaurant today and ordering steak or lobster. The preachers would come to the family dinner about once or twice a month and that was a big deal, so we'd have chicken. It was tough, because the preacher and his wife would come over and eat up most of the chicken. All us kids got to eat were the leftover chicken parts. So when I was young I never liked the preacher because of that. Everyone in our family could cook and we really had some quality meals together on Sundays.

You have to understand how I was brought up. There was never a lot of money to be made, but we found a way to make ends meet somehow. Trading was a big part of that. Maybe a hog for a type of tool you needed or a bag of flour. So there was never a lot of cash, but we learned to manage with garden vegetables, or corn, or cattle, or hogs. Trading was how we got by. We had very little cash so we learned how to trade and deal in order to make ends meet. No one had fine clothes as a kid. I never had a new pair of shoes; we just got seconds.

I remember when my Mother used to do laundry for a white family who had children and she would get shoes from them for the work that she did. We had second shoes, second pairs of pants, second shirts, second socks. They might be a little too big or too small, but it didn't matter, we still wore them. We didn't have anything else to wear. That's how we made ends meet.

I first started milking cows when I was about five or six years old. I started milking the whole herd when I was about eight or nine. All of them. That's how I developed such strong hands over the years. I built up tremendous muscles in my hands, wrists and forearms from milking about 15 cattle per day. We started working in the field when we were about six or seven years old. Chopping tobacco and stripping tobacco; it was hard work when we were only six or seven.

We never thought of ourselves as poor growing up. If you don't have anything in the first place, you don't understand what it means to be poor. You think of yourself as the richest guy in the world. When I look back, we were "rich." We had food on the table every day. We had three good meals every day. We had love and understanding in our home. I'd say that's a pretty good start right there.

T HE GLUE

CHAPTER THREE

My Mother is an amazing person, someone whom I admire a great deal. Throughout her life, in the good times and in the tough times, she has been the glue that has held our family together.

It gives me great personal satisfaction to go home to Campbellsville and see my Mother whenever Yevette and I have the opportunity to do so. It doesn't matter if it's been a week or a year since the last time we've been back, she's glad to see us and it goes without saying that the feelings are mutual.

As I said, Mother has lived in that same house out on Roberts Road since 1955. Until just recently, she used to make the quarter-mile trek down to the house frequently when Yevette and I were back in Minnesota to check up on things.

Her arthritis won't allow her to do that anymore. Nowadays when my Mother knows we're on our way home, she makes sure to come over to our house to tidy things up, put fresh linens on the bed and have it all ready for our arrival.

Mother doesn't let on to people what her age is. That's the honest to God's truth. To her it's just a number and doesn't mean a thing. Let's just say that her birthday is on October 20 and she was born sometime after 1910.

Driving a car is something that Mother never quite learned how to do. It wasn't, however, because she didn't try. She used to get in the car and drive it around the farm to see if she could get the hang of it and it was a struggle for her. Those were different times back then. A lot of women didn't drive in those days.

Mother's last attempt to master the art of driving came one day when she was out practicing in the field. Sara, who was about two or three years old at the time, was in the passenger seat. My Mother never could master working the clutch, the gas pedal and the brake. That proved to be her downfall.

They were out there putzing around in the field that afternoon and she accidentally hit the brake instead of the gas pedal. Sara's head went forward and hit the car's dashboard and I think that scared Mother. Sara wasn't hurt at all, but I think that was the straw that broke the camel's back; she figured that was enough of that.

Mother certainly understood the value of hard work and that work ethic rubbed off on us kids. With Dad usually off to work most of the day, she ran the household. She kept all of us kids in line and taught us right from wrong from day one. A patient and understanding person, she could be very vocal at times about certain situations if she felt they were important enough.

Balancing the family budget was always Mother's job too. Dad used to come home from work, give her the paycheck and she'd pay all the bills.

I remember my Dad asking my Mother many times, "Can I have a quarter, Lucy?" People today don't understand how much a quarter was back then. A quarter 50 years ago was a lot of money. So he'd ask for a quarter, and they'd argue about it for a while. My Mother would usually say something like "Columbus, I don't have a quarter to give you today. That's too much money. Here's a dime."

She understood the value of the dollar and it was a great lesson for us kids. We worked hard for what little money we had back then and Mother made sure that every penny was spent wisely. A lot of people who make hundreds of thousands of dollars today don't know how to manage it and have nothing to show for it.

It proved a point to us kids. For a young person growing up, black or white, the big question wasn't how much you made, but rather how much you saved.

It's no secret that I get my energy and strength from my Mother and Dad. They were tough-minded, strong people. My Dad suffered a stroke in 1985, and spent the last 10 years of his life in a nursing home until he died in 1995.

We all miss him dearly and I know it's been tough on Mother, but she's never complained about it. Her philosophy is to enjoy every single day that God gives us on this earth to the fullest.

It helped to have my adopted son and nephew, Hearie, to

help with things around the house and farm. Hearie has lived with my Mother for many years. Hearie's dad, my brother, Charles, Jr., was killed in a car accident back in 1964. Five of my brothers and sisters still live in Campbellsville, so they do a great job of taking care of Mother.

Mother obviously sacrificed a lot of her own wants and needs to raise us 11 kids. After I was born, the doctor told her that she couldn't have any more kids and if she did, that it could kill her. She had six more kids after me.

In addition, Mother has gone through several operations through the years. She had a nearly seven-pound tumor removed from her side, her gall bladder has been taken out and she was on her death bed once again when her appendix ruptured. She's looked death in the eye many, many times and was strong enough and spiritual enough to fight it off and survive. She just felt that the Lord was not ready for her yet.

Sometimes when I get to feeling down and out because of a tough loss or something in my life isn't going quite the way I'd like it to go, I think of my Mother and the hurdles that she's cleared in her life.

A strong faith in God has always been an important part of the Haskins family. God is number one in my life. I give thanks and praise to God every morning when I wake up and when I go to bed at night. He gives us the strength and the faith to deal with the challenges that face us in life. He's always there for us, win or lose, rain or shine.

Those beliefs are a reflection of my Mother's commitment to making the Lord a part of her children's lives every single day. She showed us the way. I remember at a very early age when we would get down on our knees and listen to my Mother pray. I've heard so many people say that when my Mother prays, even the chickens and the cows get on their knees and listen. She causes everything else around her to stop, including the wind sometimes.

Framed prints of the Ten Commandments and the 23rd Psalm looked down upon our dinner table. No meal was ever begun before the table was blessed. That's just the way it was in our house.

Even today, Mother is a real spiritual force in the community of Campbellsville and throughout Taylor County. It's not uncommon for her to reach out to sick people, no matter who they are. If someone needs help, she's there for them. I've heard her on the phone a number of times saying, "Well, we need to say a little prayer."

The mother of Brent Cox, a good friend of ours for many, many years in Campbellsville, passed away not too long ago. Brent and his wife, Betty, told Yevette and I how much Mother's prayers and support meant to them in a very difficult time. They told us that they couldn't have gotten through it without her.

My Mother still loves to raise chickens. She likes to go out and see if they've laid any eggs. She has always enjoyed having dogs around too, especially St. Bernards, which are her favorite.

I think she's had four St. Bernards in all, but she's only used two names: King and Baby. One was named King and when it passed away, the next one was named Baby, and when that one died, the next one was named King again. She's really good with her dogs and boy, they're really loyal to her. Strangers can't get within shouting distance of the house without being "greeted" by them.

With so many of our games on television these days, Mother is able to watch most of our games at Minnesota. She's my biggest fan. Mother gets a little worried about me at times when she sees me taking my sportcoat off in disgust or getting into an argument with an official over a tough call. She thinks I get a little too worked up during games and she's probably right. Mother's always right, I guess. Win or lose, when I call her she has a real soothing, calming effect on me.

My Mother's famous fried apple pies are well-known through-out Taylor County. Friends of the family routinely call her if they have some dried apples to put in a request for some. If there's a wedding, funeral or any kind of family gathering going on some-where in the county, it's not uncommon for Mother to get a call to make some of her mouth-watering dessert treats.

I don't think my Mother has an enemy in all the world. She has a heart the size of the state of Kentucky and is an incredible woman. It really says something that on Sunday mornings each and every one of her 10 children call her to see how she's doing by 10 a.m. That's at the latest. Not because we feel we have to, but be-cause we all want to.

That goes to show you just what she means to all of us. The years have passed and us kids have gone off in a lot of different directions. We've raised our own families, we took a variety of ca-reer paths.

But after all these years, one thing hasn't changed. Mother is still the backbone, the glue, of the Haskins family.

My Hero

CHAPTER FOUR

I've been fortunate enough to meet a lot of great people in my life. I've played with and against Hall of Famers on the basketball court. I've met powerful politicians, great doctors and lawyers, renowned educators, and famous actors. You name it.

But it's very easy for me to give the answer when I'm asked who my hero is. No doubt about it, it's my Dad. Looking back, he becomes even more and more important in my life every day because he took less and did more with it than any man I've ever known.

Sometimes I wonder how he could have ever raised 11 kids when the most he ever made in a year in his life was $3,500. Although he only had a third-grade education, he was a great manager and the smartest individual I've ever met in my life. My God, he could take a hog and eat the whole thing, including the squeal.

Two people that I also admire a great deal are Grandpa Shed and Grandma Lottie, for how they raised my Dad. Nowadays people think that you have to have a Ph.D. to make good decisions. That's what's wrong with the world today. We have so many so-called educators in the world today and still more problems than ever.

Today most people don't know how to manage. Although they have book sense, they have no practical management skills. Here I'm making good money and I have one hell of a time managing it. Dad didn't have the money to go to school, but he used his knowledge in order to maneuver around, take advantage of situations and make the most out of what he had to work with.

My Dad never wasted a thing. We lived on the farm, grew all our own vegetables, raised all our own meat and milked our own cows. We didn't buy any of that stuff. He taught us kids that it's not what you make, it's what you can save.

Every single day Dad studied the newspaper, and when we got a radio, he listened to the news religiously. The average person sits down and reads the sports page. Dad could have cared less about sports. He wouldn't read the funnies either. He wanted to know what was going on in the world. He could sit down and talk with anyone about any subject that they wanted to discuss.

Dad never, ever encouraged me to play sports. He never played sports and, quite honestly, was always against me playing sports. That wasn't important in his life. Working and making a living, that was the most important thing to my Dad.

I got my work ethic from Dad. That's why I've always prided myself on hard work and why I still work so hard today. He taught me a long time ago to work hard, to be honest and fair, and to always be very loyal to your employers. Those are the values I got from him.

The most important thing my Dad did for us kids was that he taught us how to work every single day on the farm. We'd get up at around four o'clock every morning and milk the cows together. We spent a lot of quality time together in the barn, when it was cold and you were still sleepy. You didn't want to do it, but you had to do it.

Back in those days you had to separate the milk and the cream as well. You had to take the milk and pour it into the separator and that was hard work. We'd work most of the day on the farm. We were usually in bed by eight o'clock so that we could get eight hours of sleep and be up and ready to go first thing the next day. There was no TV to watch. That's where I got my discipline.

My Dad was a no-nonsense guy, but a fun guy. He was someone that people really enjoyed being around. He loved to tell jokes. He also was also able to laugh at himself. A lot of people can't laugh at themselves. I feel really fortunate because a lot of people don't get to see that side of their parents; the humorous side. He was a disciplined man, but he also had his fun side too and wasn't afraid to show it.

We had a lot of fun together, did a lot of crazy things. Some of the best times I had as a kid were sitting around and listening to my Dad and my uncles reminisce and talk about things that happened in their boyhood. I'm sure that they stretched the truth a bit, but when you were eight or nine years old, you were all ears and I just enjoyed listening to them. I remember my Dad sitting around with friends like Pete Massey and Roy Bridgewater. On Sunday afternoon they'd get together and talk, tell war stories. This was on the farm after we got through eating dinner. I was all ears; I remember listening to their stories and thinking to myself how much I couldn't wait to grow up.

To this day I hate to shave. My Dad always had a heavy beard. It would grow out every day, but he'd shave only every two or three days. He used a straight-edged razor back in those days. That's what I call a man's man. I remember when I used to just stand there and watch my dad shave when I was about four or five years old. He had that soap on his face—they didn't have the modern day stuff that they have now—and he would look into a broken mirror and I'd be there watching him shave.

I was so impressed by that. One day when he wasn't around, I took his razor out, put some soap on my face and tried it. I cut my face. It wasn't a bad cut. I washed my face, put the razor away exactly the way my Dad had left it and I didn't say anything about it. Nobody noticed, at least I far as I know, and I never got in trouble for it. He would have whipped my butt for doing it if he had ever found out. It's funny looking back at it, but I was trying to be cool like my Dad.

My Dad always said that he could kick any dog off of him. He was saying that no dog could ever bite him. Most farms had a dog or two and some of them were bad dogs. Those were the ones that didn't like strangers and they'd try to bite you if you weren't careful. One of our neighbors had a dog called "Old Bob."

My brother Paul and I used to go over there all the time. They lived across the road and down a ways from us. "Old Bob" would bite almost everyone if they weren't careful. But for some reason he never bit either Paul or me. We would go over there and play with him all the time and he was a good dog around us. But he didn't like my Daddy. One day Dad came up to get us. We were up there working, messing around or doing something. I must have been about nine or 10 years old and Paul was about six or seven at the time.

When Dad jumped down off the wagon, "Old Bob" slipped around the back side, caught him by surprise and bit him. Dad was so mad that he wanted to go get the gun and shoot the dog. But Mother wouldn't let him have the shotgun to go back and shoot "Old Bob." Later on Paul and I gave Dad a hard time about it. I remember laughing and saying to him, "Dad we thought you were kicking the dog off you!" I remember him saying to us, "Oh yeah, he slipped around the wagon and got me."

"Old Bob" was a mutt, a little mix of everything. But he got my Dad that day. That was funny and we laughed about that one for many, many years. After that whenever we got around a dog with Dad, Paul or I would inevitably ask him if he was "going to kick him off today."

Yevette still teases me today about "riding so much." When we had the time after we got our first car, my Dad, Paul and I loved to just drive around the area for a good part of the day. I think that over time we looked at every farm, all the cattle and every piece of machinery in Taylor County, Green County and Adair County. We just used to get in the car and "ride."

We were nosy. We wanted to see what everyone else was growing and what kind of machinery they had on their farm. We'd stop and ask them too: How are your crops? How much milk are you getting from your cows? People love to talk and we knew that. We'd ride for three or four hours at a time. Just riding, talking and looking. I really enjoyed those times with my Dad and brother. I know that my Dad really enjoyed it too. He loved to reminisce about his childhood, where he grew up, the fields that he worked on, etc. It was fun to hear him talk about it.

The only thing I really regret is that I didn't take the time then to record, to write down, the people, the names, the places, things that went on, all the memories that he shared with us. I miss that and know that I can't ever get it back. For example, I don't know the owners of a certain farm through the years. He knew that. He shared that with Paul and me. We kick ourselves every day for not taking the time to put all that he shared with us down on paper. I don't know nearly as much as I'd like to about my family tree. He knew all that stuff. He had a great, great mind.

My Dad could have been a doctor, or a lawyer or president of the United States. I miss that knowledge that he had and wish that there was some way to turn the clock back and recapture it because the lessons he taught us as kids could be put to good use today. That's probably why I enjoy "riding" so much today.

As parents you never want to admit that your son is a man, all grown up, out on his own. My Dad was pretty realistic. And I give him more credit now than I did at the time. I was about 17 years old when he first let me drive the car to my brother Willie's house in town. I guess that's when he figured that I was growing up and he gave me a little bit more rope.

You have to understand though, that if my parents said be home by 12 o'clock, I was home by 12 o'clock. Not a minute later. It wasn't until I was a senior in high school that I was able to stay out after 12 o'clock. Very seldom did I do that. But if I did, I made sure to let my parents know exactly what time I'd be home. That was out of respect.

Dad didn't know anything about athletics. When I first started playing basketball he was totally against it. That's the opposite of what takes place today, when a lot of parents live their own successes or failures in sports through their kids.

My Dad was never like that. He resented me for playing at first because he didn't think it was important. He felt I should be working instead. After awhile he accepted me playing, as long as I did my work first. I remember a few times in the summer when I'd slip off to play ball for a few hours when I still had work to do at home. I always made sure I was home before my Dad, because if he had caught me playing when there was work still to be done he would've whipped my butt.

I honestly don't remember the first game my Dad ever saw me play. I think he came and watched about four or five of my games when I was a junior in high school. He made it to every game when I was a senior in high school. When I went to Western Kentucky, he came to most of our home games with a fellow named Dick White.

It didn't really matter that much to me that he was there to be quite honest. Don't get me wrong, I appreciated him being there, but it was no big thing to me one way or another. I've always been different in that regard. Once the game started, I didn't know who was in the gym or who was around me. I was that focused as a player and it's the same way today when I'm on the sidelines coaching. I have no idea who's in the stands or who's around me.

When I played pro basketball, we almost always invited my Mother and Dad to come visit us for a couple of days over Christmas and to see a few games. When I first entered the NBA, Cincinnati had a franchise so my parents would come and watch me play when we played there. That was about it really.

I used the money from my first pro contract to help my Dad pay off some money that he still owed on the farm. Towards the end of my playing career, I used $20,000 to pay off a second mortgage for them. I had running water put in the house, a bathroom, and bought them a car. I tried to do all those things that any good son would try to do for his parents. Yevette and the kids sacrificed a lot during those times because I didn't really make a lot of money then. But it was an opportunity for me to finally give something back to my parents who had given so much to us kids through the years.

I will never forget Christmas Day in 1985. We were at the dinner table when my Dad had a stroke. It was the last time all of us kids were all together with Mother and Dad. As usual, my Dad was at the head of the table and Mother had prepared a great feast. We had just started to eat our Christmas dinner and then I remember that Dad started quivering and he had trouble picking up his fork.

We took Dad into the living room and then called the hospital. The ambulance came and picked him up and took him to the hospital. That was the last time my Dad was ever at home. The last 10 years of his life he laid flat on his back at Metzmeier Nursing Home in Campbellsville. He never recovered from the stroke. The first year or two he recognized me when I'd go to see him, but after that he was like a vegetable. He had a pacemaker put in, had his leg amputated and he just laid there in a fetal position most of the time.

Even though he didn't recognize me, every time we went home I made sure that we stopped by and visited him. That was one of the toughest things in life for me to do. To see my Dad in that position. I never, ever thought I'd see him like that. I thought he was too tough, that he'd get back up and walk again.

My father passed away on May 10, 1995. It was a blessing. The last six months we all knew that the phone call could come at any time. The whole family had time to prepare for it. We had already picked out his gravesite at Crown Hill cemetery in Campbellsville. Even though he was like a vegetable at the end and parts of him had already died 10 years ago after the stroke, he was still alive. He was still there. On the one hand we hated to see him pass away, but on the other hand it really was a blessing.

It was hard on everybody because we knew he was suffering and there was nothing more that we could do. My Mother tried to visit him each day right up until he passed away. She was very faithful right to the end. His funeral was a time for all of us to reminisce about his life, to talk about the good times and what he meant to all of us. There were so many people who shared his life with us and it seemed like every one of them had a story to tell about him.

My Dad never met a stranger. He loved to laugh and make other people laugh. I still visit his gravesite when I get back home. It's the same place where I'll be buried. I have my spot close to him already picked out for when I pass away. I think of my Dad often, particularly when I get home. He had a tremendous impact on my life and I miss him a great deal.

F AMILY MATTERS

CHAPTER FIVE

F amily values are so important to me and that's why I've tried to instill those same values into my own children and my teams through the years. Those values have trickled down from my Mother and Dad to all my brothers and sisters.

My oldest brother Willie has worked at Parker-Kalon in Campbellsville, where they make metal screws, for the past 30 years, and he's getting close to retirement. He also helps oversee my farm in Campbellsville in his spare time.

He's very special to me because when I first started playing basketball at Campbellsville Durham High School, the all-black school in town, I used to stay with Willie and his wife, Joanne, a lot, especially after road trips.

Willie was like a security blanket for me. If I ever needed anything, he was always there for me. Willie and Joanne are very dear to me. As well as being my big brother, he was like a second father for me. He's someone I really look up to and respect a great deal.

My second oldest brother, Charles, who was named after my father, always worked for the city of Campbellsville in the sanitation department. He and his wife, Lou Willie, had four children. Charles was killed in a car accident in February of 1964 when I was a freshman at Western Kentucky. It happened between Campbellsville and Lebanon, Kentucky, which is in Marion County, an adjoining county to Taylor County. It was devastating.

I heard about it through our team manager at Western, Lloyd Gardner. A state trooper called the university and got in touch with Coach Ed Diddle. They had seen his name on the police report, recognized the last name Haskins, and called Coach to see if he was related to me.

I'll never forget it. It was a Sunday morning when Coach Diddle got the call and he asked Lloyd to talk to me to see if I had a brother named Charles. I know how tough it was for Lloyd to do. I told him "yes" and then I talked to the trooper.

Lloyd then drove me to Campbellsville to identify my brother's body. I knew about it before anyone else in my family. I went and told my Mother and Dad first, and then the rest of the family. That was one of the saddest days of my life, to lose a brother like that.

In a real classy move, Coach Diddle brought the entire team to the funeral at Pleasant Hill Baptist Church. You have to understand that this was the South and blacks and whites didn't do a whole lot of things together at that time.

It was pretty impressive to walk in the church on that day and see all these six-foot-five to seven-foot guys on hand for my brother's funeral. They were all white with the exception of Dwight Smith, who with me became one of the first two blacks to ever play basketball at Western. It was really thoughtful that they showed up and I can't tell you how much it meant to my family and me. It was really special for Coach Diddle to do that and it showed how much character and class there was on that team.

My oldest sister Lummie, who is married to Earl Webster, has a son named Greg. Lummie was always like a second mom to us younger kids. In the South in particular, parents always put the oldest kids in charge.

Since Willie and Charles got married at such a young age, Lummie was the one who was in charge of the house when Mother and Dad weren't around. She started working when she was about 12 or 13 years of age, making anywhere from 25 to 30 cents an hour.

The money Lummie made she always gave back to my Mother and Dad to help buy food and clothing for the family. She went to trade school for about a year, but she had to quit to go to work to help support the family. She didn't get the chance to get a college education, but believe me, she's one of the smartest in the family.

Today, Lummie is a floor lady, or floor manager, at the Fruit of the Loom plant in Campbellsville. She was one of the first black floor ladies ever in the plant and has been working there for 35-plus years. She's quite the lady and a great sister.

We call Eliza Mable just Mable for short. She's always been the jokester in the family. Mable's funny and witty. She used to get us together when we were kids, usually Sara, Betty, Paul, Nora and I, and tell us tremendous fairy tales. She has such a great mind, a great imagination.

Mable had the ability to just captivate you with a story. She could make up the greatest tales about the boogieman, witches, ghosts or whatever. Some of them we had heard 100 times over and over, but we still loved to hear her tell them. She used to scare the hell out of us. Everytime she'd tell a particular tale, she'd add a little something to it. They'd get scarier and scarier. It would start out as a simple tale and then become larger because of the way she'd tell it and the things she'd add to it.

Mable, who is a year older than me, would have our eyes popping out of our heads when she was finished. She'd have all of us so worked up and so scared that we could hardly sleep at night. We'd be sleeping on pins and needles, thinking that the boogieman at the foot of our bed was going to get us.

I remember when Mable got a tricycle for Christmas one year. It was a big tricycle and we had so much fun with it. One day I was on the tricycle and she was pushing me. My big toe got caught in the front wheel and it almost got cut off. It was stuck in the wheel, but she kept pushing me and I kept yelling "stop, stop!" There was so much blood that you would have sworn that it cut my whole toe off. Bless her heart, she cried so hard about that. She felt so bad.

Back in those days all they put on wounds was turpentine, vinegar and salt. Talk about setting your butt on fire! It hurt, and when my mom put that concoction on the wound, talk about a kid hollering. Wow! But I tell you what. In a day or two, there was no infection. It sounds crazy today how we cared for wounds back then, but let me tell you, it worked.

Mable has also worked at the Fruit of the Loom factory for over 30 years. When I started playing pro ball with the Bulls, she quit working at the plant to live with Yevette and me in Chicago. She was engaged at the time to her husband Jimmy Tucker. He was in the service so she came to live with us in Chicago, to help us out in any way she could. That was really enjoyable.

After about a year and a half or so, Mable moved back to Campbellsville and has been working in the Fruit of the Loom plant ever since. She and Jimmy have two wonderful daughters. The oldest, Vanessa, graduated from the University of Kentucky and is now a teacher. The youngest, Jamie, attends Taylor County High School.

Sara is the third oldest sister in my family. She's younger than I am and is a wonderful sister. She and her husband, James, live in Roswell, Georgia, and have a daughter, Kim, who is attending Georgia Tech University. James is a chemist for Kimberly-Clark.

They started dating in high school at Taylor County. Sara also worked at Fruit of the Loom until James' job took them first to Cincinnati, and now to just outside Atlanta, where they've lived for a number of years.

Paul is not only my brother, but he's also my best friend. I'm just shy of three years older than him, so he's the closest brother to me age-wise. We were always very, very close growing up. We did everything together. Although we're separated by many miles now with him living in Mariba, Kentucky, which is near Lexington, and me in Minnesota, we're still extremely close today.

I remember one Christmas when we lived in Washington County and I got a BB gun. I was about seven years old and Paul was about four. I went out to the barn to try to shoot some pigeons. I knew I was hitting these pigeons, but I wasn't killing any of them. We must have had about 25 or 30 pigeons in the barn, and for some reason, I couldn't hit any of them.

I didn't think any BB's were coming out of the gun. So I got this wild idea. Paul got a pair of Red Rider gloves for Christmas. I had him go back into the house and get his new gloves. I told him to put his new gloves on, and he said "for what?" I told him that I was going to shoot him in the hand to see if this thing was working. So he puts his gloves on and I shot him point blank in the hand. He ran around screaming and then he took off for the house. He ran into the house and told Mother that I shot him in the hand. I thought that was the end of it.

When Mother asked me what happened I told her that I did shoot him in the hand, but that he had volunteered to do it. I kept saying, "He wanted me to do it! He wanted me to do it!" Bless Paul's heart, his hand was all swollen up. Mother took the gun away from me and I started to cry. She then told me to go get a switch, which she used to whip my butt good that day. I'll never forget it. I got the gun back about a month later, but I never did kill a pigeon with it. Bad aim I guess.

I think I really helped Paul play the game of basketball, almost in a sense forced him to play. You see, I was obsessed with the game of basketball. I could not go a day without playing basketball. I just loved to play. Paul enjoyed the game, but he didn't love it as much as I did.

Growing up, wherever I went, Paul was there. He was my right-hand man. It's always been like that. We worked together in the fields, we played ball together, you name it. He just means so much to me personally. He's my brother, my best friend, and someone whom I talk to at least once every week.

Paul is someone I can trust with anything; I'd trust him with my life. He runs my farm for me. A lot of people probably think he owns the farm, that's how much pride and joy he puts into it. He makes all the tough decisions, tells me what to do and what not to do. Just like all brothers, we fuss, argue and disagree at times over things.

But Paul's helped me make some great decisions and make some great investments. He's always encouraged me to go ahead and try some things. He reminds me that nothing lasts forever in this world. We're just here for a short period of time and it's up to us to take full advantage of what we have and what we can do.

He is a guy I truly enjoy being with. We can talk about basketball, politics, social problems in the world, crime, or whatever. I think that one of the big reasons we get along so well together is that our philosophies on life really mirror each other. In addition to helping me with the farm, Paul has worked in the department of interior for the government for more than 20 years.

Betty is my fourth oldest sister. She's quite a bit younger than I am. I really didn't grow up with her since I had already started to move out of the house when she was real young. Betty is a wonderful lady who has worked at Fruit of the Loom for almost 30 years now. Betty was married to Bill Winfrey and they have a fine young son named Jerome. He's a cross country and track runner who has a chance to be an outstanding collegiate athlete.

Nora, my fifth oldest sister, went to Western Kentucky where she graduated with honors. She's still single and has worked for IBM for many years, first living in Cincinnati and now in Marietta, Georgia. Nora and Sara have always been like two peas in a pod. They're very, very close to each other.

Nora first lived in Cincinnati with Sara and her family. Then when Sara and James moved to Georgia, Nora ended up getting transferred with IBM down there too. Nora is a very dependable, very sharp, very elegant lady. She's so beautiful and so charming.

There's 12 years between my youngest brother, Merion, and me. As a result, we did not have the opportunity to spend a lot of time together. We wore about the same size clothing. When I used to come home in the spring during the time I was playing pro ball, he tried to sneak my shoes or clothes to wear. I can even remember him trying to wear my leisure suits to school.

Merion was a very good athlete who worked extremely hard. He went to the University of Kentucky and played basketball for Coach Joe B. Hall. That was a few years after they started recruiting blacks to play there.

I think Joe B. would tell you that out of all the players who played for him at Kentucky, Merion was one of his favorite guys, a young man whom he really respected. I'm sure that he'd tell you that he wasn't one of his best players. But in terms of effort, dedication and loyalty to Hall and to the program, Merion would be one of the best ever.

Merion served as team captain as a senior in 1976-77. That shows what a coach thinks of you if he's willing to give you the responsibility to be the captain of the team. He was part of Kentucky's NIT championship team in 1976 and its 1977 Southeastern Conference championship squad which advanced to the NCAA East Regional finals. He played at Kentucky alongside some great players like Jack Givens, Rick Robey and Dwayne Casey.

One of the things I regret about being away playing pro basketball is that I rarely got the opportunity to see Merion play. I saw him play only one game in high school, and only two or three games in college.

Merion now works for the Phillip-Morris tobacco company in Richmond, Virginia. He's a buyer and has done a great job for them. He has a daughter, Hope, who plays basketball in junior high and may be the next Clemette Haskins. I may be dreaming a little bit, but she's very athletic and committed to learning the game. Most importantly, she's a nice, young lady who works hard in school.

My baby sister Joyce has always devoted herself academically. She's always been a great student. She taught school in Kentucky and was a principal in the Minneapolis school district, before deciding to take some time off to get her doctorate from Harvard University.

Joyce received her undergraduate degree from Western and also has master's degrees from the University of Kentucky and the

University of Minnesota. She's single and has devoted most of her time and effort to her education and her career.

There's 14 years' difference between us, so I can't say that I really grew up with Joyce. In some ways, she's more like a daughter of mine than a sister. We're close and she still comes and spends a lot of time with Yevette and me, sometimes for weeks at a time.

All of us are close as a family. Even though a lot of miles may separate us, we try to stay in contact all the time as best we can. Physically, we try to see each other whenever we're able. It seems like that just gets tougher and tougher all the time because of our schedules.

Living in Minnesota since 1986, the thing I've missed the most is the opportunity to get back home for special occasions like Christmas, Mother's Day, Father's Day, Easter, and Thanksgiving. As a kid growing up, those were always special days in our house. We would have a big dinner together. Kids, grandkids, nieces, nephews, everyone. The first thing we would do is pray over dinner.

Those are the things that build relationships and strong families. I've tried to do the same thing with both my immediate family and the players in my basketball program. I try to let them know that family is very important. I tell my players that if they physically can't be home, they should call mom and dad on the phone. If they don't have the money for the phone call, then I tell them to write. That only costs 32 cents. The most important thing is to let some very important people in your life know that you're thinking about them.

I can't begin to tell you how proud I am of all my brothers and sisters. Each of us has made a difference in this world in our own little way. I really believe that's the ultimate compliment to my Mother and Dad for the job they did with the 11 Haskins children.

THE FIRST TIME

CHAPTER SIX

I was 10 years old the first time I ever shot a basketball. Paul and I were walking up the road one day and we saw these two guys playing basketball. So we walked across the field and started talking with two guys we had never met before, David and Buck Roberts. David, who was about four years older than me, was shooting the ball. Buck was the same age as me. They had a basketball and a goal in an apple orchard on their farm, which was about a half mile from ours.

I was standing about 25 or 30 feet from the bucket when David threw me the ball and said "try one." I caught the ball and then threw it one-handed like a baseball at the basket. It banked right in, I kid you not. So the first shot that I ever took was from 25 or 30 feet and I banked it in. I didn't know how to shoot it, but it went in anyway. David fell down on the ground and started laughing. I didn't know what he was laughing at. He couldn't even talk he was laughing so hard. Then he came over and we started to talk. I probably missed my next hundred shots after that, but I watched him shoot. I was hooked on the game immediately, and we started playing basketball after that.

I own that goal now. The exact same one that on that very day I made my first basket in. It's an old-time goal, with two extension braces on it that were used to hook it up. It had four bolts in it, two on the top and two on the bottom, that were hooked up to a wooden backboard. Two posts and planks held it up. I guess it was 10 feet, but who knows. There was no net and the court was the dirt.

Even though he was four years older than me, David Roberts became my very good friend. After we met that day, we did everything together. We ate together, we slept together. Paul, Buck, David and I used to play two-on-two baseball. How you play two-man baseball I don't know. But we made up the rules and did it. We played basketball, two-man baseball, we built hay houses, you name it. The four of us were inseparable. We had so much fun together.

There was another neighbor, Larry Clark, who was the same age as Buck and me. The four youngest—Paul, Buck, Larry and I— used to wrestle with David. We'd pile on him, but we never could make him give. He'd grab one of us and squeeze us so hard that we'd give up and then the other three would run away. Talk about fun.

David's the guy who taught me how to play basketball. He was a great shooter and I loved to watch him play. I studied his form and technique. From that first day that we met, after watching him shoot, I fell in love with the game of basketball. We started playing a lot after that day. A year later, David and Buck's father, Lester, put a light up out in their apple orchard so we could play at night. David was playing high school ball at Taylor County High School, the all-white school in Campbellsville. His brothers, Jerry and Clifford, were good high school players, so David was kind of following in their footsteps.

We didn't play in the gym at all back then. We played in the apple orchard and also in a barn loft at Jimmy and Wendell Rivers' house. They were also neighbors of ours. If it was too cool to play at night or rainy, we'd play in the barn loft.

The barn was only about 12 feet wide and about 30 feet deep. Later, when David was a senior in high school, all the guys that David played with in high school as well as a bunch from Campbellsville College would come out to this barn loft and we'd have some fantastic games. I was already good enough to play with the older guys.

We'd play until 10 or 11 p.m. many nights. Two on two, three on three, in the driveway in this barn. You had to put your foot on the wall just to get the ball inbounds. The goal hung on the loft that jetted out about 10 feet from the wall. So when you went in for a shot, especially on layups, you ended up underneath the loft. It was amazing when you think about it. I'm guessing that there were probably 25 Division I players that played in the driveway of that barn.

The fun we had in that barn was really something. Guys would drive your butt into the wall. I got a lot of burns on my shoulder from running into the walls of that barn, but you learned how to keep your body under control at all times. I own that barn now. I bought it about 10 years ago. That same barn that we played in all the time is still there. I go out there now and look at it and ask myself, "How in the hell did we ever play in here?" But we had so much fun and it played an important role in my development as a player.

I went to a one-room all-black school growing up, and as a result, I really didn't know that there was a difference between blacks and whites. I didn't know that we couldn't eat in the restaurants or go to the movies because we never had enough money to do things like that in the first place. I never had the opportunity to socialize beyond our circle of friends out on the farm, so I had no idea that I would ever be treated differently because I was black.

The first time that I realized there was a difference was when Paul, David, Buck and I went in to town to see the movie "Old Yeller" at the Alhambra Theater. I was 11 years old at the time. David and Buck's parents drove us into town to see the movie. It cost a dime to go to the movies, so the Roberts' paid for both Paul and me since we couldn't afford it. We got our tickets and walked into the movie theater together and sat down.

The movie was just about ready to begin when the usher came up to us with a flashlight, tapped David on the shoulder and told us that Paul and I would have to go upstairs. You see, the main level was for the white folks, while the blacks had to sit in the balcony. I didn't know what he was talking about, but Paul and I just went upstairs and sat down.

A few minutes later, David and Buck came upstairs and sat next to us. Pretty soon, there was the usher once again with his flashlight to tell them that they couldn't sit with us and that they had to go back and sit downstairs.

We were so excited to see the movie that we really didn't even think about it. Heck, it was the first movie Paul and I had ever been to in our lives. I wasn't worried about blacks and whites and all this integration stuff. I was excited about being at the movies. It never dawned on me that there was a separation of the two races until the movie was over and we were on our way home. We never discussed it with David and Buck, but it was obvious that they were really embarrassed and ticked off about it.

Even years later we never, ever had a conversation about it. It was never brought up in our house. There were certain things that you didn't discuss. You just accepted it and went along with life. That's what happens.

But then a younger generation came along and said, "Hey, we're tired of this. We're not going to sit upstairs anymore. We're not going to go through the back doors. We want to sit in the front of the bus." People just accepted racism until Martin Luther King and Malcolm X came along and started protesting. Blacks then stood up and said, "We don't have to accept this. We can change things because we are somebody." But at that time we just accepted the fact that we were treated like second-class citizens.

That's when I realized for the first time in my life that there was such a thing as separation of races and prejudice in the world. We never saw color in each other until that incident in the movie theater. That didn't change a thing between us though. Everything was the same. It didn't change our relationship or how we got along at all.

After David graduated from high school he played college ball at Ohio University. He stayed there and taught school and coached for a few years after he earned his degree. He eventually moved back to Campbellsville. No matter where our lives took us and how busy we were, we always stayed in touch. We were that close to each other.

David drowned in Green River Lake in June of 1972. It's a good-sized lake that lies in both Taylor and Adair counties, just about eight miles south of Campbellsville. When I got the call that he had drowned, I knew I had to go home right away. I was playing with the Phoenix Suns at the time and I was doing my summer basketball camp in Prescott, Arizona. I remember it like it was yesterday.

It's kind of funny because as kids we used to run trout lines all the time in Robinson Creek. A trout line is a line you run across the river with hooks in it. You bait the hooks and then come back the next morning to see if you caught any fish. Most of the time we'd come away with a bucket full of fish. David and Buck's dad would set out the trout lines in the evening and then Paul, David, Buck and I would come back the next morning to check on them.

It's crazy when I think about it now, because I would go in water up to my neck and I can't swim. Paul and David never learned to swim either. We used to wade in the creek to run these trout lines without a fear in the world. When I think back now, if we had gone over our heads with one step at any time, we would have drowned. There could have been a dropoff or we could have slipped. I never thought about it to tell you the truth. Even though I couldn't swim, I never feared the water.

David never learned to swim either. Buck was like a fish in the water. When we'd go in the stream he'd be doing the backstroke. It's kind of ironic. We had been in water all our lives and never learned to swim. When I heard that he had lost control of his boat, fell overboard and drowned, it brought back all those times in the water.

I was a pallbearer in his funeral. It was one of the saddest days of my life. It was shocking to lose someone who had meant so much to me all my life. David taught me not only a lot about basketball, but so much about life as well.

THE MOVE

CHAPTER SEVEN

rowing up, I didn't really get a good foundation education-wise because I was always out of school working. I didn't start going to school until I was eight years old. I went to a one-room county school for blacks until I was in third grade, and then after consolidation, moved to Campbellsville Durham in the fourth grade.

Campbellsville Durham was the all-black first through twelfth grade school in town. I was out of school more than I was in during the months of September, October and November to cut and strip tobacco. The only reason I probably stayed in school was because of Yevette's uncle, Rodney Ivery.

When I entered junior high, Mr. Ivery and H.R. Richardson, a teacher at the school, talked to my dad about letting me come to school more often. They understood the value of education and I know that my Dad realized it as well. Dad started to listen to them and he cut my workload at home down somewhat so that I could go to school more often.

They also talked him into letting me play on the school's basketball team. Dad wasn't real excited about the idea to tell you the truth, but he said it was okay with him as long as it didn't interfere with my work at home and school. The first coach I ever played for was Samuel Wickliffe in the seventh and eighth grade at Campbellsville Durham. He did a nice job with us.

In ninth and tenth grade my coach was John Whiting, who really worked with me on my shot. A great person and a close friend of mine to this day, he deserves a lot of credit for me becoming a good shooter.

We played against predominantly all-black schools at Campbellsville Durham. You could play against all-white schools when you got into the district tournament. In fact, for many years, the state of Kentucky had separate black and white state tournaments. I had two successful years at Durham, scoring 880 points as a freshman when we lost in the sixth regional final, and 874 as a sophomore when we fell in the regional semifinals.

It was after my sophomore year at Durham that I started to seriously think about actually attending all-white Taylor County High School.

I transferred from Campbellsville Durham to Taylor County at the beginning of my junior year because of David and Buck Roberts. They encouraged me and said that if I was going to reach my potential as a player and get the recognition that I deserved, I needed to make the change.

But once the possibility of the transfer was discussed, there was another larger force that drove me to want to make the move. I know now that it was God telling me that I should do this. So in the fall of 1961, I became the first black student ever to attend Taylor County High School.

It wasn't just for me, I also did it to help other people. I did it to help not only black people, but also white people and all races of people. I wanted to make people understand that we could live together and work together. All I wanted was what I was entitled to. A quality education and the opportunity to prepare for my future like everyone else.

That's not the way it was back then. Blacks didn't get treated fairly, not even close. We were looked down upon. We could not eat at most restaurants. It wasn't fair and I wanted to do something to make a difference.

I went to the school for 28 straight days before I was allowed inside. I'd ride in with Buck every day. He was going to Campbellsville College and he'd drop me off at the high school before going to his classes. Even though we were the same age, he was a couple of years ahead of me academically since I hadn't started attending school until I was eight.

After Buck dropped me off, I'd go up to the door and they'd say I couldn't come in today. I remember waiting around for 30 or 40 minutes and then being told I couldn't enter the school that day and then I'd walk back home. It was about a three-mile walk.

People in town used to talk a lot about David and Buck. They were criticized and crucified, even by their own brother-in-law, for being my friends and helping me out. A lot of people couldn't understand why Buck would drive this "nigger" to school every day. Finally with the help of state officials at the front door one day, I was allowed into school.

I want to say this about my fellow classmates at Taylor County. From the moment I walked into the school for the first time, there weren't any problems. In fact, I almost wonder if the principal, Mr. J.G. McAnelly, didn't get the whole student body together and explain to them that this might happen; that a black student might actually attend the school. I never had any problems with any other students in class, in the halls, in the bathrooms, anywhere. I never had anyone threaten to kill me, beat me up or even say anything threatening to my face.

Behind my back, I'm sure they did. But to my face, I never, ever had a student or group of students corner me and ask me "Why are you here, nigger? Why are you in school here?" That never happened at Taylor County. I can always say that and feel good about it. The entire student body, teachers and staff at Taylor County deserve a lot of credit. The majority of them really rallied behind me I think.

Sure, it was tough on me, but it was also really tough on them. I was doing something that virtually everyone in the community was against as a whole. I was stepping into uncharted territory and across boundaries that no one had ever crossed before. So they deserve to be applauded for accepting me and treating me fairly. It gave me the opportunity to get an education and be somebody. I can't begin to tell you how I felt when they voted me to be a class officer that first year. That was special.

I really think that it went so well because of the way I carried myself. You have to understand that I didn't go in there with a chip on my shoulder. I didn't go there with an attitude. All I wanted to do was to go to school and play basketball. After I was there a week or two, everyone realized that and we had no problems.

My fellow classmates were strong enough to stand up, because you know the parents of many of the students were very upset. I'm sure that a number of the parents were telling their kids "You don't want that nigger over there." I'm sure that some parents protested to the school board and the principal. I'm sure it happened. We were dealing in a different place and time.

Every teacher I had at Taylor County handled it well. They never let the distractions get in the way of their jobs. Fred Waddle, our assistant basketball coach, needs to be applauded for really doing a great job. He made me feel welcome, made me feel secure. Fred and his wife, Shirley, who also taught at Taylor County High School, were really very good to me.

Billy B. Smith was our head coach. He accepted me and did a great job under tough circumstances. But if there's one individual who stands out more than anyone else, it would have to be Fred. He probably did more for me than any one individual. He would take me home after practice from time to time, and pick me up for practice on occasion. He gave me so much support and encouragement.

There were a lot of difficult times, especially after games. I'm a very emotional person. I cried after just about every game. The things that the fans, mainly from the opposing teams, would say to me, not to mention the threats, were hard for a young person to handle. In the Taylor County High School gymnasium somebody had written "Clem Haskins High Go To Hell" on the wall behind the bleachers. In fact, I went back to the gym not too long ago, and even though it's been painted over, you can still make out the words if you look hard enough.

But I never felt any fear on the basketball court. Once I stepped on the court, I was able to wipe all that stuff out. But after the games, I remember crying in Fred's office many, many times. He and Shirley were always so supportive. They helped me along the way and I can't tell you how much I appreciated their support. Fred is now the Taylor County judge/executive and Shirley is a retired teacher. They deserve a lot of credit and I will be forever grateful for all they did for me.

I also ran track and cross country and played baseball at Taylor County as well. The main reason I ran cross country and track was because Fred was the coach for both sports and I had a tremendous amount of respect for him.

I remember going to the 1962 state track and field meet in Lexington, one of the most prejudiced cities in the whole country at that time. I remember one morning when we went to eat together as a team. There were about nine of us and, of course, I was the only black.

We walked into the restaurant and sat down to eat. I don't remember the name of the place. The waitress came up to get our orders, saw me and told some of my teammates while motioning to me that I couldn't eat there. I didn't hear her say that. But the guys then stood up, turned the table over and said "Let's go." We then all stormed out of the restaurant together.

Richard Williams, Tommy Brown...those are guys I also played basketball with. I said "That's alright, you guys go ahead and eat." They said "No, if you can't eat here, then we're not going to, either." That really, really made me feel good that those guys stood beside me.

The only place in Lexington where blacks could eat at that time was a drugstore downtown. That was the only damn place that blacks could eat on the entire main street of Lexington. So that's where we ate. I'll tell you, I learned to appreciate those guys even more after that. They were really committed to having me be a part of the program and a part of them.

That's why to this day Tommy Brown is one of my dearest friends. I think the world of him, can't say enough good things about the type of person he is. There's not a prejudiced bone in his body. He's a great guy. I mean he's for real. He has his own construction business in Campbellsville now.

I think that's one of the reasons why in the state of Kentucky, particularly in the areas surrounding Campbellsville and Taylor County, I'm respected so much today. It was tough, but I tried to handle it in a very professional manner. I got tripped and spit on, got called a nigger, a dog and a lot of other things that aren't appropriate for print. Some people even treated me like a dog.

It wasn't easy. The louder and harder that they jeered at me, however, the more it motivated me. The more names they called me, the better I played. A lot of people may have gone into a shell, but it really motivated me to play better and harder. If anything, it helped my game. I was so focused when I got on the court that nothing else mattered.

I say this often and I really mean it. I truly believe that the people who called me so many names back then are responsible for making me a pro basketball player and the person I am today. It motivated me to work harder, to work on my game more, especially in the offseason to become a better player. So in one sense it was bad and tough to handle. But on the other hand, it pushed me to become not only a better basketball player, but also a stronger person. I was more focused and more determined the next day in practice, or the next game or the next season. It not only made me work harder than anyone to become a better player, but also made me tougher so that no one or situation can intimidate me.

I was proud of the fact that there were five blacks at Taylor County High School by my senior year; my brother Paul, Joseph Rowe, Don Smith, Charles Graves and me. I helped clear the way for them to go to school there. Don't get me wrong. It still wasn't easy for them by any stretch of the imagination. In fact, in September of 1963, the community's entire school system was integrated. But I think that it took something like I went through to help bring people together and pave the way for change.

MAKING HISTORY

CHAPTER EIGHT

I remember that there was a lot of security at the first game I played for Taylor County High. You could cut the tension in the air with a knife. We played St. Augustine and we won the game 58-39, but the final outcome wasn't what most people will remember from that night.

There were a lot of threatening calls and letters before the game. "Nigger, we're going to kill you if you play tonight," things like that. But you have to understand that I never, ever worried about that. When I played basketball, I was so focused on the game. I was tripped, knocked down, spit on and kicked in high school, but I really never worried about the danger until the game was over. Once the game started, I blocked all of that out of my mind and just concentrated on basketball.

I must admit that it was a relief to get that first game over with. But the tension remained for every game, especially the first time we played a school. The road games were always interesting. You name it and someone in the stands probably said it about me. Often we were jeered when our bus pulled up to the gymnasium. When we traveled we couldn't go into the restaurants and eat, so Billy B. and Fred would have to go in and get the food and then bring it back on the bus.

The guys on that team will always be special to me. In addition to Tommy Brown, there was Gary Seaborne, Richard Williams, Randy Shreve, Billy Netherland, Dale Newton, Gary "Tootsie" Minor, Norman Perkins, Lloyd Graham and Samuel Cox. They put up with a lot of grief, but showed a tremendous amount of character and class through it all.

We finished my junior season with an overall record of 29-4, and Billy B. was named the Coach of the Year in the South Kentucky Athletic Conference (SKAC) after we won the title with a 9-2 mark in league play. Along the way we defeated Campbellsville High School, 77-63, to win the Christmas Invitational and beat Greensburg, 58-57, to take the SKAC Tournament crown. I was named to the all-state team after averaging 24.6 points per game.

I remember the night during my junior year when I scored a school-record 51 points against Tompkinsville High School. We won the game 94-60, and I sat out the last three minutes of the game. That was one of those nights where I couldn't miss against a team that had really motivated me. I made 20-of-23 field goal attempts and 11 free throws in the contest. I had one of those phenomenal games against a team that had really ticked me off for some of the things they had said about me. Because of that I wanted to get as many points as I could and the guys did a great job of getting me the ball to do it.

I remember that "Tootsie" kept feeding me the ball all night. Tootsie was a five-foot-five guard for us and boy, was he a tough little player. I think that Gary was more excited about me breaking the school record than I was. He couldn't shoot a lick. All he could do was pass the ball. I still give him a hard time about that. Gary is now the superintendent for the Taylor County School system.

Our game against Campbellsville Durham that year was also interesting. Yevette, whom I had started dating the year before when we were sophomores, was a cheerleader at Durham. She was very understanding of why I needed to make the move to Taylor County and it was never a problem between us.

What a lot of people don't understand is that my decision affected a lot of people, not just the whites in town who didn't want me to go to school at Taylor County. In the eyes of a lot of blacks, I was a traitor because I left the all-black school in town, Durham, to go to the all-white school in town. This was not a one-sided thing. There was racism on both sides of the fence. Blocking all of that out once I stepped on the court, I helped lead us to a 64-47 win over Durham.

We went on to beat Campbellsville in a thriller, 47-46, to win the 21st District championship. It marked our third straight win that season over our crosstown rivals. Then we defeated Larue County, 75-66, in our first game of the 6th Regional tournament, before falling 72-71 in the last seconds against Bloomfield in the finals.

I had made a shot with 26 seconds left in the game to put us on top, 71-70. I will always wonder if I took the shot too soon, but the opportunity was there and I went after it. Down by one, Bloomfield then ran the clock down and won the championship when Billy Keeling hit the game-winner with three seconds left.

Despite scoring 30 points and grabbing a school-record 30 rebounds, the thing that I remember most was seeing Billy B. sitting by himself in the corner of our locker room after the game. I felt like I had let my coach down. We had come so close to our goal, but just couldn't quite get over the hump.

That set the stage for our senior season in 1962-63 when we made school history by becoming the first team in Taylor County High School history to make it to the state tournament.

After an 8-2 start, we reeled off 25 straight wins before dropping a heartbreaking 65-64 decision to Lexington Dunbar in the state tournament quarterfinals. Despite having just two starters back from the previous year, Tommy and I, we finished the season with a 33-3 overall record, which made us the winningest team in the state of Kentucky that year.

It was made all the more special because I got to play alongside my little brother Paul, a six-foot-four freshman who started at center for us. Senior Kraig Carroll, a six-foot-two guard who moved to Campbellsville from Fort Knox, Kentucky, and Don Smith, a six-foot-one sophomore forward-center who came from Illinois, were also key newcomers for us.

En route to the state tourney we won the SKAC Tournament and regular season titles for the second straight season. I averaged 26.7 points and 18.0 rebounds per game and was named to the Scholastic All-America team in the process. In addition, I was selected to the all-state team for the second straight year as well.

We showed that we meant business right from the start that season by routing St. Augustine, 84-18, in the opener. I had 30 points, Tommy scored 21 and Don poured in 19 in his first game for us.

Adair County took us into overtime in our second game before we escaped with a 59-54 win on our home floor. I hit a jumper to tie it up right before the end of regulation and then we won it in overtime as I finished the game with 31 points.

We tasted defeat for the first time that season when we lost 50-46 in overtime at Greensburg to fall to 2-1 on the season. Tommy,

Kraig and I all fouled out of the game. I scored 21 points, but was awful to tell you the truth. Behind Tommy's 27 points, we bounced back with a 62-54 win over Elizabethtown Catholic to start a six-game win streak.

Our final defeat before the 25-game winning streak was a 58-54 loss at top-ranked Louisville Seneca, who went on to win the state title later that year. The buildup for that game was tremendous and there was a standing-room-only crowd on hand in their gym.

Seneca had two great players in Wes Unseld and Mike Redd. Mike, who I outscored 28-26 and outrebounded 21-8 in the game, was named Mr. Basketball in Kentucky that season. We were both two-time all-state selections. He was a great high school player, but unfortunately, he never had much of a career beyond high school. Wes, who was only a junior that season, went on to a Hall of Fame career in the NBA. In fact, we ended up being teammates with the Washington Bullets in my final two seasons in the league.

We had four players in double figures as we defeated Greensburg, 76-70, to win the Campbellsville Invitational Tournament for the second straight year. I led the way with 22 points, followed by Tommy and Don with 16 apiece, and Kraig with 12. Paul just missed double digits with eight points in the game as we showed the kind of scoring depth we were going to need come tournament time.

Senior Dale Newton, a scrappy five-foot-nine guard, junior Joe Rowe, a six-foot guard, and junior Charles Graves, a five-foot-ten guard, really started to give us some good minutes the second half of the season.

Ahead by just one point at the half, 30-29, I scored 13 of my 30 points in the third quarter to lead us to a 68-51 win over Adair County in the SKAC Tournament title game in Columbia, Kentucky. Tommy had 14 points and Kraig scored 12, and Joe turned a few heads with the way he handled the ball. The victory was our 12th in a row and raised our overall record to 20-2 on the season.

I scored 42 points in our second-to-last game of the regular season, an 89-35 rout of St. Charles. In my final home game, I scored 27 points in a 67-53 win over Louisville Male as we ran our record to 26-2 and registered our 18th straight win. Tommy was right there once again with 19 points, while Joe had 13 points of his own.

It would be an understatement to say that we entered district play on a roll. We kept things going on the right track with a

52-47 win over Adair County on their home floor. I had 25 points and Joe scored 15 points. It was the fourth time we had beaten them that season. In the semifinals we beat Greensburg, 74-62, and I scored 39 points.

Durham, my old school that had upset Campbellsville in the first round, was our opponent in the finals. I scored 22 points and Tommy chipped in 20 as we easily won the district title for the second straight year with a 70-49 win.

We opened the regional tournament with a 67-50 win over St. Joseph. In the semifinals I scored 33 points and Tommy chipped in 23 as we chalked up our 31st win of the season and 23rd in a row with an 81-62 win over Fort Knox.

For the second straight year we had advanced to the 6th regional final. The previous year's one-point defeat at the hands of Bloomfield was certainly on my mind as we prepared for the long-awaited rematch with Elizabethtown Catholic and their star player Tom Hendrix in the Campbellsville City High School gym.

It was a crazy scene that night. The gym was overflowing with fans long before the start of the game. I guess they estimated that they turned away about 2,000 fans, some of which stood in line for about two hours. Paced by Paul's seven first-quarter points, we took control of the game from the opening tip and led 15-4 after the first quarter.

We never trailed in the game and the closest Elizabethtown Catholic ever got to us after that was four points as we came away with a hard-earned 66-58 win. We held Hendrix to just 14 points on the night. It was a great team effort from top-to-bottom.

I scored 28 points in the final and finished the three-game regional tournament with 86 points. I was joined on the all-region team by Tommy, who scored 12 points in the championship game and had 51 in the tourney, and Joe, who only scored 11 points in three games, but did a great job handling the ball and playing defense.

It was time to celebrate. For the first time in school history, Taylor County had made it to the state tournament at Freedom Hall in Louisville. It's actually called the "Sweet 16." Believe me, going to the "Sweet 16" in the state of Kentucky is just as big of a thrill for a kid as playing in the NCAA Final Four in college.

It would be an understatement to say that tournament fever gripped Taylor County. I remember that the merchants and businessmen of Campbellsville and Taylor County purchased new blazers for us to wear. There were parades and pepfests, and a lot of the merchants in Campbellsville just closed up shop and headed for Louisville figuring there wouldn't be any business anyway.

This was the "Big Show" in the state of Kentucky and media pressure was intense. There were a lot of great players in the tournament that year and a lot of the talk was centered around who was the best player in the state, Redd or Haskins.

I remember when we arrived in Louisville and I read a column by *Courier-Journal* sports editor Earl Ruby where he quoted Benny Edelen, a veteran referee, as saying that Haskins is "so good he'll make people forget the Big O before he finishes his sophomore year (in college)."

I was like wow! The Big O that he was referring to was none other than Oscar Robertson, a star player in the NBA at the time who ended up becoming one of the greatest guards in basketball history. Even though that was a great honor to even be mentioned in the same sentence with the Big O, I knew I couldn't worry about all the hype. It was time to get down to business.

I remember how big I thought Freedom Hall was, especially to a bunch of farmboys like us. Our eyes were wide open and our jaws just dropped when we walked into the place. I remember asking my dad, "How much hay do you think we could store in here?"

We easily won our first game, 57-43, over Breckinridge Training. We were just too strong and physical for them. I scored 19 points and had 13 rebounds, but most importantly, Billy B. didn't play the starters a whole heck of a lot of minutes so we'd all be well rested for the next game.

My high school career and our 25-game winning streak came to an abrupt end when we lost, 65-64, in the quarterfinals to Lexington Dunbar in front of a standing-room-only audience of 17,500. We had played in front of big crowds before, but let me tell you, that was really an experience for a bunch of high school kids.

Dunbar shot 56 percent from the field in the game. At times it seemed like they just couldn't miss, especially George Wilson, who was 10-of-15 from the field and finished with 21 points. I can still remember one shot they made that rolled across the rim and it seemed like it hit something and then fell in. They also had a basket that shouldn't have counted that in the end cost us the game.

I scored 25 points and was named to the all-tournament team. Kraig and Joe had 13 and 11 points, respectively. We played a good basketball game, but got beat by a very good, very athletic team. Dunbar almost became the first all-black school to win the state title, but they lost 72-66 to Louisville Seneca in the championship game.

It's the dream of every kid who plays basketball in the state of Kentucky to someday play in the "Sweet 16." Going to the state tournament with Taylor County High School is one of the highlights of my career; high school, college or pro. Coaching Minnesota to the Final Four in 1997 was an incredible thrill, but my experience of playing in Kentucky's "Sweet 16" back in 1963 ranks right alongside it to tell you the truth.

During my four years of high school basketball, I scored 3,325 points. That still ranks sixth on the all-time Kentucky boys high school scoring list. Remember, this was before the three-point shot. God only knows how many points I would have scored with the three-pointer in effect.

It was a great honor to have my high school basketball jersey number 22 retired on December 5, 1995. I also was inducted into the Kentucky High School Athletic Association Hall of Fame on March 15, 1988.

But more important than jump shots and honors, through my success on the basketball court and the way I carried myself, I was able to break down racial barriers to help make the place where I grew up and still call "home" a better place to live for future generations.

A FRUITFUL SUMMER

CHAPTER NINE

I t seemed as though the college recruiters were at every game my last year at Taylor County. No matter what time of the day or night, the phone never stopped ringing.

I was contacted by about 130 schools from coast to coast. Of course, there were a number of schools in the South that I couldn't even think about going to because I was black.

Legendary Coach Adolph Rupp's Kentucky program was one of the best in the nation year in and year out. The school had yet to integrate at that time, however, so it was not an option for me. I'm not sure how that would have affected my decision, but it sure hurt not to have the opportunity to go there simply because of the color of my skin.

I struggled with the decision. I knew that I wanted to play somewhere close to home so my family could see me play. Eventually, I narrowed it down to Louisville, Western Kentucky, Purdue, Indiana, Morehead, Eastern Kentucky, Cincinnati, Ohio University and Dayton.

But in the end I decided to sign with the University of Louisville. Peck Hickman was the athletics director and head coach there, and John Dromo was the assistant coach who spent a lot of time recruiting me. When I visited the campus, they introduced me to the great quarterback Johnny Unitas and Lenny Lyles. They were both former Louisville football stars who were playing with the

Baltimore Colts in the National Football League at the time. I was impressed by that. They had also signed some other good players already and that probably helped sway my decision more than anything else.

After I signed the grant-in-aid, one of the Louisville newspapers said that the "manhunt ends." I was relieved when it was over and done with. I'm sure my entire family felt the same way.

The best thing in the world that ever happened to me, and it was a mistake on Louisville's part, was having me go to summer school there right after I graduated from Taylor County. I went the first four weeks and cried just about every night. I was so unhappy. I was a country boy who was really homesick in the big city.

After the first summer session was over, I told my Mother and Dad that I didn't want to stay there. Then I told the coaches at Louisville that I was checking out and wouldn't be coming back. Obviously Peck and John were very upset, but it was a mistake on their part by having me go to summer school and then not spending any time with me. They tried to get me to stay, but my mind was made up.

It's ironic because Peck was a great player at Western in the thirties. In fact, he was inducted into the Western Kentucky University Hall of Fame in 1997.

Western Kentucky had recruited me hard and I had planned on going there all along. I felt good about Coach Ed Diddle and he had a great staff in place. Ted Hornback was an assistant coach at that time who had really recruited me hard. He became the athletics director at Western a few years later. I felt comfortable in Bowling Green. What can I say, other than that it was just the right place for me to be.

My parents and I called Western Kentucky and told them I'd be there in the fall. I would join fellow Kentucky high school all-stater Dwight Smith of Princeton Dotson, a six-foot-five guard, as the first black basketball players ever at Western Kentucky. Looking back, it ended up being one of the greatest decisions I've ever made in my life.

That summer I had the opportunity to play in the Kentucky vs. Indiana all-star games. We won both games and it was a great experience. Three of my teammates in those all-star games—Dwight, Wayne Chapman, a six-foot-six guard from Davies County and Pearl Hicks, a six-foot-seven forward/center from Clay County—would also end up being teammates of mine at Western. Wayne actually signed with Kentucky, but ended up transferring to Western after his freshman year in Lexington.

We were joined by Mike Redd, Tom Hendrix, Charles Taylor of Owensboro, Lewis Couch of Carr Creek, Bill Chumbler of Lowes, Jim Hengehold of Erlanger St. Henry and Bob Mattingly of Louisville DeSales. Our head coach was Jim Morris of Flaget and Morton Combs of Carr Creek was the assistant coach. Let me tell you, that was a pretty impressive collection of high school players on one team.

I also played in the annual East-West game in Lexington. With Mike as a teammate, we led the West to an easy 80-67 win. I was named MVP of the game after scoring 19 points and hauling down 17 rebounds.

A good friend of mine, Dick White, a Western Kentucky graduate and a former all-conference player for the Hilltoppers in the '50s, worked at the Fruit of the Loom plant in Campbellsville. The plant, which my oldest brother Willie helped build, opened in 1948. Up until the summer of 1963, however, no blacks had ever been employed there.

I broke Dick's heart when I decided to go to Louisville. We used to play ball together a lot and had talked for years about me going to Western Kentucky. That was my first choice all along, but I made a mistake.

Dick deserves a lot of credit for staying with me, for standing by me during a time of great racial tension. He's a great person who ended up driving my parents to Bowling Green for all of Western's home games during my career. He even took my Dad to some of the road games as well.

Anyway, Dick was the son-in-law of the boss at Fruit of the Loom. His wife, Patsy, was the daughter of Everett Moore, the president. Dick set it up for me to get a job at Fruit of the Loom and it was time for me to break down another barrier.

I became the first black to ever work at the Fruit of the Loom plant the summer before my freshman year in college. Don't get me wrong. It was by no means a glamorous job. But the key was that a black was actually working in the plant. Up to that point, Fruit of the Loom had been a great opportunity for the white community, but not the entire community.

I worked in the basement grading spools of yarn. We would separate the good spools from the bad spools, throwing the bad ones away. I did that for three summers in a row with a guy named Jargo, who became a dear friend of mine. He was killed in a car wreck in Florida years later.

Jargo was so quick with his hands. The production schedule called for us to grade about 50 spools per hour, but Jargo could do about 200 in an hour. I was not even close to as fast as he was. We had so many to do per day. Since he was so fast, we were able to work for an hour and then goof off for an hour.

We made minimum wage, which was between $1.25 and $1.75 an hour. But we had a lot of fun. We used to slip off during the day and go fishing in City Lake right in Campbellsville. No one complained because we had a certain amount of work to do each day and we always got it done. He loved to fish. In fact, he was on a fishing trip when he was killed.

I was not out in the plant, and as a result, I was kind of isolated from the rest of the workers. There were no incidents, no problems with me working there. Jargo and I would do our jobs and come and go each day. We were not involved in the shipping and receiving, or on the production line. Because of the job I did, no one really said anything about having a black work there.

To be honest with you, since Dick White hired me and he was the son-in-law of the boss, they couldn't say a whole lot. They probably knew that if they said something, they'd be gone.

It was so much fun to work with Jargo for three summers. I remember that we got a 20-minute break every morning at 10 o'clock. The Dairy Queen in town was only five minutes away and we'd go there every single day on our morning break. We'd usually get a milk shake and a hot dog. Often that 20-minute break would become 30 or 40 minutes before we'd get back to the plant.

Then at noon we had 30 minutes for lunch. Many times we'd go get a boat and fish for lunch. Like I said, Jargo loved to fish, just absolutely loved it. If the fish were really biting, we might not get back to work until one o'clock or one fifteen. When quitting time came at four o'clock, we used to get the boat out once again for some more fishing. That was really fun and I miss him. We got to be real good friends. Here's a guy that had only about a fourth or fifth grade education. He was married, had children and was just an average guy.

When I think about it, I had no life jacket on and to this day I can't swim. Jargo could swim, but I don't know if he would have been able to save me if I had fallen in. City Lake is a real deep lake.

I can't even count the number of times I was out there with no life preserver on.

When I go back home today and drive past that lake, I often look out and think how we used to go out in that little 16-foot boat with nothing but a paddle. If that boat had ever capsized, I would have been dead and gone. I had no fear as a young man; I never thought about death. The thought of drowning never crossed my mind.

I'm sure that some people said some things about Jargo for working with and hanging out with a black guy. But he never, ever treated me with anything but class. We had so much fun and did a lot of things together.

At that time, I didn't realize the significance of being the first black to work there. Four of my sisters have worked there and three still do. As I mentioned earlier, Lummie, Mable and Betty have worked there for several years. My brother-in-law, Jimmy Tucker, Mable's husband, works there now too. Sara also worked there for a few years, as did Paul and Yevette for a couple of summers.

Fruit of the Loom has not only been good to the Haskins family, but to Taylor County as a whole. The plant provides jobs for an estimated 3,000 people, both black and white, with an approximate monthly payroll of over $5 million. It's huge. People from seven or eight surrounding counties drive to the plant each day to work. Some probably have a commute of 50 or 60 miles each way. It's really unbelievable. It's the number-one industry in town. I wear Fruit of the Loom every day. That's the only underwear and T-shirts we buy in the Haskins house.

I headed to Bowling Green and Western Kentucky University in the fall of 1963. Dwight and I were not only roommates, but we quickly became the best of friends as well. He was a wonderful person, and because of what we went through as the first black players to ever play there, I think that the bond between us was that much stronger. We needed each other.

That issue aside, it was an adjustment in and of itself just to go to college. The classwork was so much tougher than high school. It required so much more studying than I had ever imagined. I was also on my own. Mother was no longer making me three meals a day. Dorm food didn't even compare to what she made for us at home.

On top of that, Yevette had gone to school at Kentucky State and we missed each other a lot. It's tough when you're used to seeing someone that you love and care so much about every day, and then all of a sudden she's 165 miles away. We used to write all the time and try to visit each other when we could.

It was hard for me, but a guy named Prince Fant deserves a pat on the back for helping me to get through some of the tough times. He worked as a cook at the university and became a very good friend of mine. He and his wife, Joanne, had me over for dinner at their house many times. That really meant a lot to me.

I used to go and visit Prince whenever he was working. No matter how busy he was, he always had time to listen to me. When Yevette would come to Bowling Green to visit, Prince and Joanne would provide her with a place to stay at their house. I want to thank them for opening their home to Yevette and me. We will be forever grateful for their kindness and generosity.

Back then it was an NCAA rule that freshmen were not allowed to play on the varsity team. It's not like today when freshmen can come in and play right away. In a lot of ways I think that it was the best thing for me that first year. It allowed me to get adjusted to school and the life of a college student.

I really enjoyed playing pool in my spare time and I became pretty good at it. My favorite game was bank. That's where the ball has to be banked in off the sides of the table before dropping into the pocket. Believe it or not, I actually won some tournaments in college.

Dwight, Pearl and I highlighted a very good freshman team in 1963-64. We worked hard together and became very close over the years. We played 16 ballgames that season against other freshman teams as well as junior college teams. I averaged 24.9 points and 14.9 rebounds per game. We were 14-2 that year, with our only losses coming against freshman teams from Tennessee Tech, 75-72, and Austin Peay, 84-71.

The freshman games were usually played right before the varsity games. Our games would start at around 5:30 and on most occasions we'd have 10,000 people watching us play. When the varsity would play after our game, there were usually about 5,000 fans there. The interest, the excitement, the anticipation that that group of freshmen brought to the campus was amazing. Obviously, a lot of fans were probably intrigued to come and watch two blacks, Dwight and I, play the game.

Dwight and I were kind of isolated. We lived in our own dormitory with the rest of the team and were with our teammates and coaches who accepted us with open arms. I did run into racism in my classes. I had professors who did not like me because I was black, and I felt that they penalized me grade-wise because of it.

I had one teacher, and I don't want to mention any names here, who was so prejudiced that she flunked me. That may be one of the reasons she lost her job. There was another professor who was going around bragging about the fact that he had all these basketball players in his class and that he was going to flunk us all. It was a prejudiced statement because he wasn't talking about the whole group, but about Dwight and me. A lot of that went on with professors back then.

I also had some outstanding professors who had a profound impact on my life. I used to visit with Dr. John Scarborough, the dean of the education department, at least once a week. After class we'd talk about school, basketball, you name it. He was an ex-coach who taught me a lot about life and helped mold me both as a student and as a man. He used to always tell me, "Clem, there is no free ice cream." That's a slogan that I still use today. In fact, I have a sign with that slogan on it hanging in my office today.

Dr. Tate Page, another ex-coach who was a dean at Western, and Dr. Norm Deeb, a professor in the education department, were also very influential. I wasn't a great student, but I worked my butt off in college. I never missed a class and I asked a lot of questions of them. They always had time for me and they helped me so much as a student.

I have so much respect for them as educators because they took the time to talk with young people, regardless of who they were. That's something I really feel is lacking in our school system today.

Dwight and I really didn't have a lot of problems on campus with people protesting against us being there or threatening us. We would hear it at games, though. It was especially bad, terrible really, when we played on the road. The Western Kentucky fans always treated us with respect. Sports have a way of bringing out the best and the worst in people.

People love a winner. It's as simple as that. It's always been like that in sports. People don't give a damn if you're black, you're poor, you're rich, you're white, you're purple. As long as you can field a winning program and put an exciting team on the field or the court, people will support it.

With all the prejudice that was going on at that time, a team with two blacks on it was still filling up the arena every single night. Why was that? Because they all wanted to see a winner. For the four years that Dwight and I were there, and the next four years that Jim McDaniels was there when they also had some great teams, you could not get a ticket to a game at Western. We sold the place out. It was the toughest ticket in town.

Let me set the record straight, though. For a lot of people, the cheers for Clem Haskins were all on the basketball court. It did not happen in the community, when I walked downtown, went into a clothing store, or whatever. I still couldn't eat in most restaurants in town. So it was false hope. They supported me on the basketball court, but they didn't want me eating at the same restaurants or going to the same movies as their sons or daughters. When I was on the basketball court, everything was OK until the game was over.

Tom Payne became the first black ever recruited to play basketball at the University of Kentucky in 1969. A lot of people don't realize it, but the year after Dwight and I went to Western, Rupp offered Wes Unseld a scholarship to attend Kentucky, but he turned it down and went to Louisville instead. Butch Beard also turned down Rupp's offer the next year and joined Unseld at Louisville.

There's no doubt about it that Dwight and I helped pave the way for that to happen. A few years after Dwight and I went to Western, Vanderbilt was also integrated. Western Kentucky University was the leader in the South in integration.

The success Dwight and I had as basketball players, and probably more importantly the way that we handled ourselves in the classroom, on campus and in the community, helped pave the way for other blacks in the South. I think that all the barriers I broke starting way back in high school, had a dramatic impact on helping to integrate the state of Kentucky.

CLEM THE GEM

CHAPTER TEN

I was itching to play for "real" by the time my sophomore season rolled around. We had a great freshman team, but now it was time to see what we could do against the big boys.

Coach Diddle decided to retire as coach prior to the season and he was replaced by former Tennessee Tech coach John Oldham, who was an All-America player at Western in 1949. I was disappointed at first because I can't tell you how much I wanted to have the opportunity to play for Coach Diddle. He coached from 1922-64, an amazing 42 seasons in all. He coached 1,062 Hilltopper games, won 759 of them and captured numerous championships along the way.

Coach Diddle, who passed away in 1970 at the age of 74, was and still is a legend at Western. His 759 career victories still ranked fourth on the all-time college basketball's winningest coaches list after the 1996-97 season, behind only Dean Smith, Rupp and Henry Iba.

One of Western's great traditions started with Coach Diddle. He always clutched a red towel on the sidelines during every game. He chewed on it, he waved it to get the fans going and he used it to signal to players on the court. You see a lot of coaches with towels on the sidelines nowadays, but he was the first to do it.

Fans at all Western sporting events still wave red towels today. In fact, my wife Yevette brought a bit of that tradition with us to Minnesota. You can always spot her behind our bench at Williams Arena waving a gold Play Hard! towel.

Even though Coach Diddle had retired, his presence was still felt. He still came to every practice and he and his wife lived right with us in the Diddle Dorm. That was the dorm on campus where the basketball players were housed. Coach Diddle was our alarm clock at exactly seven o'clock, and not a minute later, every single morning.

You know that Coach Oldham and the rest of the staff couldn't help but tap into his vast knowledge and understanding of the game. With the utmost respect, every one of us players still called him "Coach."

I'll always be thankful to Coach Diddle for giving me the opportunity to play basketball and go to school at Western Kentucky. He had not only the guts and courage, but also the foresight to recruit Dwight and me to break down the color barrier in the school's basketball program.

Dr. Kelly Thompson, the president of Western Kentucky at that time, also deserves a lot of recognition for helping to integrate not only the basketball program, but the entire campus as well. He befriended Dwight and me and welcomed us with open arms. He always encouraged us to hang in there and told us how happy he was to have us there.

Given the controversy surrounding us being there in the first place, it couldn't have been an easy thing for Dr. Thompson to do in his position. But he was man enough to stand up for what was right. I can't begin to tell you how much that meant to both Dwight and me.

We were a close-knit team, both on and off the floor and that really helped us to get through the tough times. We really cared for each other. Coach Oldham was a big key in helping that to happen. He was a guy with high morals, a very honest, wholesome person. He never lost his composure; if he did, I never saw it. The harshest words I ever remember him using were, "gosh dang."

He was the right fit to be our coach and to lead our team. We were a high profile group of young men. Dwight Smith, Pearl Hicks, Hamilton Watkins, Billy Warren, and I were very highly recruited out of high school. If they rated recruiting classes back then like they do today, we probably would have been one of the top classes in the country.

I also met a great guy named Steve Cunningham who I was fortunate enough to play two years with. A year ahead of Dwight and me, Steve was a big, solid guy who was a key player for us down low. We had a lot of good guys in the program who accepted Dwight and me. There might have been some resentment initially because we were good players and that took some playing time away from some other folks. But I think our ability spoke for itself and that made it much easier for the guys to accept us. We worked hard and were unselfish players.

We finished my sophomore season with an 18-9 overall record. We advanced to the second round of the National Invitation Tournament (NIT) at New York's Madison Square Garden where we lost to Army, and Dwight and I were named to the OVC all-conference team. I averaged 23.4 points and 10.9 rebounds per game and was named OVC Player of the Year.

A catchy nickname that I'm still called even today was created that season by Ed Givens, who was the sports information director at Western back then. Ed had been a teammate of my high school coach, Billy B. Smith, during his college days at Union University in Jackson, Tennessee. A great guy, Ed is now the sports information director at Middle Tennessee State.

It was during a time when nicknames that rhymed were popular. A couple of the more popular ones at that time were Earl "The Pearl" Monroe and Nate "The Skate" Archibald. Ed wanted to come up with something that the media and fans would remember to help promote me for All-America honors.

Ed came up with Clem "The Gem" Haskins and it stuck. It caught on right away and kind of mushroomed from there. I kind of liked it to tell you the truth. It made me feel good when people would yell it out. It's funny, because even today, I'll be in the airport somewhere or in a restaurant when we're on the road, and someone will still call me Clem "The Gem" after all these years.

It was ridiculous, but I could flat out shoot the basketball. I figured that anywhere from within 25 to 30 feet was in my range. I always felt that I was a threat to score once I got over the halfcourt line.

They talk so much about double-doubles nowadays. That's where a player hits double figures in two statistical categories in one game. Heck, a lot of people forget that I averaged not only 22.1 points per game during my college career, but also 10.6 rebounds per game as well. So I averaged a double-double every night.

I was as hot as a firecracker when we played Middle Tennessee on January 30, 1965. That game was one of those typical nights when you get hot. I could have kicked it in the basket that night. I hit 25 of 33 shots in the game. That's a lot of attempts, but that's a lot of makes too. Somebody figured out that if the three-pointer was part of the game at that time, I would have hit seven of ten three's and had 62 points in the game. I shot some from so far out that night that I swear they must have been from beyond 30 feet from the hoop.

The 55 points scored and 25 field goals made in one game are still Ohio Valley Conference and Western school records. The thing that I really like to talk about though was that I also had 11 rebounds and seven assists, and most importantly, we won the game, 134-84.

Playing in the NIT my sophomore year was one of the highlights of my college career. Back in those days, the NIT was a bigger tournament than the NCAA's, mainly because of the media exposure the event received because it was played in New York. Unlike today, where early round games are played at campus sites and then the semifinals and finals in New York, all the games back then were played in Madison Square Garden.

We beat Fordham, 57-53, in our first game in New York. They were the city champs so I think a lot of people were surprised that we won. They had a tremendous ballclub and, quite honestly, after we beat them we expected to go on and win the whole thing. We figured as much since we had just defeated the best team in the East at that time.

We played Army in the next round and they had a big guy named Mike Silliman from Kentucky. So he was fired up to play Western Kentucky. He was a big guy, about six-foot-six and 230 pounds, but he seemed closer to a rock-solid 270 or 280 pounds. He was wider than John Thomas and Courtney James from our 1997 Final Four team combined. He was really put together and quite a player. Army wound up beating us, 58-54 in a great game. That was really a hard-fought game from start to finish.

That was a great experience for me to go to New York City for the first time in my life. I will never forget when we got off the bus and looked up at the tall buildings. You've got to understand, we were a bunch of hillbillies, a bunch of country boys. We almost got our tonsils tanned by the sun from looking up so long with our mouths wide open. That was unbelievable and so much fun.

I remember hearing about how many killings there were on the New York City subways that year. I don't remember an exact number, but I think there were like 50 or 60 unsolved murders that happened in the subways. It was really scary and we were told to not ride the subways.

So what did we do? Of course, we all went out and bought

ourselves a knife. There were 10 of us on the trip and we were really going to be bad now. I remember Coach Oldham saying that whenever we went anyplace in the city to make sure we went as a team, to always go in groups of two, three, four or whatever. Never go out alone.

We all had our pocket knives and we thought we were really going to cut up New York City. It's funny looking back at it now, because when we were walking around, if anyone had said "boo" there would have been 10 guys who would have dropped their knives and run off because we were so scared.

It was a great experience and it's neat to think back at how much fun we had. We had the time of our lives. I remember the coaches asking us the first day if we wanted our meal money or should they set up a training table in the hotel for us. Right away all of us dumb guys wanted the money, we wanted the cash.

So the first day the coaches gave us two dollars for breakfast, three for lunch and five for dinner. Ten dollars for the whole day. We thought that was a lot of money. Talk about an education for young people. We took our ten dollars and right away headed across the street to a restaurant to eat. We all had something like two eggs, bacon, hash browns and orange juice.

Being a bunch of dummies, of course, we never bothered to check the prices. You should have seen our eyes when we got the check from the waitress. Since we had spent most of our money on the first meal we ate only one more time the rest of the day. We wound up going over to a deli where we bought some lunch meat and bread. We brought it back to our rooms and sat around and made bologna sandwiches.

Boy we were really living it up in New York! But in reality, it was a great education for us. We got together the next morning and told Coach Oldham that we didn't want meal money the rest of the time and that we wanted him to set up the training table right there in the hotel.

I also remember going to church on Sunday in New York and meeting Norman Vincent Peale, a world famous minister. We went to his church, met him and had our picture taken with him. He's written a lot of books. I got on his mailing list and I used to receive all his literature. That was one of the highlights of the trip.

Everything about New York was exciting. It was downright intimidating to be in a place that was so big. That was the first time any of us had ever been to a city that big, the first time we ever stayed in such a nice hotel, the first time we had ever rode on a subway, the first time in Madison Square Garden…there were a lot of firsts on that trip.

There was a photo from our second-round game against Army in Madison Square Garden that was on the cover of *Look* magazine. It won a bunch of awards for being the top sports photo in the country that year.

It had all five of our starters boxing out for the rebound and Dwight, a tremendous rebounder, up above the rim rebounding the ball. You could see the smoke hanging throughout the rafters of the arena, like a fog. Of course that was a different era and smoking was allowed in the arena. I remember guys sitting there watching the game while smoking these big, fat cigars. It was a fantastic, incredible photo.

There were several times that first season on the varsity where we ran into racism on the road. I remember in Tennessee once where, because of Dwight and me, the whole team had to move to a different hotel. We always stayed together though and that's a real credit to both my teammates and the whole coaching staff. In several places we knew that people were talking about us behind our backs as we checked into the hotel.

I've always thought that it was ironic that racism could find its ugly way into religion of all places. One of the things that Coach Oldham always talked to us about was going to church on Sundays. When we were on the road on Sundays, we always went to church together as a team. That's the kind of thing that I still try to do with my players today. It was good for me then and I believe that it's good for my players now.

I remember one Sunday when our whole team went to a church in Tennessee; I don't remember the city. A lot of the regular members of the church didn't show up because there were two black guys there. Of course, those two blacks were Dwight and me. From that point on, I realized that some people just aren't going to make it into the pearly gates of heaven, even if you go to church every week and put your money in the collection basket.

I've learned a lot of things in my life. The Lord doesn't care if you're black, white, yellow, purple or whatever. That experience showed me that even a church, a place where you're supposed to go to worship and give thanks to God, can be a place where prejudice exists. It showed me that prejudice can and does exist in virtually every aspect of our society.

GO BIG RED

CHAPTER ELEVEN

My sophomore season had only whetted my appetite for bigger and better things. The NIT experience had reaffirmed my feelings that I knew we had the chance to be a special team, one that could contend for the national championship the next two years.

But there were more important things to take care of first. One of the greatest days in my life was May 22, 1965. That's the day that Yevette and I were married in a small ceremony in Bowling Green. Dwight was my best man, and my sister Sara was the maid of honor. It ranks right alongside the birth of our three children as one of the most exciting and rewarding days in my life.

We lived in a little village that was reserved for married students our last two years at Western. They were old army barracks that they had converted into little apartments. The rent was $25 a month. My teammate Joe Mac Hill and his wife, Anne, lived right across the street from us. Joe Mac was a six-foot-two guard/forward for us. Yevette and I are still very close to them.

Our first child, a girl whom we named Clemette, was born on November 28, 1965. I had the demands of school and basketball, and Yevette was working as a secretary in Western's physical plant office, so Clemette stayed with my Mother and Dad in Campbellsville until after I graduated. Yevette only made $47 per week on the job, so there was no way we could afford a babysitter. It was tough, but we tried to get back home and be with her just as often as was humanly possible.

Coach Oldham was someone that always stood by me and encouraged me to hang in there. I remember when I went to tell him that I was going to get married.

He said to me, "Well I wish you wouldn't, but you won't be the first guy in college to get married or the last, so I give you all my best." Then he asked me, "Do you love her?" And I said "Yes." He thought for a second or two and said, "Then all I ask you to do is to be a good husband and a good father. Be honest and fair at all times."

Coach Oldham always gave me great advice. Sound advice that I still use today with my own family and players. He was not only my coach, but also one of my best friends and someone that I have the utmost respect for.

We opened the 1965-66 season with six straight wins, before falling 72-69 to Vanderbilt in our own tournament. We then reeled off seven more wins in a row in which our margin of victory was at least ten points or more in each game to run our record to 13-1 on the season. Then we were absolutely drubbed by Dayton, 77-57. I can't explain that one, except to say that maybe it was something that we needed heading into the homestretch of the season.

We were on a mission after that loss and we finished the regular season with 10 straight wins, most of them decisive. The only victory that was by less then double digits was a 72-67 win over Eastern Kentucky.

With a starting lineup of Dwight, Steve and me, along with Wayne Chapman and Greg Smith, a six-foot-five forward who was Dwight's younger brother, we had gone a perfect 14-0 to win the OVC championship. I was named OVC Player of the Year for the second straight season. We finished the regular season with a 23-2 overall record and were on a roll heading into postseason play.

We beat a very good Chicago Loyola ballclub, 105-86, in the first game of the NCAA's at Kent, Ohio. We were huge underdogs going into the game, but we played extremely well. The whole team did. Dwight scored 29 points and I had 25 as we shot 56 percent from the field for the game, including 62 percent in the second half alone. Greg not only had 19 points, but also ripped down 15 rebounds for us. We got back to Bowling Green that night, and let me tell you, that was what college sports are all about.

There were probably about 5,000 people waiting for us at the airport when our plane arrived, but it seemed more like 15,000 or even 20,000. There were so many people and they were so excited, that when we landed, they were actually physically charging the plane. They wouldn't let the plane taxi off the runway.

Many people who are heroes have the incredible ability to control crowds and control people out of sheer respect. Coach Diddle was one of those people. He was like a Martin Luther King, Jr. or a John F. Kennedy. They were all great men, people whom I really admire. We were trying to taxi off the runway for about 30 or 40 minutes, but the crowd just wouldn't allow it. They kept rushing toward the plane. It was complete chaos.

Finally, Coach Diddle took charge. From the bus, using his loud, thundering voice without the aid of a microphone or even a megaphone, he told the crowd that, "We're going to take this bus out there and get the boys, and you all stay right here."

When the bus pulled up to the plane, Coach Diddle got out and told the throng that had followed it on its path out to the plane "Goddamn it, get back, so we can get these boys back to the arena. You all follow us back to the arena." Everyone backed away, we got off the plane, boarded the bus and then the whole crowd followed us to the arena. He was 70 years old at the time, but he was still very much in control.

So we get back to the gym, and it was well after midnight by then, and the place was just packed. There was not an empty seat in the house and we celebrated for I betcha two hours at least. The crowd was just on fire. That was fantastic, a moment I know I'll never, ever forget.

We played Michigan and the great Cazzie Russell in the next round at Iowa City. We lost, 80-79, and it was the ripoff of all time. We outplayed Michigan the whole ballgame and had a 79-78 lead with 11 seconds to go when there was a jump ball. Greg was jumping against Cazzie, and of all things, they called a foul on the jump ball. A pushoff on Greg.

Cazzie hit both free throws, then I missed a last-second shot and we lost by one point. Our dream of a national championship had vanished into thin air just like that on a phantom call.

Greg had gotten the tap on the jump and we had the ball. He tapped it right to Steve Cunningham. We had the basketball and the game. That just wasn't right. It was a non-call. We should have just played on. For the official to so blatantly determine the outcome of a basketball game like that was just plain wrong. His name was Steve Honzo, a big-time referee from Philadelphia.

We looked at the films later that night and our worst nightmares were confirmed. Greg's arm was not on Cazzie's shoulder and holding him down as Honzo had said when he made the call.

In fact, his arm was about as far away from Cazzie's shoulder as it could get.

On the last shot, I drove down the right side and pulled up from about 12 to 14 feet and it was short. I had the chance to win it and missed it. But it never should have come down to that.

I remember that Steve had an exceptional game and Wayne really played well too. Steve led us with 24 points and Wayne, the father of former Kentucky star and current NBA player Rex Chapman, had 22. They were the keys to the game for us, along with a little five-foot-ten guard named Butch Kaufman who came off the bench and really played well.

Dwight, a tremendous guard who was probably the most valuable player on our team at the time, guarded Cazzie and did not play one of his best basketball games. In fact, he fouled out of the game after scoring only seven points. I had 15 points and 12 rebounds, but really didn't have a great game either. Dwight and I had mediocre to average performances, to be quite honest. In spite of that, we still had a chance to win the game.

It was like a morgue in the locker room after the game. We replayed the tape over and over again and you could see that it was a bad call. With all the media coverage today, the controversy wouldn't have died down so easily. Paul Just, the sports information director now at Western Kentucky, still has frame-by-frame photos of the jump ball in his office.

Cazzie and I both ended up playing in the NBA, but we really never talked about that game much. Every once in a while I reminded him about how the game ended. I'd rib him about how fortunate they were to win it. But you can't blame the players for that. It was the referee who made the call.

I think we also felt a lot of pressure to win the game because we knew that if we beat Michigan, we would have played Kentucky in the next game. One of the things that the three blacks on our team—Dwight, Greg and I—lived and dreamed about was the opportunity to play Kentucky. When Dwight and I graduated from high school, they wouldn't recruit or accept blacks at their school.

I think we overlooked Michigan somewhat by looking ahead to a matchup with Kentucky. That probably got us beat more than anything. The Wildcats had Pat Riley, who has gone on to a wonderful coaching career in the NBA, Larry Conley and Louie Dampier in their lineup, among others. It was our lifetime dream to get the chance to play against Kentucky and beat them.

Kentucky beat Michigan to advance to the Final Four where they lost in the championship game to Texas Western. Texas Western, now called UTEP, made history by starting five blacks en route to the title.

At that time, in the NCAA regionals you played a consolation game. Despite the heartbreaking loss to Michigan, we showed a lot of character and class by coming back to beat Dayton, 82-68, in our final game to finish 25-3 on the season. That win also avenged our 20-point loss to the Flyers earlier in the season.

With four of five starters returning for my senior season in 1966-67, we knew that we could make another run at the national title. Steve had graduated, and those were big shoes for us to fill, but Butch moved into the starting lineup and did a great job for us.

After a very good high school career at Taylor County, my brother Paul was a freshman at Western Kentucky when I was a senior. The toughest thing for a younger brother to do is to follow in an older brother's footsteps, especially if that older brother has been very successful. There are too many comparisons between the two.

It was the best thing for my youngest brother Merion to go to Kentucky and I know that it was extremely hard for Paul to play at Western Kentucky. It was tough to follow me at Western because I set such a standard that it was tough for anyone to top.

Paul was a role player in college, but the expectations placed upon him were just too great. It would have been the same for Merion if he had decided to go there. I'm not really in love with the University of Kentucky, but he definitely made the right decision because there was no way he could ever have lived up to the standards I had set.

They were good players in their own right. Paul, a letterwinner at Western in 1968, 1969, and 1970, played extremely well for the Hilltoppers as a sixth, seventh or eighth man off the bench for most of his career. Merion was the same type of player for Kentucky.

I can't tell you how great it was to have Paul at Western for my last season. But at the same time, I know that it was a trying experience for him to play there.

We opened the 1966-67 season with a disappointing 76-70 loss to Vanderbilt. We were shocked. But once again I think the setback may have been the best thing for us, even though we lost

Dwight for a couple of games with an ankle injury. There had been so much optimism and speculation about our chances to win it all going into the season, but the defeat brought us back down to earth in a hurry.

A dose of reality then set in, we got down to business and proceeded to win 16 games in a row heading into a game with Murray State on February 6 at Diddle Arena. That's the game when I fell to the floor and broke the navicular bone in my right wrist, which is my shooting hand.

When it happened, the first person to my side was Dwight. He picked me up off the floor. I realized something was seriously wrong, but up until that time I had never been hurt before. It would be incorrect for me to say that I knew immediately I had broken my wrist. It was extremely painful, but at the time I thought I had just sprained it badly and that I would be OK.

I remember how quiet the crowd was. They were concerned because I was never a guy who would stay down. If I got knocked to the floor, I would always hop back up right away. But this time they could tell that something was seriously wrong. It was kind of like the break heard all around Bowling Green, Kentucky.

Everyone knew that it was something that would affect our whole season, our ability to compete for the national title. I was averaging about 27 points and 10 rebounds per game at the time. You just don't replace that.

After going to the sidelines, I did go back into the game. We won the game 88-79 in overtime and I scored seven big points in the overtime playing with a broken wrist.

After the game I went into the shower, and when the hot water hit the wrist, it was like it just blew up. Within 10 minutes after I got through with my shower my arm was swollen all the way from my fingertips up to my elbow. Then I couldn't even bend my wrist.

That's when I realized for the first time that I had really seriously hurt something. The x-rays later that night didn't show a fracture, but I was told that it would take a week or two for the swelling to go down before they'd be able to tell for sure whether it was broken.

Then I went down to Nashville to see Dr. Pinky Lipscomb. He was the Vanderbilt University team doctor. A lot of the teams went to him back then because he was really ahead of his time in dealing with various fractures, operations and so on. He had treated Pearl who had suffered a similar injury. Dr. Lipscomb was very highly respected. He diagnosed the fracture and casted it up.

It was obviously a big blow to us as a team and to the whole community. But it was also a major setback for me personally because it was my senior year and I had worked so hard for us to get into the position to be able to compete for the national title. I thought we had a great shot at winning the whole thing.

When I broke the bone, we had only lost one game. I never thought about individual goals, about becoming the first player in history to be named MVP of the league three straight years which eventually happened anyway.

I wasn't interested in any of the personal honors. We had set so many goals as a team and were on the right track when I suffered the injury. My main concern was to try to get myself physically and mentally ready for postseason play. I was upset that it happened, but I had to try to put that out of mind and get ready for the NCAA Tournament.

Soon after I suffered the injury, I received a letter from Kentucky's great player Pat Riley, who I had read about in the newspaper, but had never played against or even met. I still have that letter today. It reads:

Clem:
Although we have never really met on or off the court, but came mighty close last year at Iowa City (when you got rooked by Michigan), the reason I am writing this letter is because I want to tell you I am sorry that you had the misfortune of an injury when you were playing at your greatest.

Clem, only a player of outstanding ability such as yours can really know what disappointment is, especially at a time like this. Believe me, I know what it is like and sympathize with how you must feel. With you having a great year personally and your team heading straight for the NCAA Tournament, it really is a bad thing for you, your team and Coach Oldham.

Seeing that UK is not going anywhere this year, believe me I would rather see Western come out of Kentucky because you all deserve it, especially you.

So again, Clem, I am sorry it had to happen to you at the height of your varsity career when you are having such a great one. Hope you can still play like they say because even a left-handed "Gem" is better than none.

Pat Riley

I was surprised to get the letter from him and it shows how much class he has always had as a person. That gave me a tremendous boost on the road to trying to get back on the floor before the start of postseason play.

Coach Oldham was always like a father to me. I absolutely loved pecan pie and it's still my favorite today. Back then people around Bowling Green used to make pecan pies and send them to me. Well I started gaining a little weight from eating all these pies and it especially wasn't good when I broke the wrist. Coach wanted to make sure that when I got back into the lineup, I was in shape and ready to go.

When we went down to Nashville every Wednesday to see Dr. Lipscomb, we used to go to a place called Morrison's Cafeteria. They had great pecan pie and, of course, that's what I always ordered. We got back one night after a trip to Nashville, he dropped me off and then for some reason he decided to circle around and come back to our place.

Coach walks into our place, opens the refrigerator and sure enough sees a whole pecan pie in there. He grabbed it and on his way out said, "You don't need anymore pie, you're gaining too much weight." So he stole my pecan pie, took it home and ate it himself. That wasn't the last time either. He was the guy responsible for either stealing or hiding all my pecan pies!

Mike Fawcett, a 5-10 junior guard, was the guy who replaced me in the starting lineup after I broke the wrist. He was one of those guys who broke a few curfews and messed around a little bit back then. I used to keep him out of trouble, stayed after him a lot.

I could get on guys and they wouldn't get offended by it because they respected me both as a player and as a person. They respected me enough to straighten up and do what's right. Now Mike had to really step forward for us.

That was tough to sit and watch from the sidelines, especially when you're watching your college career ticking down to its end. The guys did a great job of pulling together to win four of our next five games.

In fact, after beating Murray State for our 17th consecutive win in the game in which I broke my wrist, they won four more in a row to set a new OVC record with 21 straight wins.

Mike, who had scored a total of 36 points all of the previous season, registered 38 points in those four games alone. Butch turned it up a notch too, averaging 17.5 points per game in those four wins. Dwight and Greg were sensational too. In the four games the Smith brothers combined to score 136 points and grab 116 rebounds.

The final game of that winning streak was a 71-62 win at Eastern Kentucky that sealed our second straight OVC championship. When we returned home, an estimated 5,000 fans greeted us at about 1 a.m. at Diddle Arena to celebrate the title. I didn't play in the game, but it was an accomplishment that I was every bit as proud to be a part of.

After missing five games, I returned to the lineup with my right wrist heavily bandaged and had 16 points, eight rebounds and six assists in a 116-76 win at Austin Peay. In fact, I took the opening tip from Greg, drove down the floor and scored the game's first basket just three seconds into the game. Dwight and Wayne led the way for us with 27 points apiece in the game.

Then I played in the regular season finale against Middle Tennessee. It was an emotional night for us seniors to play our final home game in Diddle Arena. But I think "Senior Night" had an even greater significance for Dwight and me. We had been through so much together the past four years and had become the very best of friends through a lot of adversity. It was satisfying to know that we had blazed a trail for other blacks, not only at Western, but also throughout the South.

We beat Middle Tennessee, 55-46, to end the regular season ranked third in the nation with a 23-2 overall record. I scored only five points in the game, all from the free throw line. I missed all seven of my shots from the field in the game. It marked the first time in my career that I didn't make a field goal in a game.

In reality, I was about a third of the player that I was before the injury. I had to shoot and handle the ball predominantly with my left hand. Later on in my pro career I really think it helped me become a more complete player because I was able to shoot and handle the ball that much more effectively with either hand.

Our dreams of a national title vanished in a hurry when Dayton beat us, 69-67, in overtime in the first round of the NCAA Tournament at the Coliseum in Lexington, Kentucky. We led 35-25 at the half, but just couldn't put the game away. Dayton, paced by Don May's 26 points and 20 rebounds, actually had two chances to win it in regulation before the buzzer sounded.

After I had tied the game up at 67-67 on a driving layup with 31 seconds left in the overtime, a guy named Bob Hooper hit a 20-

footer with three seconds remaining to win the game for Dayton. Dwight led us in scoring with 18 points, Butch had 17 and Wayne added 12. It was a frustrating end to my college career. I made just three-of-fourteen field goal attempts in the game.

Dayton ended up going all the way to the finals where they lost to UCLA. So you can imagine what kind of team we had that year when we lost to Dayton with me basically playing left-handed.

I truly believe that if I hadn't broken my wrist, we would have won the national championship. We were the only team in the country that could have beaten UCLA that year. UCLA at that time had Lew Alcindor (now Kareem Abdul-Jabbar), Lucius Allen, Lynn Shackelford and Mike Warren.

If anybody in the country could have beaten UCLA it was us, because we could shoot the jumper. You couldn't drive on those guys. If you tried, Lew Alcindor had a field day blocking shots. But we had a bunch of guys who could stick it from anywhere on the floor and that's what you needed to do in order to beat them.

To this day, I honestly believe that we would have won two national championships if we hadn't gotten screwed against Michigan in 1966 and if I hadn't broken my wrist in 1967. But that's the way it goes.

It was tough to see my college career come to an end. I was a consensus All-America selection as senior after being named to a number of All-America teams in each of my three seasons at Western. Lew Alcindor, Elvin Hayes of Houston, Wes Unseld of Louisville and Jimmy Walker of Providence were the other first team Associated Press All-America team selections.

I remember getting a congratulatory telegram from Kentucky Governor Edward T. Breathitt. That really felt good, especially knowing what I had gone through both on and off the court as a black man growing up in a very prejudicial state. The first paragraph of the telegram reads: *"Your selection as an All-American does honor to you, your university and the Commonwealth of Kentucky."*

In addition to the All-America honors, I still am the only player to ever be named OVC most valuable player three consecutive seasons. My 1,680 career points ranks second on the school's all-time three-year list. In three seasons we chalked up an impressive 66-15 overall record, including a 48-6 mark the last two seasons alone. Throw in our 14-2 record on the freshman team and that's an 80-17 record over four seasons. Not too shabby.

On September 13, 1991, I received a big honor when I was an inaugural inductee into the Western Kentucky Hall of Fame. That was a year after being inducted into the Kentucky Athletic Hall of Fame where I joined an elite membership that includes Muhammad Ali, Adolph Rupp and Paul Hornung among others.

But more important than statistics and honors, we had a tremendous amount of closeness and unity on the teams that I was fortunate enough to be a part of at Western. We were real close both on and off the court.

Coach Oldham, and his assistants Gene Rhodes and coach Buck Sydnor, were a good staff for that group of young men. They did a fine job of molding us together as a unit.

The guys on the team accepted Dwight and me under trying circumstances and that's a real credit to them. The two main reasons were because of the way we carried ourselves and the way we blended in. I became real close to Dwight, his brother Greg, Pearl Hicks, Billy Warren, Wayne Chapman, Norm Weaver, Mike Fawcett, Butch Kaufman, Joe Mac Hill and Steve Cunningham …there are just so many guys from my days at Western that I'm still close to even today. That's what make sports, especially a team sport like basketball, so special.

We had a great team. To give you an indication of just how good we were, I was a first-round draft pick who went on to play nine years in the NBA, Greg was a great rebounder in the NBA with the Milwaukee Bucks and Wayne, who ended up coaching Kentucky Wesleyan to NCAA Division II titles in 1987 and 1990, had a long career in the American Basketball Association (ABA).

Quite honestly, Dwight, who was a first-round pick of the Los Angeles Lakers, may have been the best pro out of all of us if he hadn't been killed in a car wreck shortly after our senior year.

I'll never forget that day: May 14, 1967. His sister, Kay, was also fatally injured in the crash and Greg was driving the car. Kay was a freshman majoring in sociology at Western. Dwight had just been drafted by the Lakers. They were coming back to campus after spending Mother's Day with their parents in Princeton.

I was on a trip to Hazard, in eastern Kentucky. On the way back to Bowling Green I heard the news report about the accident on WAKY, a Louisville radio station. Tears filled my eyes. I was in shock and had a hard time driving my car.

It happened on U.S. 41A, 10 miles south of Madisonville, Kentucky. The coroner said that the car hit some high water and overturned in a ditch containing several feet of water. Greg managed to escape from the car after it went into the ditch. It was presumed that Dwight and Kay drowned. It was estimated that more than 3,000 people attended the double funeral on May 18 at the Caldwell County gymnasium in Princeton.

I still get choked up just thinking about it. Dwight was a great person, a great friend, and I still miss him dearly. That was an emotional time for all of us. But we came together as a team—coaches, players and staff—and helped each other through a very difficult time. I think of Dwight often and the impact he made on my life in four short years at Western.

THE NEXT LEVEL

CHAPTER TWELVE

I experienced the same type of feelings and emotions after my last college game when we lost to Dayton in the NCAA Tournament, as I had four years earlier after the high school state tournament loss to Lexington Dunbar.

The last time I took my jersey off in high school I cried like a baby. I didn't want to take it off. I was in the locker room at Freedom Hall in Louisville, Kentucky, for an hour or two after the game. Coach Smith and Coach Waddle had to come and get me. I thought my whole career was over.

I was a high school All-American and I didn't know if I was good enough to play at the next level. I almost passed out in the locker room in Louisville that night because I thought that might be my last game.

I felt lost. I felt alone. I felt empty. I kept asking myself, "Boy, I love this game. Is this the last game I'm ever going to play?" That was in high school.

After we lost to Dayton in overtime in my last college game I felt empty again. Was pro basketball in my thoughts? You have to remember that at that time there were only 12 teams in the league so there weren't a lot of jobs to be had.

I didn't know if I was good enough. Dwight and I used to talk about pro basketball from time to time. There weren't as many nationally-televised games back then, so we didn't get the chance to see a game every week. It's not like today.

When a game was on television, it was usually the Boston Celtics against the New York Knicks, or you might see the Philadelphia 76ers. We had the opportunity to see a game a couple of times a year. I had never seen a game in person though.

Dwight and I used to talk to each other about someday just getting drafted and being able to go to camp. Then later on in life we'd be able to tell our sons or daughters we got drafted and went to training camp. That's the honest to God's truth. That's all we ever talked about.

We didn't talk about actually *making* the team, but just about the experience of getting drafted and having the opportunity to go to training camp and maybe play in a few exhibition games. To be able to play with or against Bill Russell, Wilt Chamberlain, Jerry West, Elgin Baylor, Oscar Robertson, Bob Cousy, K.C. Jones, all the household names that we had heard about.

It wasn't like today. I never dreamed about being a professional basketball player. The kids today all assume that they're going to play in the NBA. That was never, ever my number one priority. I wanted to play in the pros, but in my heart I wasn't sure if I was good enough to make it. So I can't sit here and say that I always dreamt about playing in the NBA.

That's why I get so irritated with young players today. In their minds they're already driving a Rolls Royce or a Cadillac, and wearing $500 shoes and a $1,000 suit. They just assume they're going to be a pro and the agents they deal with build them up so much that they don't know the difference.

Coming out of high school I didn't know if I was good enough to play in college, much less become an All-American. Then after college I didn't know if I was good enough to play in the NBA. That's why I never lost sight of what was really important in college. I was by no means a straight-A student, but I worked hard at it and I can't tell you how proud I was to receive my bachelor's degree in 1967 and then my master's in 1971 from Western.

The summer after my senior year at Western, I was working in the field at home with my dad, my brother Paul and John Parker, a neighbor of ours, when I heard that the Bulls had drafted me. To tell you the truth, I didn't even know that the draft was being held that day. The draft back then was no big deal like it is today. Don't get me wrong, I was really excited about being drafted.

I went and called Coach Oldham at Western and he said that the Bulls had indeed drafted me with the third pick in the first round and that I needed to call them right away. Jimmy Walker from Providence was the first pick. He went to the Detroit Pistons. Earl "The Pearl" Monroe from Winston-Salem State was the second pick. He went to the Baltimore Bullets.

Walt Frazier of Southern Illinois went to the New York Knicks with the fifth pick of the first round and Pat Riley was taken by San Diego with the seventh overall pick.

I was also the Kentucky Colonels' top pick in the American Basketball Association's inaugural draft. The ABA was beginning its first season in the fall of 1967. The league was just getting going and they were pretty disorganized at the time. They had no general managers in place, no one who was really in charge.

So Coach Oldham gave me the phone number and I called the Bulls. They congratulated me and told me how happy they were to have me and all the usual stuff like that. Jerry Colangelo was the man responsible for drafting me for the Chicago Bulls. He was the team's director of scouting at the time. After my senior season in 1967, I remember seeing him at the Final Four at Freedom Hall. I had no idea who he was.

I was walking into the arena and this guy approached me. It was Jerry. He asked me, "Are you Clem Haskins?" and I said, "Yes." Then he said, "Would you like to play pro basketball?" and I said, "Oh I'd love to play pro basketball. All I want is for someone to give me the opportunity to play. If someone gives me the opportunity, I think I can make their ballclub and make them very proud."

I think that my attitude really impressed him. I wasn't some cocky kid who thought he was going to come in and turn the league on its ear right away. He knew that I truly did love the game above all else.

You have to understand that my hand was still in a cast when they drafted me. I wore a cast from February until the first week of August. The cast came off about three weeks before the start of my first training camp with the Bulls.

My agent, Bob Pierce, was the brother-in-law of Dr. Kelly Thompson, the president of Western Kentucky University. Bob was an attorney in Bowling Green.

Bob did it for free. As I said earlier, one of my favorite sayings is, "There's no free ice cream." If something is free, or it sounds too good to be true, you better check it out, because it probably is. He had no experience and it probably cost me some money.

That summer Bob and I went to Chicago together to sign my contract. The Kentucky franchise in the new ABA never really entered into the picture. Of course, we probably could have used it for leverage if I had had an experienced agent. This was before the real bidding wars between the two leagues heated up though.

Dick Kline was the general manager and owner of the Bulls at the time. He basically explained to Bob that their offer to me was about what everyone else was making and that it was a good contract. Bob had no experience whatsoever in dealing with contracts of this nature. I didn't know beans.

I signed a three-year contract that called for me to make $12,500 the first season, $17,000 the second and $23,000 the third year. I also received $1,000 in bonus money in each of those three seasons for a total in bonuses of $3,000.

Right after I signed the contract I thought I was the richest guy in the world. I hardly had a dime in my pocket and all of a sudden I was holding a $1,000 check. That was quite a bit of money back then, especially for me. I felt good. I was happy to be able to sign a contract for that much money.

The first thing I did was give my Mother and Dad quite a bit of the money. How much I don't recall. I helped pay for their farm. That's what I did with a good portion of my money those first three years, to help get them out of debt. I also bought Yevette and myself some new furniture and a new car. Clemette was two years old when we went to Chicago for my first NBA season.

I also got involved in a business venture back in Bowling Green with a guy named Bennie Jaggers. It was a men's clothing store called "The All-American Shop." The store's slogan was, "You don't have to be an All-American to dress like one." Let's just say that my involvement in the business was short-lived.

Needless to say, I didn't keep Bob as my agent. He worked with me on that first contract and that was it. I didn't really know him that well. Coach Oldham and President Thompson both knew that I needed someone, so they put it together to have Bob represent me.

I never had any kind of relationship with Bob, but I needed an agent and I didn't know anybody. In the same situation today, as the third pick overall in the draft, I would have had any number of agents looking to have me as a client.

That's both good and bad. Some agents today are very good and do look out for the best interests of their clients. Still others are nothing more than bloodsuckers looking to make a quick buck. They fill the ears of these young kids with grandiose thoughts of millions of dollars, jewelry and fast cars. It really makes it tough on today's college players to try to figure it all out.

I was a few years ahead of the big dollars. You can't help but think about the type of money these young kids make today. Before the present salary cap was put into place, the third pick in the draft four or five years ago could expect to sign a deal in the $40 to $50 million range for a five or six-year contract.

It's kind of tough to swallow because I could kick in more jump shots than most of these kids can shoot in today. It's just amazing what these players are making and most of them can't shoot a lick. Most of them are more worried about dunking the ball.

But times have changed and I know that I have to try to understand that. The game has changed and so have the players. I was just a little bit ahead of the times. But I thoroughly enjoyed my time when I played.

Financially, today's players should be set for life. Unfortunately, that's not always the case. Some of them waste their money, spend it foolishly and walk away from the game with very little left. That's sad to say when they make millions of dollars nowadays and they're not financially secure when their careers are over.

I don't understand that. But I'm disturbed and concerned about the future of the game. More and more young kids want to skip college altogether and go right into the pros to make the big money. The pressure starts with the parents, the coaches and the agents. The NBA is going to keep taking the players. They don't want to help the college game. They want to help themselves.

So I really think we have some serious problems to take a look at with the young guys jumping straight from high school to the pros. Although I don't think it'll ever happen, I'd like to see some restrictions to prevent that from taking place.

I think that they should have to stay in college for at least two years. There should also be an age limit of 20 or 21 years of age before you can make the jump to the pros. I don't want to deprive anyone of an opportunity, but I think it'll give some of these young guys the chance to grow and mature both physically and mentally. They need to know how to deal with the money, the drugs, and the women. It would give them a couple more years to grow up in college. That's just Clem Haskins' philosophy.

Once again, it gets down to the agents as one of the major problems. Don't get me wrong, they're not all bad. But many of them are not concerned about the best interests of the player, but rather their own interests; to make as much money for themselves as they can. They may say they want to help them, but they're out to sign the guys to contracts so that they can grease their palms as much as possible.

NBA rookie contracts are pretty standard today. It's all pretty much locked in with the salary cap depending upon when you get drafted. That's why I would never advise my players to ever pay an agent to negotiate their first contract. Anybody can do it. It's pretty much carved in stone. I can give them the figures. I wish the kids coming out today would understand that and stop giving their money away.

But the thing that they do need agents for is to help with endorsement opportunities and how to deal with their money. They need some help with how to invest their money properly. A good accountant or investment firm can help with that as well. The toughest thing is to find someone they can trust, because they'll certainly have lots of "friends".

A lot of times people have these great get-rich-quick investment opportunities. My first question to them is always, "If it's such a great investment opportunity, how much of your own money do you have invested?" Basically what I'm saying is don't expect me to put my money into the deal if you don't have any of your own in it already.

Basically, they're trying to get rich with my money. That's where young people make some terrible mistakes. I've seen guys get robbed and taken to the cleaners financially to the point where they're broke because some agents who are supposedly so smart have gotten them into some real bad investments.

I played with a number of guys who walked away from the game with nothing. It's sad. The money that I made from the game I made sure I invested myself with a lot of research and care.

I signed only three contracts during my pro career. Herb Rudoy from Chicago, who is still an agent today, negotiated my second contract. I received advice from Larry Fleisher, who later became head of the players' association, on my third and final contract.

The first two were three-year contracts and the last one was a four-year deal. I had only fulfilled three of the four years on the last one. Physically my body was shot after nine years in the league and I knew it was the end of the line for me.

As I said, I only had my cast off for about three weeks when I went to my first training camp in Chicago in the fall of 1967. Was I nervous going into it? You bet I was. Other than what I had read and heard about, and seen a couple of times on TV, I didn't know much about these guys and what I was going to be up against.

I've never really been afraid of a challenge. I never doubted my ability once I stepped on the court. All I wanted was the opportunity. I had worked long and hard enough to prepare myself to make my shots, to make the plays. I was mentally tough enough to compete. You couldn't intimidate me.

That's what I try to instill in my players today. When I look back, I had all of the ingredients to make it. I was tough-minded and I worked harder than anyone else. I had no fear out on the court. I had the mental toughness to compete and not back down from anybody no matter how big or strong they were.

I had a lot going for me, more than I probably realized at the time. On the second or third day of training camp, I got into my first fight. Guy Rogers, a veteran player who was a great guard, called me a "damn rookie." It's kind of ironic, but after the Bulls' management saw what I could do, they ended up trading Guy.

Anyway, I hated the word rookie because back when I played it was a putdown when someone called you that. It's not like that today. Back then some of the veterans made you feel like you didn't deserve to be there. You had to carry the equipment bags and take all the crap. I didn't like doing all that stuff, but out of respect for my teammates, I did it anyway. I didn't have any problem doing it for certain guys, but some others rubbed it in.

But after that day when I didn't back down from Guy, I think they realized that they had their hands full. They knew that I wasn't going to back down from anybody. It wasn't real smart on my part because I didn't really know how to fight. But they knew that I would compete. It really wasn't much of a fight. The rest of the guys broke it up pretty quickly. But I got instant respect from my teammates.

That's what I try to tell my players today. A lot of times it's not who won or lost the game, it's about whether or not you competed. Don't get me wrong. I'm certainly not advocating fighting on the basketball court in any way, shape or form. That's not how you get respect. When things get tough on the court, however, you can't tuck your tail and run. It's not all about winning, but whether or not you competed. I mean really competed with everything you have. That's so important.

I never carried myself with a chip on my shoulder. I was very humble and I think that's another difference from many of today's players. Jerry Sloan, now the very successful coach of the Utah Jazz, was in his second year with the Bulls in 1967-68. We roomed together on the road my first year and he's someone whom I have the utmost respect for.

When I came into the league I was what you would call a "Greenhorn." I had no idea how to play defense. I was a great college player, but I didn't know anything about how to get over a pick on defense. Those were things that we never went over in college. We had such great teams at Western that we just simply overpowered people.

You see, in pro basketball you never broke things down. It was a different deal altogether from college ball because there's a lot of one-on-one situations. There's a 24-second clock and you can't play any zone defenses. The shell drill, the four-on-four and two-on-two drills; we didn't do those things my first year in the pros. So everything we learned we did on our own.

Jerry really helped me a lot. He used to talk to me, showed me how to set screens and how to get over picks. I watched him play defense and tried to pick up on his technique, his style, and apply it to my game. I got beat up a lot at first simply because I didn't know how to play defense, but his advice really helped me to become a better defensive player.

I remember one game that first year when we played Detroit and I had to guard the great Dave Bing, the leading scorer in the NBA at the time. I not only bottled him up on the defensive end of the floor, but I scored 16 points as well and we cruised to a big win.

Having Jerry as a roommate really helped me get through some tough times early in my career. That's the thing that I respect so much about him and that I will cherish for as long as I live.

My wrist was really weak and small when we first started camp. I still couldn't shoot the ball the way I wanted to. I had a rubber ball that I used to help get the strength back in my hand, wrist and forearm. I would squeeze it constantly and then rotate the wrist back and forth. It ached like a toothache.

It hurt bad, but it was mind over matter. I got myself mentally ready, but physically my wrist wasn't ready to play. Finally, we went and got it x-rayed and that showed that the fracture had never healed. They wanted to perform surgery, but I wanted to know what else they could do so that I could play.

The doctor told me that I'd have to play in pain all year if I didn't have the surgery. If I had the surgery, I would have been sidelined for the whole season. My first question was whether or not I could do any further damage to the wrist if I continued to play. Once I was assured that was not the case, I played my whole rookie year with a fractured right wrist.

The pain was so bad that I could hardly bear it. So every three or four weeks I would get a shot of novocaine into the wrist. It was a long needle, as big as a toothpick. Man was that painful. I can't even describe how bad it hurt. After they did it, I could hardly move the wrist for two days. Then it started getting flexible and the pain went away. But oh boy, 25 to 30 days later the pain would be back and we'd have to do it all over again.

I wanted to play. Looking back I'd say that it was the right thing to do. I didn't risk doing any further damage to the wrist, and if I hadn't done it, I might never have had the opportunity to play nine years in the NBA. Who knows what might have happened?

We were awful though, that first year. Especially at the beginning of the season when we lost our first nine games to open the year and 15 of our first 16 games overall. I took the losses real hard. I'd be crying in the locker room just like in high school and college after we lost.

I wanted to win, and at the same time, I wasn't playing a whole lot either. I also wasn't used to losing so much. In three years at Western, our combined record was 66-15, including 48-6 the last two seasons. So I lost more games in the first month or two of the season with the Bulls than I had over three years of college ball.

I remember in the middle of another nine-game losing streak when our coach, Johnny "Red" Kerr, came up to me in the Sheraton Hotel in Boston after we had just got whipped by the Celtics for our sixth straight defeat. He said, "Hey rook, you can't take these games so hard. Remember that we've still got a lot of games left to go. It's a long season and you can't be crying every time we lose. Who knows, we may not win another game."

Johnny was kidding of course, but I got the message loud and clear. We couldn't do anything about the games we had lost, but he was telling me we still had to get geared up for the rest of the games on our schedule. That you can't worry so much about what happened yesterday. You learn from your mistakes, but you have to start preparing for tomorrow.

I can laugh about it now, but that conversation really helped prepare me for the rest of my career. That's kind of how I looked at things after that. It kind of snapped me out of it. You have to go out and work your butt off every game and try to get yourself prepared to play both physically and mentally. But you can't control everything around you during the game. Just get yourself ready to play.

After that talk I just went out and did my best. If it was good enough to win, that was great. If not, it was over. I just tried to build upon the positive things and look ahead to the next game.

Then we turned things around and made a late run to make the playoffs even though we were only 29-53 overall for the season. We traded Guy for Flynn Robinson from Cincinnati and that made a difference. I started playing more at the end of the year as well. We lost to the Los Angeles Lakers four games to one in the first round of the playoffs.

Life in the NBA at that time was far from glamorous. Those were tough budgetary times for the league. I remember how disappointed I was with some of the conditions in training camp. We stayed at the Lawson YMCA in Chicago, which had adjoining rooms. That meant that two rooms and four people had to share a common bathroom. That's not easy for a bunch of big, tall basketball players.

Then our training camp practice site was about as bad as it could get. We worked out at the Settlemen House near DePaul University. It was an antiquated place that had the old wooden backboards. One goal was about nine feet, six inches high, the other was about ten feet, five inches tall. So one was too low and the other too high.

When we traveled, we flew commercial airlines and sat in coach. That's hard on the big guys. We didn't stay in the best hotels by any stretch of the imagination. Sometimes our flight time schedule would be determined upon whether or not management could save a day's per diem by waiting an hour or two later. The per diem that first year I was in the league was $8 per day.

I'd go on a 10-day road trip where our per diem was $80 per player and come back with $40 in my pocket. I was very conservative. I saved money. I wouldn't go out and eat at a steak house, but tried to be smart, and shopped around to save some money.

I learned how to do that through my teammate Bob Boozer. To this day, he's still the tightest guy I know. He's so tight that when he walks, he squeaks. He taught me how to save some money on the road. We're still great friends so I know I can give him a hard time.

In many ways, we were treated better in college. We had better facilities and better trainers in college. The first time the Bulls trainer, Joe Proski, tried to tape me, he almost cut my ankle off because the tape was so tight. So I started taping myself.

It's funny to think back to those times because 30 years later Joe is probably one of, if not the finest trainers in the league. He's with the Phoenix Suns now. He's a super guy. We joke about it now, but back in those days he couldn't tape a lick.

It was quite the experience that first year. There were only 12 teams in the league at that time. I remember how exciting it was to go into Los Angeles, New York, Detroit, and wherever we were going to play for the first time.

I'll never forget the first time I played in Los Angeles. This was before the Fabulous Forum was built; at that time the Lakers' home games were played in the Los Angeles Memorial Sports Arena. Much like today, a lot of movie stars would be at the games. To watch an actor like Tony Curtis or an actress like Jane Russell at the movies, and then see them at our game was incredible.

That was wild stuff for a little old boy from Kentucky. I was like, "Gee whiz, this is really something." I wasn't in the starting lineup at the time and I didn't mind it because I wanted to sit on the bench and watch all the stars.

I actually had one of my best games as a rookie in the Sports Arena against the Lakers. They were an outstanding team with players like Elgin Baylor, Jerry West, Gail Goodrich and Mel Counts to name just a few. We were down by about 20 points and I came off the bench to hit eight straight shots to bring us back. I ended up getting fouled with two seconds left in the game and the score was tied.

I go to the free throw line, and at that time in the NBA, it was three shots to make two. I shot the first one and it was short. Then the Lakers called a timeout. After the timeout, I went back out there and shot the second one too long. Then we called a timeout. Was my ass tight? Yes it was tight.

So then I went to our bench and our guys were saying, "Rook, just make the free throw," which is probably the worst thing they could have said to me at that time. Now I could really shoot the ball. Remember that I've already hit eight straight from the field in this game.

I went back out there for the third and final free throw attempt. All I was telling myself was that I shot the first one short and the second one long. So now let's put this one just over the front of the rim. Well, I shot it short again, Elgin rebounded it and called timeout with two seconds still left.

Nowadays we have the clocks with tenths of a second at every arena. When I was fouled there might have actually been closer to three seconds left. The Lakers got to take the ball out at halfcourt after the timeout. I'll never forget what happened next as long as I live.

During the timeout the Lakers had set up a play where Mel Counts would break from underneath the basket off a set of picks and take the inbounds pass. Mel, by the way, would end up being a teammate of mine a few years later in Phoenix. The ball was thrown inbounds toward Mel, and for some reason Reggie Harding, our seven-foot center, decided to come over the top of Mel and ended up hitting him in the back of the head.

The ball was actually thrown over Mel's head and out of bounds. I'm not sure what Reggie was thinking at the time, because Mel had absolutely no chance to ever catch that ball. Of course, the refs called the foul. Mel then stepped up to the free throw line, hit a free throw and we lost the game by one point.

I took losses hard, but I took this one especially hard. I had played my ass off. I had brought us back from a big deficit. Looking back, there are turning points in one's career. In that game, I earned respect, showed my teammates that I could really shoot the basketball and proved that I belonged in the league.

After the game I was off in a corner of the locker room by myself crying. Then something really special happened. One by one, every guy on the team came over to me and patted me on the back. Every single player on the team. Most of them said something like, "That's OK rook, you'll be alright."

They started saying "rook" in a different tone. Soon after that, they started calling me "Clem" instead of "rook." I was paying my dues, earning their respect. That one game meant a lot because I had laid it all on the line for them. I'll tell you one thing. I never, ever missed three free throws in a row the rest of my career.

I really believe that things always work out for the best. My philosophy is to try to take a potentially negative situation and turn it into something positive.

I always took a lot of pride in my ability to shoot free throws. When I got fouled, in my head I was automatically chalking up two points for us before I even got to the line. I shot 79 percent from the line in my career, and never shot any lower than 83 percent in each of my last five seasons in the league.

There were some great players and great people on the first team in Chicago. In addition to Jerry, Bob, Flynn and Reggie, we had Jimmy Washington, McCoy McLemore, Keith Erickson, Erwin Mueller, Barry Clemens and Dave "The Rave" Schellhase.

The starting guards that first year in Chicago were Sloan and Erickson, the forwards were Boozer and Washington, and the center was Harding. Schellhase, Robinson and I were backup guards, McClemore and Clemens were reserves at forward and Muller backed up Harding at center.

I played in 76 games and averaged 8.9 points, 3.0 rebounds and 2.2 assists per game during my first year with the Bulls. But if you went back and looked at the last half, or two-thirds of my rookie season, I averaged in double figures.

Being a rookie in the NBA was different back then. At that time rookies had to pay their dues before getting any extensive playing time. Most rookies didn't start. That's just the way it was. Usually you'd come off the bench to give one of the veterans a break or to give a couple of good, hard fouls late in the quarter.

That was an adjustment for me after starting and playing almost every minute of every game in both high school and college. That may have been compounded by the fact that I was primarily a point guard in the NBA after playing mostly forward in college. I had to handle the ball more out front, something that I really wasn't accustomed to doing.

I was a little tentative at first, but a game against Cincinnati helped turn things around for me. We were down by two points when I rebounded the ball with 18 seconds left, dribbled the length of the floor and then hit a jumper from the corner to send the game into overtime. The next night against San Diego I scored 28 points. I was on my way.

IT DOESN'T GET ANY BETTER THAN THIS

CHAPTER THIRTEEN

During the offseason, we always went back to Campbellsville to help out my family after the season was over. We had to get the tobacco out, get the hay up, milk the cattle and take care of things on the farm. More than anything, it was always good just to get back "home."

It was harder for me to help out on the farm as much after my rookie season with the Bulls. Shortly after we were eliminated by the Lakers in the playoffs, I went in and had the surgery to repair my wrist. I was in a cast for about four months once again. I got it off a month before the start of my second training camp. So in a 24-month period, my right hand was in a cast for about 10 of those months.

I'm really proud of the fact that, after my rookie year, I had six straight seasons where I averaged in double figures. Keep in mind that this was before the days of the three-point shot. My averages would have been even higher if that rule was in effect when I played.

But I think my stats reveal that I was a consistent player and I prided myself on that. Not only making shots, but also being a good passer and being consistent with whatever the coach asked me to do. I tease Cotton Fitzsimmons, who was the coach my first two years in Phoenix, from time to time that he did me an injustice because I was always a point guard. He never gave me the chance to be a shooting guard.

I played point guard in the NBA with two of the slowest shooting guards to ever play in the league; Jerry in Chicago and Dick Van Arsdale in Phoenix. Jerry and I still joke about being the slowest backcourt in the history of the NBA. But we made the playoffs two out of the three years I played in Chicago with Jerry, and then we won 48 and 49 ballgames in each of our first two seasons in Phoenix with Dick.

I was a very good shooter, but most of the time during my career I was the fourth or fifth option as a scorer on the team. As the point guard, I knew that it was important for me to sacrifice some of my offensive numbers in order to get my teammates around me involved.

In Chicago my job was to get the ball into the hands of Bob Boozer, Bob Love and Chet Walker. In Phoenix it was Neal Walk, Connie Hawkins, Paul Silas and Dick. So I was always the fourth or fifth option, but I was still able to get my 15, 16, 17 points a night.

It shows that I was a pretty good shooter because I didn't always get a lot of looks at the basket. My shots usually came off second, third or fourth options, or off a putback after a rebound from time to time. In addition to being called, "Clem The Gem," I was also called the "Kentucky Rifle." But, gee whiz, I never really had the opportunity to display that because I was always trying to get my teammates involved.

When I got traded to the Washington Bullets at the end of my career, I had the chance to play with a great point guard in Kevin Porter. All you had to do was get open and he'd get the ball to you.

I was really able to enjoy my last couple of years with the Bullets because I was no longer the primary ball handler. We had Kevin, Jimmy Jones and Dave Bing. So I had the chance to run the floor a little bit and just shoot it when I was open. That was a lot of fun.

For the first six-and-a-half years of my career I was a starter. I moved into the starting lineup about halfway through my first year with the Bulls and stayed there until they traded me to the Suns where I started all four years. My last two years in Washington, I was basically a third or fourth guard.

I really prided myself on coming to play every night. I missed very few games in nine years because of injury or illness. A couple of times early, and then late, in my career the coach may have decided not to play me on a given night for whatever reason. But when it came time to play, I was always there.

Dick Motta replaced Johnny Kerr, who went to Phoenix, as our coach at the start of my second season in Chicago. Dick came to Chicago after coaching at Weber State University. I averaged

17.2 points, 4.5 rebounds and 3.8 assists per game for the Bulls in my second season in the league. We finished 33-49 overall and missed the playoffs after ending up fifth in the Western Division, but we picked up two key players in Bob Love and Bob Weiss.

Everything really started to jell during my third season with the Bulls in 1969-70 when I averaged career highs in virtually every statistical category. I averaged 20.3 points and 4.6 rebounds per game, and also ranked third in the league with 7.6 assists a game. We tied for third in the Western Division that season with a 39-43 record and then lost four games to one to Atlanta in the first round of the playoffs. I set a team record with 13 assists in our 131-120 playoff win over the Hawks.

That was a great year. Dick ran the high-post offense, we had two great players in Chet Walker and Bob Love, and our first-round draft pick in 1968, Tom Boerwinkle, was a very good passing center. It made it possible for me to score a lot of points because teams had to double up on Chet and Bob. That opened up a lot of scoring opportunities for me. In fact, I hit a team-record 11 straight field goals in a game against Detroit in Cobo Arena.

One of the things I'm most proud of though, is ranking third in the league in assists that year. Lenny Wilkens from the Cleveland Cavaliers was first at 9.1 per game. Walt Frazier of the New York Knicks was just in front of me at 8.2 a game. Cincinnati's Oscar Robertson averaged 8.1 per game, but he didn't play in the minimum 70 games during the season to be eligible. That's some pretty good company to be in with right there.

After the season I was traded to the Phoenix Suns. I was coming off a great year, but the timing of the trade was good. I signed another three-year contract and I got the chance to rejoin Jerry Colangelo, who had gone from Chicago to Phoenix to get the expansion franchise started. He was the general manager there and ran the whole show. Cotton Fitzsimmons was a rookie NBA coach, fresh out of a successful college coaching job at Kansas State.

I wasn't bitter about the trade at all. It was good to move from Chicago to Phoenix, a new environment and a new franchise. Their system under Cotton fit my style of play. I was extremely happy in Chicago, but it's just part of the pro game that you have to accept to make it work.

The trade enabled me to better myself financially. I went from $35,000 for the first year, to $45,000 in the second year and then to $50,000 in the third and final year of the deal. Something like that.

It wasn't phenomenal, but it was better from that standpoint.

Clemette was almost five years old then and hadn't started school yet, so that made the move a lot easier. Our second child, Lori, was born that summer in Bowling Green. Both times I was traded during my career it was in the off-season, so that made it so much easier on our family. We'd have the whole spring and summer to adjust. We had time to sell our house and get relocated.

We finished 48-34 in 1970-71 and 49-33 in 1971-72 and somehow missed the playoffs both years. Connie Hawkins, Paul Silas, Dick Van Arsdale, Neal Walk and I were the starting five. Those were two great teams that really deserved to get into postseason play. I averaged 17.8 points, 4.0 assists and 4.7 rebounds per game my first year with the Suns, and then 15.7 points, 3.4 rebounds and 3.7 assists the second season.

The Suns then replaced Cotton with Butch van Breda Kolff prior to the 1972-73 season, my third year in Phoenix. He was an excellent coach, but he only lasted seven ballgames. We were 3-4 before Jerry Colangelo let him go and hired himself as coach.

Jerry was the general manager and coach for the rest of the season. We had a 35-40 record with him as the coach and finished 38-44 overall and out of the playoffs for the third straight year. I averaged 10.5 points, 2.2 rebounds and 2.6 assists per game that season.

After the season Jerry realized that he should stay in the front office and give up coaching. Don't get me wrong. He's a wonderful man and a good friend, but he just wasn't cut out to be a coach in the NBA.

Prior to the 1973-74 season, our son, Brent, was born. That gave us three great children, a real houseful. Clemette was seven at the time and Lori had just turned three.

Jerry ended up hiring a rookie coach straight out of college for the third time in my career. He brought in John MacLeod who had done a good job at the University of Oklahoma. We finished the season with a 30-52 record and missed the playoffs again. That was my fourth and final season in Phoenix after averaging 11.1 points, 2.7 rebounds and 3.2 assists per game.

Jerry did me a big favor by trading me from Phoenix to the Washington Bullets where I had the pleasure of playing for K.C. Jones my final two years in the league. He sent me to a team that was capable of making a run for the NBA title. They needed my services. The Bullets needed a shooter, a scorer, and that was something that I could certainly deliver.

Looking back, I wasn't bitter about either time that I was traded during my pro career. I was happy and pleased. Both trades helped me both as a player and financially as well. Both trades helped prolong my NBA career. I had the opportunity to play with and against many of the greatest players to ever play the game.

I was able to do my thing coming off the bench for the Bullets. I got the chance to play with a great player like Phil Chenier, and with the two big guys up front and a pair of Hall of Famers in Elvin Hayes and Wes Unseld.

We finished the 1974-75 season tied with Boston with an NBA-best record of 60-22. For that, each of us received $18,000, which was more than I made in each of my first two years in the league. We advanced to the NBA Finals that season and that was a wonderful experience.

Our starting five that year included Phil and Kevin Porter at the guards, Wes and either Truck Robinson, Mike Riordan or Nick Weatherspoon at the forwards and Elvin at center. Then there was Tom Kozelko, a very good friend of mine, Jimmy and me to round out the top 10 players on the team.

Golden State beat us in four straight games for the championship. Elvin scored at will on the inside for us, while Wes and Truck also did a great job up front. Our backcourt, however, was completely crippled by the time we met Rick Barry and the Warriors for the title. Phil had hurt his back and couldn't play, I had pulled a hamstring and could only play about half speed, and Jimmy was out with a serious knee injury.

In the Eastern Conference semifinals we beat the Buffalo Braves, four games to three. The series featured one of the greatest frontcourt matchups of all time: Elvin against Buffalo's Bob McAdoo. Those two were amazing and it was a sight to watch them go after it. It was a tremendous series and we came out on top to advance to the finals.

We lost Jimmy, a great six-foot-four guard for us, in the Eastern Conference finals against the Boston Celtics, a series that we won four games to two. He went up to block John Havlicek's shot, tumbled over in the air after getting the block, caught his leg and snapped it. He tore up his knee pretty bad and that pretty much ended his career.

We were heavily favored to beat Golden State in the finals,

but just the opposite happened. Simply put, we just didn't have enough scoring punch in the backcourt to stay with them.

It was a great run and we were good enough to win the NBA title. It just didn't happen. We had the best record in the league that year over 82 games and proved that we were the best team, but physically we couldn't play anywhere near our best against Golden State.

It was one of those things you dream of. It doesn't matter what level you're playing at—high school, college or pro—you want to win a championship. We made it into the championship round, but unfortunately we couldn't take the final step toward the title because of injuries.

It's frustrating, but when I look back at my playing and coaching career, I honestly feel that injuries have cost me a national championship or two as a player back at Western Kentucky, an NBA championship at Washington, and the NCAA title as a coach at Minnesota.

After going to the Finals in 1975, we came back the next season thinking that we had a great shot to win it all. We finished the regular season 48-34 overall, and in second place in the Central Division. But then Cleveland upset us four games to three in a great first-round series.

I only played 55 regular-season games my last year in the league. Physically, I couldn't play any more than 15 to 18 minutes a game. I had tendinitis in both knees real bad. I was the fifth or sixth guard on the team behind Chenier, Porter, Bing, Riordan and Kevin Grevey.

That's when I had the chance to sit and observe K.C., and one of his assistants Bernie Bickerstaff, coach the game. They allowed me to have some input on the game, let me make suggestions from time to time. We talked about substitutions and things like that.

I think that's really when I had the chance to sit back, analyze the game and think once again about a career in coaching someday. Because of my experiences, I think I see things out on the court and am able to make adjustments as well as anyone. It was great to sit, watch and evaluate the game. That's when I knew in my heart that I wanted to be a coach.

A CLOSER LOOK

CHAPTER FOURTEEN

I had a wonderful nine years in the NBA. I played in 681 regular season games and scored 8,743 points and had 2,087 rebounds. I played for some great coaches, and with and against some of the real legends of the game.

Two names jump out at me right away: Bill Russell and Wilt Chamberlain. When you talk about records and championships you start with those guys. Wilt holds most of the records and Bill has so many championships.

The greatest guards to ever play the game are Oscar Robertson and Jerry West. If you think there are two better guards playing today than those two guys, I tell you what, let me see' em. These kids today are good players, but they couldn't carry those two guys' jocks.

Elgin Baylor was another great player. It's incredible to look back now and realize that I had the honor to play on the same court as those guys. Connie Hawkins was one of the greatest talents of all time. He was 27 years old when he came into the league as a rookie. He was blackballed from college basketball and the NBA for seven years after being unfairly connected to a point-shaving scheme at the University of Iowa in 1961. He was eventually cleared of any wrongdoing. He played with the Globetrotters for a few years before he was allowed into the league. I also had the privilege to play with a couple of Hall of Famers in Elvin Hayes and Wes Unseld.

I remember a funny story about Bill Russell that involves the first time during my rookie year that we played against Russell,

John Havlicek, Sam Jones and the great Boston Celtics in an exhibition game at the University of Illinois.

The veterans didn't care much about exhibition games. They just kind of went through the motions. I had 25 points in the first half. I was really lighting it up. We were up by 15 or 20 points in the second half. I was hustling, trying to get every bucket that I could.

Early in the third quarter, I hit the high post and cut to the bucket with the ball. Russell came out of nowhere it seemed and blocked my shot. They threw it down to Havlicek and he shot a layup at the other end.

I'm thinking to myself, "That's OK." A couple of minutes later, I came off a screen at the high post and Russell swatted my shot again. You have to understand, this guy was phenomenal. We don't have anybody in today's game even close to Bill Russell. I'd like to see another one someday in my lifetime.

So after a great first half, he blocked my first two shots of the second half. He was just letting me know that the rookie should enjoy what happened in the first half, but the old man was there now so don't bring that stuff around here anymore.

I'll never forget that. Russell was a guy that no matter where he was on the court, you could feel his presence. He was the leader of some of the most dominant teams in the history of the game. It wasn't a matter of how many shots Bill blocked every night. It was his mere presence out there on the court.

When you went to shoot the ball and no one could alter your shot, it was easy to have all the confidence in the world. But when you had a guy like Bill out on the court someplace, you were looking over your left shoulder, your right shoulder, out of the corner of your eye, knowing that he could come and block it at any time.

He obviously didn't physically block every shot, but his presence was felt. It caused you to miss so many shots and that alone helped Boston win so many games and so many championships.

Today, there aren't any players like Bill Russell who have an impact on the game like he did. Today's players run faster, jump higher, they're quicker and are better athletes. But they're not the players Bill Russell and Wilt Chamberlain were.

Like I said, about all they used rookies for at first was to draw fouls and give fouls. You'd go in right before the end of the quarter and hammer somebody to send him to the free throw line, especially if the other team had someone who was a poor free throw shooter. Then you'd have the chance to get the ball back and hopefully get two points for one, or if he missed both free throws, two for zero.

I remember when Wilt and the 76ers came to Chicago early in my rookie season. There I was, a three-time All-American who had a great college career and only lost six games total over my last two years at Western.

But the first time I played against Wilt, a guy I had read and heard so much about, I couldn't believe that all of a sudden I was on the court with him. I tell you, I couldn't pee a drop before the game started. Then when the game started, I almost peed my pants I was so excited. I was actually on the same floor with the greatest player I had ever been around. My first impression was that he was sooooo big.

I went into the game for one reason and that was to foul Wilt because he was a poor free throw shooter. So lo and behold, we shoot, miss it and there's a long rebound. They rebound the ball and Wilt, who could run like a deer, gets behind everyone and takes the outlet pass at the other end of the court at about the free throw line.

I proceeded to grab Wilt at the free throw line and in the NBA you have the continuation rule. He has the ball and I grabbed him around his neck trying to get the foul. He took the ball and me all the way to the hoop for a thunderous dunk. After he dunked it, I flipped all the way over his back, to the floor and he caught me.

You know, Wilt is really a nice guy. I was scared to death. I'll never forget it. He patted me on the butt and said, "Rook, you're going to be OK." Then he stepped to the free throw line and made the free throw to complete the three-point play.

When I went to the bench, all my teammates were saying, "Why didn't you stop him!" I said, "Stop him my ass. I weigh 205 pounds and he took me to the bucket like I weighed an ounce!"

Wilt was just so powerful. I don't think that people really ever appreciated his strength. Today, they would be in awe of his great physical size and strength. His arms were huge. But he also played with grace, with finesse. He didn't use brute strength like a Darryl Dawkins did or like Shaquille O'Neal does today. If he had wanted to be nasty like some guys, there's no telling what would have happened.

Wilt led the league in scoring and rebounding many seasons during his career. But most people aren't aware that he also led the league in assists in 1967-68, with 8.6 assists per game. He had the complete game. He could absolutely do it all.

There's a funny story I like to tell about Wilt. Toward the end of his career, people were starting to say that he couldn't score anymore. That was why he was passing the ball so much. So Wilt decided, against us on December 16, 1967, in Chicago, that he was going to put that theory to rest in a hurry.

Wilt proceeded to score 68 points against us that afternoon, still a 76ers team record. He hit 30 of 40 shots and was 8-of-22 at the free throw line, and had 34 rebounds in 48 minutes. He wanted to show the world that he could still score.

He set the all-time record with 100 points with the Philadelphia Warriors against the New York Knicks on March 2, 1962, in Hershey, Pennsylvania. He also hit 35 field goal attempts in a row over a four-game span during the 1966-67 season.

So when you talk about NBA records you start with Wilt Chamberlain. He either still holds, or at one point has held most of the league's all-time records.

When I first started playing in the league, the structure and organization wasn't there. My first pro coach, Johnny "Red" Kerr with the Chicago Bulls, was an ex-NBA player who relied on his own instincts quite a bit.

Johnny was a great storyteller and a fun guy to play for. He gave me an opportunity to play as a rookie, to get my feet wet in the league. Like most rookies at that time, however, I didn't play a lot early in the season. But he played me quite a bit over the final 40 or 50 games of the season and that gave me the opportunity to get some valuable minutes and prove that I was worthy of being a first-round draft pick.

After my first season in Chicago, John left to go to the expansion Phoenix Suns, so Dick Motta became our head coach fresh out of Weber State University. Dick came in and brought a little more organization, more structure to our team.

I played my final two seasons in Chicago for Dick. We ran the high-post offense under him and we used some of the same disciplined offensive principles back then that I still use today.

Everyone thinks that you control the other team with your defense, but basically it's with your offense. That's one big thing that I think I learned from playing for Dick. You can control your opponent with your offense. As long as you have the basketball, they can't score.

As a result, we had one of the best defensive teams in the NBA during those two seasons. We not only had some great defensive players on the team like Jerry Sloan, but we controlled people because we did such a great job of running our half-court offense. We rarely shot the ball quickly and made sure that our opponent had to really work on the defensive end of the floor.

That's kind of my philosophy today. If you can catch and pass and execute on offense, and get good shots and be in position to rebound, then you have the chance to control people. That's why the scores stay low at times. You make them play defense. Then at the end of the year the statistics make it look like you're a great defensive team. But in reality it's because of your great offensive structure.

When I was traded to the Phoenix Suns, I played my first two seasons there for another former college coach in Cotton Fitzsimmons. He had some great teams at Kansas State and it marked the second time in my career that I broke in a rookie coach right out of the college ranks.

Cotton was a very good coach and I probably picked up more from him about playing man-to-man defense than anyone. I had been playing basketball since I was 10 years old and it was the first time that I had ever heard "jump to the ball and force the backcut." Believe it or not, as long as I had been playing, I had never heard that terminology before.

I really think that the teaching aspect of coaching in the NBA really changed when college coaches like Dick and Cotton first started getting a shot in the league. They not only brought structure and organization, but also a teaching element and a work ethic that I believe had been sorely lacking in the league.

Dick and Cotton really helped start that trend and I think they deserve a lot of credit for their impact on the game. It's no surprise that they're still involved in the NBA today.

So I played two wonderful years for Cotton with the Suns. We ran the triangle offense under Cotton and won almost 100 games in those two seasons. Out of all the coaches I've ever played for, I probably have more respect for him than anybody. I really like him personally as a coach, a man and as a friend.

Cotton and I were playing golf together recently and talking about some of the old times. We used to ride to practice together, go to the games together and argue about things a lot. I was the point guard and he'd want me to run the show. I didn't always agree with him, but in the end, he was right because he was the head coach and I respected him so much.

We had a great relationship and we still do. Cotton, Paul Silas and I used to live in the same neighborhood, within a block of each other. A funny story about Cotton and I is that we used to go to the dog races together in the summer at Black Canyon Racetrack. It would be Cotton, his first wife Nancy, Yevette and me.

Since back then we didn't make a lot of money in the NBA, we used to pool our money together, $30, $40 or $50 and then bet on the dogs. Now Cotton being the coach, he wanted to pick every race. So we'd get to arguing about that.

There was a great dog at the track at that time called Chisholm. He was a horse, the Secretariat of dog racing in our minds. Chisholm had won so many races in a row. Then he went into a slump and he couldn't win a race. But Cotton being Cotton, he wanted to keep betting on Chisholm. But I didn't want to and we'd argue about that.

It would get to the point where we wouldn't speak for days because we were arguing over dog races. Then Yevette and Nancy would get us together for ice cream, or whatever, we'd laugh at each other and make up again. Those are the relationships you don't have in the NBA today. You don't have those coach and player relationships anyplace.

Cotton and I still get together quite often today. He's now married to a wonderful lady, Joanne, and they are both great friends of ours.

Throughout my career, I helped break in Dick, Cotton and then John MacLeod from the college ranks to the pros. John was a well-structured, disciplined, hard-working coach who had many successful years in Phoenix.

To be honest, our philosophies did not mirror each other. We didn't see eye to eye on many things. I had been in the league seven years and I had a way of doing things that he didn't agree with at the time.

To tell you the truth it was frustrating to have to break in three rookie coaches, because as a player you had to make the adjustments to each one's style and approach to the game. But I have to thank each of them for giving me the opportunity to play. I started every ballgame in two seasons for Dick in Chicago, every game for two straight seasons with Cotton in Phoenix and then every game during my last year with the Suns under John.

K.C. Jones was a real player's coach, the type of guy you loved to play for. He had a super assistant coach in Bernie Bickerstaff at that time. They were two of the finest coaches I ever played for in my career. They really know how to get the very best out of their teams.

K.C. let you play your game. He has a great knowledge and feel for the game. He's one of the winningest coaches in the history of the NBA and for good reason. We had a great two years in Washington and it was a great situation for me to finish my career.

I didn't run into racism as much in the larger cities of the NBA, but you did see it when we played in exhibition games prior to the start of the regular season.

Much like they do today, exhibition games are played in a number of smaller cities throughout the country. I'll never forget when we played an exhibition game in Auburn, Alabama, when I was with the Bulls. That was a bad scene.

We stayed at a hotel outside of town and I remember that they didn't want to serve the blacks on the team in the restaurant. Growing up in the South I had seen it all, but some of the other guys on the team really reacted to it. It could have been a nasty scene, but we handled it in a professional manner and nothing really came of it. We just got up and left to eat somewhere else.

We also had a bad experience at a restaurant in a hotel with the Bulls once in Winston-Salem, North Carolina. We were there to play Earl "The Pearl" Monroe and the Baltimore Bullets. There were things that happened on both sides. Things that were said that shouldn't have been said by both parties and so on. Once again, it could have been an ugly scene. Thankfully, however, cooler heads prevailed, we got up and walked out of the place.

It's really sad though when you think about it; to know that for no other reason than the color of your skin you weren't treated fairly. It's a hurtful thing. But by growing up in a racist community and state—like most cities and states in the South at that time—it didn't affect me as much as some other players.

I remember one day in Boston when I was with the Phoenix Suns. We were taking a cab over to the Boston Garden for the game. It was Neal Walk, Dick Van Arsdale, Mel Counts and me. I was the only black guy in the cab. I sat in the back seat over in the corner.

We had one guy in the front seat and three of us in the back. The cabbie didn't realize that he had a black guy in his cab. He started talking about the Celtics and the black guys on the team. He also talked about the places in the city where he wouldn't go and pick up the "spades," the "spicks" or the "niggers."

So we asked him what he thought of the Celtics that year. His reply was, "They have too many niggers on the team. I really liked them before they brought in all those niggers. That's why I won't go over and pick up those niggers. All they want to do is cut your tires." This was our whole conversation for 20 minutes from the hotel to the arena.

Neal, Dick and Mel were so embarrassed and really hurt. When we arrived at the arena and got out of the cab, I told the other three that I'd pay for this one. It was about a $10 cab ride. Back in those days we always went over to the arena on our own. Three or four guys would ride together and then the team would reimburse you for the cost.

I'll never forget when I walked around the cab and the cabbie saw me for the first time. I told him, "You know it's amazing, you really have to watch what you say. You never know who's listening to you."

Then I said to him, "You have a lot of forgiveness to ask for before you die, because I know where you're going if you don't change your thoughts and feelings. I don't want to go in the same direction you're heading. Here's $10, you don't deserve a tip. You get your life, your act, together before you die because you have a lot of hatred in your heart." Then I gave him the money and walked away.

He was devastated. It was a bad experience, but I also think it was good for those other three guys in the cab to hear it, to know how a lot of people really felt. I think they were surprised and impressed that I could hear all that crap and not get pissed off and stayed under control.

The cabbie wouldn't have said those things if he knew I was in the cab, but he still would have felt it in his heart. Me being there wouldn't have stopped him from feeling the same way. I'm glad he said it. He said what he felt in his heart.

My hope is that maybe that experience changed his life a little bit. Hopefully he came to the realization that it's wrong to feel that way about another human being.

I didn't hear as many racist remarks in the NBA like I did in college. I'm sure that there was lot more than I realized, but I had gone through so much of it already that I had programmed myself to tune a lot of it out. I had been hearing it ever since I was a young boy. A lot of other people were more sensitive about it, but I had learned how to deal with it.

Jerry was great to have as a roommate my first year in the league. The impact he had on my game, especially on the defensive end of the floor, was tremendous. Man to man, friend to friend, we didn't see color in each other. We've remained very good friends to this day. He helped me out a lot that first year. I was searching for advice and direction, and he gave that to me as a friend. Not because he's white and I'm black, but because he's a friend who happened to be white.

Shoe contracts back then were never like they are in the NBA today. Pro Keds were just coming on the market in the late '60s or early '70s. When I was in my second or third year with the Bulls, Doug Black, who worked for Pro Keds, offered a pair to me, Bob Love, Chet Walker and Jerry Sloan.

Bob and Chet wore the shoes, but I don't believe that Jerry ever wore them. I had worn Converse all my life and the Pro Keds were just a little bit too heavy of a shoe.

Some three or four weeks later, Doug came by and asked us how we liked the shoes. I was being honest and I told him that I thought they were just too heavy and that I was going to stick with my Cons. To make a long story short, Doug then gave Bob and Chet like $2,500 or $3,500 as a shoe contract for the rest of the season.

I guess it was just another story of me being a day late and a dollar short. They wound up making a little money to wear those shoes and I was left out in the cold. That's the closest thing that I came to in my whole NBA career to having a shoe contract. I wore Converse most of the time during my career. At first I bought my own shoes, but then later on, Converse started giving us shoes to wear.

My last year in the league with the Bullets I made $90,000, the most I ever was paid in my nine years in the league. To give you an idea of how that stacks up with today's game, the minimum salary a player could receive in 1996-97 was $247,500 for a veteran and $220,000 for a rookie. The average salary was $2.2 million. Wow! Timing is everything I guess.

K.C. lost his job after the 1975-76 season and they hired Dick Motta, who of course, had coached me at the beginning of my career in Chicago. I went back to training camp in the fall of 1976, but physically I just couldn't go anymore.

They put me on waivers and I had a lot of teams call me. The Lakers and the Indiana Pacers were two that expressed a lot of interest, but I realized right then and there that my career was over. So I went back to the farm and spent the next year serving as a scout for the Bullets.

I left with no regrets. A lot of times some players try to hold on. But I realized that it was over. I didn't look back. I didn't blame anybody. I didn't want to go to any other camps or play for any other teams. I never played in any old-timer games or pick-up games. When I walked away from that last game, I put my pro career behind me. It was over.

When I started playing basketball, I did not anticipate playing even one year in the league. God had really blessed me. I had nine wonderful seasons in the NBA and now it was time to move on with my life.

S WITCHING GEARS

CHAPTER FIFTEEN

T here's always an emptiness when you quit something that you've enjoyed so much. But my philosophy is simple: you must have something to do to occupy your time and your mind.

Basketball was my life since I was 10 years of age. I had always been a competitive person. Suddenly I couldn't play anymore. I had made up my mind that the day I walked off the court for the last time, that was it. There was no looking back. I had played nine wonderful years in the NBA, but I realized that it was over.

So I went back to the farm in Campbellsville. Farming gave me the opportunity to work every day, stay busy and it kept my mind occupied. Bob Ferry, general manager of the Bullets, also had me do some scouting that season as well.

That kept me involved with the game. It was also a time when we could get our kids settled down in school back in Campbellsville. Clemette was in the sixth grade at the time. The fun part about it was that she played basketball for the Taylor County High School varsity team. She was the team's third guard as a sixth-grader. That was a real treat to have the time to be able to watch her play.

Lori was six at the time and in the first grade, while Brent was three years old. That was a fun year to be able to spend time with the kids and see them grow. It was a good year in that I was able to settle my thoughts and get my head squared away.

I think that's why I made the adjustment so quickly. I had something to turn to. Once you finish a career, whatever it may be, you need something to do, and farming was my way out.

Then in the spring of 1977, Dr. Kelly Thompson, the former president at Western Kentucky who was working with the school's College Heights Foundation, hired me to work in the Continuing Education Center at my alma mater. I will be forever grateful to him for giving me the opportunity to go back to Western.

I was involved with providing accommodations for groups on campus and tending to their needs in my new job. We had a hotel on campus that I managed and I worked out of the president's office.

We bought a home in Bowling Green that summer. I really had gone to Western just to work in the Continuing Education Center, but then that fall I started working as a volunteer assistant basketball coach for Jim Richards, who was Western's head coach at the time.

The thought of a career in coaching began to appeal to me even more during my last season with the Bullets. Now this was an opportunity to work with someone who was a very good teacher, someone who really knew the game.

Jim was a very good coach, but he just didn't have the players to work with his last few years. We finished with a 16-14 record that season and then he resigned in the spring of 1978.

He went out on top, however, after leading us to the "Sweet 16" of the NCAA Tournament where we lost to Magic Johnson and Michigan State. We had upset Syracuse, 87-86, in overtime in the first round. I was really disappointed to see Jim step down as coach. I was looking forward to working two or three more years with him so that I could learn the ins and outs of the game from him.

In April, Gene Keady was hired as the new head coach. He had been an assistant coach under Eddie Sutton at the University of Arkansas. To be quite honest, the job was offered to me first. But I realized that I was not ready for a head coaching job at that time and I made one of the best decisions in my life by turning the job down. Just because you played basketball, doesn't mean you're necessarily ready to coach the game.

I did have the opportunity to work under a great coach like Gene. It was the best thing for my career to have the opportunity to work under two great basketball minds like Jim and Gene.

Before he took the job, Gene asked me if I'd be willing to be his top assistant. That's basically why he got the job because I agreed to work with him and remain a part of the program. So it worked out great.

After being the subject of an intense recruiting battle my senior year in high school, it was interesting to be on the other side of the fence as a coach. The first recruit I ever signed was Kenny Ellis, a six-foot-four, guard-forward out of Winter Park, Florida. He went on to have a fine career and become a four-year letterwinner for us.

When I first started coaching, I used to demonstrate to kids. But I stopped doing that, because I could hit 20, 30, 40 or 50 shots in a row. I think it had a reverse effect on the kids. I got the message loud and clear when one of my players told me, "Coach you can make those shots and you can make those plays. We can't do that."

It was intimidating to them. I was playing the game, instead of concentrating on coaching the game. I was trying to coach the way I played the game, instead of trying to look at things subjectively and utilize each players' own strengths and weaknesses. I tried to make everyone play like me. That was a terrible mistake on my part.

In Gene's first year as head coach in 1978-79, we finished with a 17-11 overall record. After defeating Morehead State, 90-85, in the first round of the Ohio Valley Conference Tournament, our season ended with a tough 78-77 loss to Eastern Kentucky.

We followed that up with a 21-8 overall record and a berth in the NCAA Tournament in 1979-80 after beating Murray State, 54-51, in the OVC Tournament championship game on our home court at Diddle Arena.

We didn't have to go far for the NCAA Tournament since the Mideast Regional was being held in none other than Diddle Arena. Our season ended when Virginia Tech came in and beat us, 89-85 in overtime, after we led by 18 points at the half. I really think we started looking ahead to playing Indiana in the next round and we got away from doing the things that gave us the big lead in the first place.

It was quite a stretch drive that we went through that season en route to the title. We beat Murray State on the road by one point, 56-55, in our third-to-last regular season game. Then we topped Middle Tennessee, 81-79, at home in three overtimes, before we lost at South Carolina, 73-65, in two overtimes in the regular season finale.

In the semifinals of the OVC Tournament we just slipped by Eastern Kentucky, 84-83, in overtime, to advance to the finals where we beat Murray State for the third time that season.

Sophomore Craig McCormick, a six-foot-ten center out of Ottawa, Illinois, really came on and had a great season for us. He earned All-OVC honors after leading us in scoring and rebounding, and showed that he was going to be a force to be reckoned with in the future.

Shortly after the NCAA Tournament ended, Gene accepted the head coaching job at Purdue University. He had a 38-19 record during his two seasons in Bowling Green, an OVC title and a trip to the NCAA Tourney. Those were two wonderful years with him at Western and he remains one of my closest friends and colleagues to this day.

Gene brought a lot of structure, discipline and organization to the program. He showed me how to construct a daily practice schedule, as well as how to deal with and implement a variety of game situations and strategies. He's a great teacher and those are the things I learned from him more than anything.

When I first started working for Gene I hated the fact that he wanted us to run such a disciplined offense. We always used to disagree, because I wanted us to run up and down the floor and shoot. I had that pro mentality, that pro background.

I was upset at him because he wanted us to pass the ball around on offense 25 times and shoot a shot every two days. I wanted us to make a pass and then shoot it right away. We didn't agree on that, but he was the head coach and I respected his decisions.

Behind closed doors we may have disagreed, but out on the court you have to have solidarity. So I always supported him on the court, even though I didn't agree with that philosophy at the time.

Now my teams are probably more disciplined than his are. He teases me about that a lot. That's the beauty and the joy of working with someone like Gene Keady. I try to pass along the same things to my assistants now. Your program must have organization and discipline in order to be successful.

He's always been the toughest damn guy for me to beat. I would rather coach against anybody in America than Gene Keady. He's that good, and his teams are that well-prepared. It's hard for me to beat him. We mirror each other so much.

I fear no one, but I respect Gene Keady. I know that when we play his team, I better have my act together and my kids better be physically and mentally ready to play because it's going to be a war out there.

That's the attitude that I try to bring to my players and teams. When people get through playing us, they may have won the game, but they know they've been in a war.

I want the opposing team to say that they don't want to play Minnesota again because they're well-organized, they're well-coached and they're disciplined. They're not going to beat themselves. They come to play. That's the way I approach coaching the game and much of that can be attributed to the two years I worked with Gene Keady.

Gene is a good friend and someone that I have so much respect for because he still has so much respect for the game. He still makes sure that kids do what they're supposed to do: the discipline, the attitude, the mental approach to the game. Those are the things that I look at and why I think he's one of the very best coaches in the game.

THE TIME IS NOW

CHAPTER SIXTEEN

Basketball has been in my blood since I took that first shot in David and Buck Roberts' apple orchard when I was 10 years old.

I realized after my playing days were over that through coaching I could make a difference in young peoples' lives. I know that if they play for me for four years I can give them life skills, survival skills, that will help them become better young men. Not necessarily better basketball players, but better young men that are prepared for life.

It's important for me to be able to give something back to this great game and the kids who play this game; to preach to them the difference between right and wrong. I feel like in my heart I've been able to do that over the last 20 years.

So after one year as a volunteer coach under Jim Richards and two years as the top assistant to Gene Keady, I was ready to accept the head coaching job at Western Kentucky.

When Gene left for Purdue, the job was immediately offered to me and they gave me the time I needed to make the decision. I went to Yevette first to get her feelings about what I should do, because there's more to it than just being able to provide a living for your family.

I wanted to make sure that she fully understood the pressures, the headaches and the heartaches that go with this job. The things that she would hear about me and what people would say about me. Was it worth all that to become the head coach at Western Kentucky University?

Being a head college basketball coach is not as glamorous a job as everyone thinks. I had been around long enough to know that we had to be together on the decision or it wouldn't work out, wouldn't be worth it.

I really admire all coaches wives. They are the unsung heroes. Once the game starts and we're on the court, I don't hear the booing, the guys questioning my coaching philosophy, my substitution pattern. I don't hear it, but my wife can hear all that stuff. But for a coach's wife to have to sit through that and take it, it hurts. It hurts a lot.

I wish more fans out there would think before they open their mouths. There is some wife, brother, son, daughter or family member who doesn't want to hear someone talk about their relative like that.

Yevette agreed that she had tough skin and that she could deal with it. She's the first person I talked to once I was offered the job. Because I knew what she would have to go through.

I never felt that they handed the job to me because I was a former All-American there who went on to play in the NBA, although I'm sure that some people felt that way to a degree. I felt like I got the job because I paid my dues. I had been an assistant and had come up through the ranks. I deserved the job and felt I was the best guy for the job.

That's the way I've always operated. What's mine, what I deserve, I want. I earned the right to be the head coach, to succeed or to fail. That's the way I always looked at it.

Four days after Gene resigned, on a cold, wet Sunday afternoon in the middle of April, I was introduced by President Donald Zacharias at a news conference in the Wetherby Administration Building as the new head men's basketball coach at Western Kentucky University.

I was 36 years old and on top of the world. It was a dream come true for me. They even had Mrs. E.A. Diddle on hand at the news conference to present me with the traditional Hilltoppers' red towel.

With the appointment at a salary of $37,000 per year, I became the first black head men's basketball coach in the history of Western Kentucky University and the only black head men's basketball coach in the Ohio Valley Conference at that time. In fact, I was the only black to ever serve as a head men's Division I basketball coach in the state until Kentucky named Tubby Smith as its head coach in May of 1997.

That's mind-boggling. It's sad, but those are the facts. I hate to point out black and white differences because we're all Americans. We shouldn't judge each other based on the color of our skin. I hope somehow things can and will change. People shouldn't get jobs because they're white or black. People should be measured on whether they're qualified or not. As I said earlier, that's why I was ready to become the head coach at Western. I was qualified.

There are some very qualified black coaches out there who have paid their dues and deserve head jobs and only need an opportunity. That is the key word: opportunity. That's all I've ever preached.

I'm so glad that I got the opportunity to coach and that I was able to prove to people that I could do the job. Sure, I made my share of mistakes like anyone does when just starting out. It doesn't matter if you're white or black, there's no substitute for experience. I'm a much better coach today, hands down, than I was when I started out in 1977.

I can remember checking into hotels with the team, going up to the front desk and having the receptionist ask me, "Where's the head coach?" They assumed he would be white. I remember my trainer at Western, Bill Edwards, pointing at me and saying, "Coach Haskins is the head coach."

Those were the types of things that I had to deal with. It was the same thing with officiating. I think I got cheated a number of times because of the color of my skin. They would never admit to that, but I think I got screwed so many times it's not even funny. My God, how could I win? There I was, a young guy trying to coach my butt off and win games, and I got no calls whatsoever. I thought it was totally unfair.

In every basketball game, it only takes one or two close calls to go against you to turn the game around. I look back at some of the tapes now and we were fortunate just to even be in a lot of those games. It proved to me that I was doing one hell of a job. If my teams weren't so well prepared back then, we would have really been in trouble, because I got absolutely no help from the officials.

Don't get me wrong. I don't think they intentionally meant to be racist on the court. It's just the way it was. They were just going to give the other team the benefit of the doubt. I'd like to sugarcoat it and say it was because I was a rookie coach, but it happened during my first year there, my second year, my sixth year— it just never stopped. I feel it was because I'm black; no question about it. It's sad to say those things, but I got hammered. We're talking about facts of life.

One of the first things I did after moving into my office at Western was to erect a larger-than-life portrait of Coach Ed Diddle, who had passed away in 1970, on my wall. For all he had done for Hilltopper basketball, I thought it was appropriate.

Ann Handy was my secretary at Western and she did a wonderful job helping me when I became the Hilltoppers' head coach. She helped out so much with the organization of the office and a variety of administrative duties. I couldn't have done it without her, and she's still a very dear friend of the Haskins family.

My former coach, John Oldham, was the athletics director at Western at the time and I got great support from him. When Jim Richards resigned as basketball coach, he moved into an assistant athletics director role at the school.

Jim was very helpful to me in my rookie year; I talked to him quite a bit. I could ask him just about anything; about defenses, matchups and so on. I just liked to pick his brain. When you're young and just getting started, you need someone to lean on. He gave me a lot of insight and really helped me survive that first season.

I had a real young staff to work with that first year. One of my assistant coaches was Ray Hite, who had played for Dean Smith at North Carolina. He was brought on board by Gene and I kept him on my staff. I also hired Dwayne Casey, who had played college ball at Kentucky. It was his first full-time coaching job. They were young guys who really did a nice job for me.

Even though we lost four starters from our NCAA Tournament team of the previous year, I felt deep down that we had a very good team returning in 1980-81. I actually was involved in recruiting all those guys and then I wound up being their head coach.

Craig McCormick, who was coming off an All-OVC sophomore season, and Rickey Wray, a six-foot-eight senior from Hickman, Kentucky, were my centers. Craig was not only a good shooter and rebounder, but he also was a good passer for a big man. He was just a good, solid fundamentally sound player.

Tony Wilson, a six-foot-seven sophomore from Lexington, Percy White, a six-foot-six sophomore from Washington, D.C., and

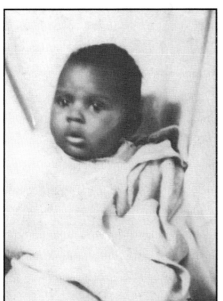

Clem Smith Haskins at three months.

Who is this handsome guy? I'm 11 years old here.

This photo was taken shortly after I was baptized in the Green River. I was 10 years old. (front) Betty Lou Haskins, Nora Haskins; (middle) Amy Runyon, Johnnie Maddox, Jesse Buck Williams, Libby Maddox, Mable Haskins, Pinky Williams, me, Louise Bridgewater, Rev. J.D. Runyon; (back) Columbus Haskins, Mary Lou Massey, Lucy Haskins, Henry Maddox.

I was selected the Most Athletic Boy in the 1963 senior class at Taylor County High School. (photo courtesy of Taylor County High School Cardinal)

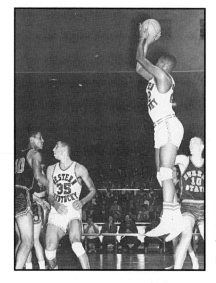

I hit this jumper in our 71-59 victory over Murray State in the 1966 Ohio Valley Conference Tournament at the Convention Center in Louisville. (photo courtesy of Western Kentucky sports information)

This picture of our starting five in 1966-67—me, Wayne Chapman, Dwight Smith, Butch Kaufman and Greg Smith—was taken outside of Grice Hall shortly after I fractured my right wrist. (photo courtesy of Western Kentucky sports information)

I took a lot of pride throughout my career, not only in my ability to shoot the ball, but also in my ability to find the open man.

A happy household. Yevette, Lori, Clemette, Buffy our dog and me at home in Phoenix on July 4, 1971 — Lori's first birthday.

Washington Bullets teammate, Elvin "The Big E" Hayes, never knew what hit him when I beat him in this game of pool back in 1975.

Yevette and Brent join me courtside before a Washington Bullets game in 1976.

The 1978-79 Western Kentucky coaching staff: Assistant Coach Jay Williams, Assistant Coach Ray Hite, Head Coach Gene Keady, and me. (photo courtesy of Western Kentucky sports information)

This family photo was taken just after I was announced as the Western Kentucky head coach on April 13, 1980. Mom and Dad are seated. Standing (left to right) are Mable, Betty Lou, Willie, Yevette, me, Joyce, Paul, Sara, Nora and Lummie. Merion couldn't attend due to a work commitment that took him out of the country.

It was a real thrill in my first year as head coach to be able to cut down the nets after our 71-67 win over Murray State in the Ohio Valley Conference Championship game. (photo courtesy of Western Kentucky sports information)

In the huddle during the 1981-82 season. The players are (left to right): Craig McCormick, a three-time All-OVC player for us, Bobby Jones, now an assistant coach at Minnesota for me, Gary Carver, Kenny Ellis, Shawn Giddy and Darnell Phillips. (photo courtesy of Western Kentucky sports information)

I didn't get many breaks from the officials when I first started coaching. Here I'm fighting for my life with referee Ben Dunn and UAB Coach Gene Bartow in our 64-56 loss to the Blazers in the 1985 Sun Belt Conference Tournament. (photo courtesy of Western Kentucky sports information)

A three-time All-American who led Western Kentucky to a pair of Final Four appearances, Clemette was honored on "Senior Night" before her last home game in 1987. It marked the first time I had been back to Western since I took the job at Minnesota. (photo courtesy of Western Kentucky sports information)

I'm as proud as a Dad can be on the day that Clemette was named head women's basketball coach at the University of Dayton. (photo courtesy of the University of Dayton sports information office)

Clem Haskins Blvd. in Campbellsville, Kentucky.

The 1989-90 Golden Gophers: (front) Academic Counselor Jim Hale, Assistant Coach Silas McKinnie, Assistant Coach Al Brown, me, Assistant Coach Don Evans, Assistant Coach Dan Kosmoski, Trainer Roger Schipper; (middle) Student Manager Doug Turner, Connell Lewis, Arriel McDonald, Nate Tubbs, Walter Bond, Kevin Lynch, Melvin Newbern, Mario Green, Student Manager Travis Glampe; (back) Student Manager Joe Favour, Student Manager Guy Andrews, Rob Metcalf, Richard Coffey, Jim Shikenjanski, Bob Martin, Ernest Nzigamasabo, Willie Burton, Junior Graves, Student Manager Tom Ostrom. (Wendell Vandersluis)

After falling 93-91 to Georgia Tech in the 1990 Southeast Regional Final, about 2,000 fans showed up to say "thank you" at the airport. (Wendell Vandersluis)

"Senior Night" in 1990 was an emotional evening at Williams Arena as we said goodbye to five seniors — Willie Burton, Jim Shikenjanski, Melvin Newbern, Connell Lewis and Richard Coffey — who had helped to rebuild the Golden Gopher program. (Wendell Vandersluis)

Giving back to the community has always been an important facet of my basketball programs both at Western Kentucky and at Minnesota. Here I'm joined by Ernest Nzigamasabo in 1990 on our annual holiday trip to the University of Minnesota Children's Hospital. (Wendell Vandersluis)

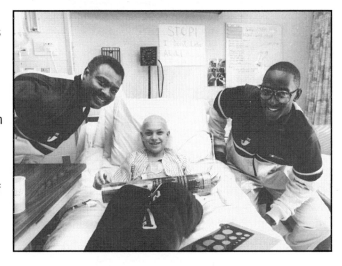

Voshon Lenard and I hug after we beat Georgetown, 62-61, to win the 1993 NIT title. Voshon was sensational throughout the entire tournament en route to being named NIT MVP. (Wendell Vandersluis)

My assistant coaches —Dave Thorson, Dan Kosmoski, Milt Barnes—and I show off our new hardware in Times Square after winning the 1993 NIT crown. (Wendell Vandersluis)

The 1994 USA Junior World Championship Qualifying Team Gold Medalists: (front) Richard Price, Trajan Langdon, Steve Wojciechowski, Stephon Marbury, Eric Harris, Albert White; (middle) Athletic Trainer Wayne Barger, Assistant Coach Clint Bryant, me, Assistant Coach Mike Montgomery; (back) Mike Maddox, Robert Traylor, Issiah Epps, Tim Young, Shareef Abdur-Rahim, Tremaine Fowlkes. (Wendell Vandersluis)

Lenny Wilkens, Charles Barkley and I enjoying the 1996 Olympic Games opening ceremonies. (photo courtesy of USA Basketball/Andrew Bernstein)

It was a real thrill when Bishop Desmond Tutu showed up at one of our "Dream Team" practices. The whole team is signaling "Peace to the World." (photo courtesy of USA Basketball/Andrew Bernstein)

Vice President Al Gore came down to our locker room at the Olympic Games. (photo courtesy of USA Basketball/Andrew Bernstein)

It was a genuine honor to be able to join the likes of Bobby Cremins, Jerry Sloan and Lenny Wilkens on the 1996 USA Olympic Team coaching staff. (photo courtesy of USA Basketball/ Andrew Bernstein)

A few instructions for "Shaq" before he checks into our Gold Medal game against Yugoslavia. (photo courtesy of USA Basketball/ Nathaniel Butler)

I came back out on the raised Williams Arena floor to thank the crowd following our 67-66 win over Illinois which clinched a tie for the 1997 Big Ten title. I was so excited that I even blew kisses to the crowd shortly after this photo was taken. (Wendell Vandersluis)

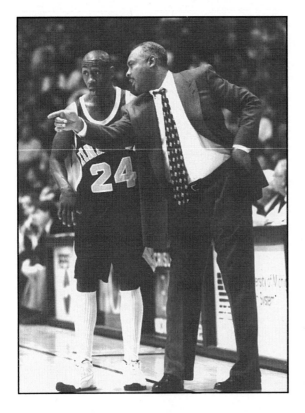

Giving instructions to 1997 Big Ten and NCAA Midwest Regional MVP, Bobby Jackson, in our game at Michigan. Bobby would later make the winning free throw with 2.9 seconds remaining to give us a 55-54 win that clinched the Big Ten title. (Wendell Vandersluis)

1997 Big Ten Champs!!! (Wendell Vandersluis)

My wife and best friend, Yevette, on the plane heading back to the Twin Cities after we clinched the Big Ten title. (Wendell Vandersluis)

The scoreboard tells the story at the 1997 NCAA Midwest Regional in San Antonio. Minnesota is on its way to the Final Four for the first time in school history! (Jerry Lee)

I invited former Golden Gopher and Boston Celtics great, Kevin McHale, to talk to our team before we headed into the 1997 NCAA Tournament. A great guy, Kevin is currently vice president of basketball operations for the Minnesota Timberwolves. (Jerry Lee)

I was fortunate to win most of the National Coach of the Year Awards in 1996-97. Here I received the Associated Press Coach of the Year Award and Wake Forest's Tim Duncan the Adoph Rupp Player of the Year Award the day before our national semifinal game against Kentucky. (Wendell Vandersluis)

The 1996-97 Big Ten and NCAA Midwest Regional champions: (front) Student Assistant Coach Hosea Crittenden, Program Aide Brent Haskins, Academic Counselor Alonzo Newby, Assistant Coach Larry Davis, Head Coach Clem Haskins, Assistant Coach Bill Brown, Assistant Coach Charles Cunningham, Trainer Roger Schipper; (middle) Student Manager Brett Bresnahan, Bobby Jackson, Charles Thomas, Aaron Stauber, Eric Harris, Russ Archambault, Student Manager Kevin Ellich; (back) Jason Stanford, Jermaine Stanford, Courtney James, John Thomas, Trevor Winter, Kevin Loge, Miles Tarver, Quincy Lewis, Sam Jacobson.(Wendell Vandersluis)

We have the greatest fans in college basketball at Minnesota and they packed "The Barn" to the rafters to welcome us home after we beat UCLA to advance to the 1997 Final Four. (Jerry Lee)

My family is my pride and joy. Yevette and I are joined by Clemette, Brent and Lori. (Wendell Vandersluis)

I've got the best seat in the house at Williams Arena. (Wendell Vandersluis)

Kenny Ellis, my first recruit who was entering his junior season, were my forwards.

Kevin Dildy, a six-foot-three junior from Chicago, Mike Reese, a six-foot-three senior from Hopkinsville, Kentucky, and Bobby Jones, a five-foot-ten freshman from Macon, Georgia, were my guards. Bobby was a big-time recruit for us going into my first year as head coach. His high school team had won the national championship his junior year and had gone undefeated two straight years. He ended up doing a tremendous job of quarterbacking our ballclub for four years. In fact, he's now an assistant coach for me at Minnesota.

We won the first ballgame I coached, 73-69, over Bill Foster and South Carolina in our own Wendy's Classic at Diddle Arena. Craig led the way for us with 21 points and 11 rebounds. Believe it or not, I became the first coach at Western to win his first game since Coach Diddle beat Adairville, Indiana, 103-7, in the 1922-23 season opener.

I'll never forget that first game. I invited my high school coaches—John Whiting from Campbellsville Durham and Billy B. Smith from Taylor County—to the game. It was a very exciting and emotional night for me, but it was just the start of things to come.

A lot of good things happened to us and me personally that first season. We finished the season 21-8 overall, won the OVC title and advanced to the NCAA Tournament. I was named the OVC Coach of the Year and NBC-TV honored me as the National Rookie Coach of the Year.

We put together a nine-game winning streak at one point in the season. On the flip side, we never lost back-to-back games all year long. With four players in double figures, we clinched the regular season OVC title with a relatively easy 66-44 win over Murray State at Diddle Arena. An All-OVC selection for the second straight season, Craig had 12 points and 15 rebounds in the game. Tony and Mike scored 11 points apiece, while Percy came off the bench to score 10 points. That win clinched the homecourt advantage for the OVC Tournament.

We beat Austin Peay, 82-71, in the semifinals of the OVC Tournament in Diddle Arena. Tony Wilson, who was called "TWA" which stood for Tony Wilson Airlines because of his outstanding jumping ability, scored 15 points to lead us to the victory. Kenny came off the bench to scored 13 big points, all in the second half.

Then in the championship game we defeated Murray State, who we had split games with during the regular season, 71-67 to take the title. Bobby, who was named to the OVC all-freshman team, put the win on ice with two clutch free throws with 23 seconds left. Percy had 18 points in the game and was joined by Tony on the all-tournament team.

It was a great feeling to go up there and cut down those nets and know that we were the Ohio Valley champs and on our way to the NCAA Tournament in my first year of coaching. I proved to myself that I was worthy of being the head coach. Yes, I was still green and had a lot to learn. But I was on my way.

Gene Bartow's UAB team beat us up pretty good in the first round of the NCAA Tournament in Tuscaloosa, Alabama. The final score was 93-68. They were a big, strong, very athletic team. A loaded team. In fact, they almost beat Kentucky in the next round.

We were disappointed to get beat by 25 points, but it was a wonderful experience for our players and for me as a rookie head coach. The travel, the media attention and the mental preparation is all different in the NCAA Tournament. My inexperience hurt us, but our opponent was also an outstanding team. I'm a good coach in postseason play today because of the experiences I gained back then.

Believe me, everybody wasn't happy about having a black head coach. It's sad to say, but even with us winning the title that first year, a lot of people still weren't happy. Even in our hometown of Bowling Green there was some discontent. I was an All-American at Western Kentucky and you'd think that everyone would have been overjoyed. Not true. It's been like that throughout history. That's just the way it is.

A lot of people were happy because we were going to the NCAA Tournament, but for others the hatred and prejudice was still there, solely because of my skin color. On the outside they were happy, but on the inside they would've rather had a white coach. Winning didn't change things; the prejudice was still there.

That's what I've been working all my life to change. Give people their just due. Don't worry about the color of their skin. Can a person do the job? That's all I think is important. I'm a man first who happens to be black. I'm not bitter, but those are the types of things that I'm still disappointed about.

I've always said that you must please yourself first and foremost. If you can look in the mirror and say that you gave it your all, that's all you can ask. I may not be the smartest person in the world, but I gave it my all and felt good about what we accomplished.

It was very satisfying to have such a great first season. We didn't vary much from the system that Gene had put in place. I added a few new ideas and wrinkles, but we pretty much stayed with the things that had been so successful for us all along. I really think that made the transition that much easier.

I was a workaholic and NCAA rules were different back then regarding how much you could practice. School started late in August, so I started conditioning right after Labor Day and we went right on through the season from there. If I had to do it over again, I probably wouldn't work them so hard, to tell you the truth. It was too much and I learned from that.

But they were prepared both physically and mentally. Preparation has always been the key with my teams. I pride myself on having my teams well-prepared. If you beat my team, it's because you're better. I've had that mentality all my life. You have to prepare to win.

It was a great group of young men to coach. We had our share of problems like all teams do, but they really made my first season easy in a lot of ways and that's a real credit to those guys. The key ingredient was that we had great depth. We played nine or 10 guys all season long, the same thing I like to do today. We were able to overcome a lot of adversity and have a super year.

That first team of mine will always be special. Throughout a coaching career, there are a lot of teams that you grow close to and become fond of for various reasons. Not necessarily because they won a lot of games or championships, but because of the people who made up the team. It wasn't the closest I've ever been to a team, but they gave me an opportunity to coach and be successful.

If you pray to God, not for selfish motives but for the right things, then good things will happen to you. We need to be ready so that when the Lord presents us with opportunities, we're ready to follow his lead. In this case, the opportunity for me was to go back to Western Kentucky and become the head basketball coach.

NEVER SAY DIE

CHAPTER SEVENTEEN

My second team at Western Kentucky in 1981-82 went 19-10 overall. We were regular season co-champions in the OVC and just missed a second straight NCAA Tournament appearance when we lost by two points, 54-52, to Middle Tennessee in the OVC Tournament championship game at Diddle Arena.

We lost to a very good Middle Tennessee team coached by Stan Simpson for the title. For those of you who don't remember, after they beat us, they went on to beat Kentucky in the NCAA Tournament. They ending up losing to Louisville in the second round. That says something right there and it made the OVC and us look pretty good too.

Ironically, we then had to go up and play Gene's Purdue team at Mackey Arena in West Lafayette, Indiana, in the first round of the NIT. So just a little over a year later, here's a matchup between the former head coach and his successor.

Like I said, Gene has always been one of the toughest guys for me to coach against and it started right away with this game. But I tell you what, I was really proud of the way our guys played against the Boilermakers. We lost, 72-65, but they knew they were in a battle the whole way.

We suffered some heavy losses to graduation after that season, guys who had been the nucleus of our program for four years. Craig was named to the All-OVC team for the third straight season after finishing his career with 1,354 points. You just don't replace a player of that caliber overnight, especially a talented big man in the middle like that. Kevin and Kenny were going to be sorely missed as well.

It was a transitional period for our program because we were not only rebuilding, but we were also moving into a more competitive league in the Sun Belt Conference. As a result, we finished 12-16 overall in 1982-83, 12-17 in 1983-84 and 14-14 in 1984-85. To make matters worse, we lost in the first round of the Sun Belt Conference Tournament two out of those three years.

To add injury to insult, I suffered a knee injury during the 1983-84 season during one of our practices. I spent some time in the hospital recovering and then had to coach from the sidelines sitting in a wheelchair.

The Sun Belt Conference was underrated. Old Dominion, Virginia Commonwealth, UAB and South Alabama were four strong teams in the conference. We struggled for three years in that league because we didn't have the players, and the other teams were just flat out better than us. It was as simple as that.

VCU had two great players in Calvin Duncan and Rolando Lamb, two of the finest guards on one team that I've ever gone up against. That team never got the recognition that it deserved. Coach J.D. Barnett did one whale of a job at VCU.

Gene Bartow also did a great job at UAB. We found that out firsthand when they trounced us in the 1981 NCAA tourney. He was loaded with great players, did a wonderful job of coaching, and as a result, they were always very difficult to beat. Cliff Ellis at South Alabama had a super player as well in Terry Catledge who went on to play several years in the NBA.

Coach Paul Webb at Old Dominion had guys like Mark West, who is still playing in the NBA, and Mark Davis. Lee Rose did a tremendous job at South Florida too and had a great player on his team in Charlie Bradley.

So it was a very tough league with a lot of great talent at that time. Combine that with the transition our own program was going through, and it made the road pretty rocky at first for us. I was always proud of my guys through those tough times. They played hard every night out.

We played Georgetown and their outstanding center Patrick Ewing three straight years and almost pulled off a huge upset over John Thompson's team during the 1982-83 season. We played valiantly but lost, 70-66, in overtime at Diddle Arena.

That was the season after Georgetown had lost to North Carolina with Michael Jordan, James Worthy and Sam Perkins, in the national title game by one point. In 1983-84, John and Patrick got their national title by beating Hakeem Olajuwon, Clyde Drexler and Houston's Phi Slamma Jamma.

We also went through an eight-game losing streak during the 1983-84 season in which all eight defeats were by four points or less. We were getting closer and closer to getting over the hump.

The bottom line is that we needed to get good enough to overcome poor officiating. I've always felt that if my team is at least even with our opponent talent-wise, I'll win the game nine times out of ten. We didn't get any breaks from the officials our first three years in the Sun Belt Conference and it killed us. Looking back at some of the tapes of those games, it's incredible to see some of the ridiculous calls that cost us games.

Regardless, our fans were getting impatient. There was talk going around, "Can he win in this conference? Can he go out and recruit good enough players? Can this guy coach?"

We quickly silenced the critics in 1985-86 when we had a 23-8 overall record, finished second in the Sun Belt with a 10-4 conference mark and advanced to the second round of the NCAA Tournament.

The difference? We recruited our tail ends off and that's a real credit to our entire staff. I had the pleasure of working with some great assistants at Western.

Ray remained on my staff for a few years after Gene took the Purdue job. Ray's thing, his pet peeve really, was making sure that guys boxed out on every shot that went up. He used to always say to me, "Coach, we have to box out, we have to box out" over and over during a game. He and his wife, Pattie, are still very good friends of ours. Donnie McFarland also did a tremendous job for me.

Don Evans had as much to do with our success as anyone. He was our team manager when I became coach, then I promoted him to a graduate assistant coach and then to a restricted earnings coach. Don's someone who is very loyal. I trust him a great deal. He handled a variety of duties and actually joined me when I took the job at Minnesota.

David Farrar joined my staff in 1984 after spending the previous five years as an assistant coach at Mississippi State. He is a tremendous defensive coach. He and his wife, Lochia, who is an outstanding lady, have two wonderful daughters and Yevette and I still stay in touch with them.

Dwayne, who will always be dear to me, was on my staff from day one. He did a great job in a number of areas, especially in the area of recruiting. He was the main man in the recruiting wars and helped turned the tide for us by bringing in so many great players.

Each and every one of those guys who was a member of my coaching staff at one time or another, played a major role in our success that season. It felt good to once again have a team that we had a legitimate chance to win with each time we stepped on the court. There's no substitute for talent.

Clarence Martin was a six-foot-eight, 225-pound junior center from Alexander City, Alabama, for us that season. He was someone that I respected a great deal because he battled back from a serious knee injury to become a key player for us. The doctors told him that his career was probably over, but he spent a full year in rehabilitation and came back.

He was a real inspiration to his teammates because of everything that he had gone through in his life. His father was a policeman who was shot and killed, and then his mother passed away about six months later. His last two years in high school he drove a school bus to make money for the family and he helped raise his sister and brother.

Clarence was already a man by the time he got to Western. His grandfather and grandmother told me, "If you take care of him and help be a father to him, we'll let him go to Western Kentucky." He was inexperienced as a basketball player. In fact, both Alabama and Auburn were recruiting him for football.

I think that Clarence was really one of the big things that helped turn the program around because we were able to get the big guy we needed to play the center spot for us. He was a big-name recruit and provided a springboard for us to be able to land some other top players.

Kannard Johnson was a six-foot-nine, 220-pounder who was a junior for us in 1985-86. He was out of Cincinnati. Kannard committed to Western in early February during his senior year at Taft High School when he was averaging about 25 or 26 points and maybe 10 or 12 rebounds per game. Then he went on a tear where he probably averaged close to 35 points and 20-plus rebounds the last 10 games of the season. Then every school in the country was after him.

I remember Dwayne and I went to see him play one night when he scored 55 points and had like 35 or 36 rebounds. He was amazing and the arena was jam packed. I told Dwayne, "This is the night we're going to lose this young man."

But his mother stayed with the commitment and Kannard came and had a great career for us at Western. She told me that lots of schools had offered her money. She told everyone to take a hike and said that Western Kentucky had been recruiting her son all along and that was where he was going to go.

I will always have a soft spot in my heart for Tina and Kannard; I have a lot of love and respect for them for staying with their commitment. If anybody needed the money, it was her. They had four kids living in one bedroom. They didn't have a kitchen, just a small stove to warm food. She told me, "Kannard is going to come to school and play for you. You're going to make a man out of him. He needs a father figure."

When I left to take the job at Minnesota, I promised Tina and Kannard that I would go back and be a part of the ceremony when they retired his jersey at Taft High. I remember that I got a great big hug from her when I did go back and we both cried. She said, "You're a man of your word." That was one of the happiest days of my life.

Another big, and I mean big, recruit for us was Tellis Frank, a six-foot-ten, 225-pounder out of Gary, Indiana. He was a junior for us in 1985-86 and, along with Kannard and Clarence, formed a front line that I felt was as good as anyone's in the nation.

We had solid depth up front with Bryan Asberry, a six-foot-six, 240-pound wide body also out of Gary, Indiana, Fred Tisdale, a six-foot-six, 205-pound sophomore from Russellville, Kentucky, and Steve Miller, a six-foot-seven, 215-pound sophomore from Lexington.

The backcourt was led by Billy Gordon, a six-foot-one, 180-pound senior from Jackson, Mississippi, and Ray Swogger, a six-foot-three, 195-pound junior from Buffalo, New York, by way of Erie Community College. A six-foot, 180-pound sophomore from Owensboro, Kentucky, James McNary was also a key performer for us.

We opened the season with seven straight wins, including a 71-58 win over Auburn in our own Wendy's Classic. Despite 28 points from Billy, the streak ended with a hard-fought 73-70 loss at Louisville. Bryan added 15 points and James dished out 11 assists, but we turned the ball over 22 times in the game and that was our downfall.

Billy hit a 15-footer with five seconds left in overtime to give us a big 75-72 win at nationally-ranked UAB. In the rematch in front of a sellout crowd at Diddle Arena, Billy scored 20 points and Tellis had 17 points and 12 rebounds to lead us to an 81-75 win over Bartow's Blazers. I remember that some idiot threw a candy bar out of the stands at one of their coaches and Gene almost pulled his team off the floor. I was able to calm the crowd down, however, and the game continued.

We moved up to No. 19 in the Associated Press national poll, the first time in 15 years that Western had cracked the top 20 in the country. A 51-46 win over Jacksonville was our 10th straight win on the season and left our overall record at 18-3. Kannard had 18 points and Clarence hauled down 14 rebounds in the victory.

That was an exciting time at Western and especially in the Haskins household, as Clemette, a junior guard, was helping lead the school's women's team to yet another memorable season. She received All-America honors as the Lady Toppers made it to the women's Final Four for the second year in a row. The hardest part was that my schedule didn't allow me to see nearly as many of her games as I would have liked to.

We finished the season with a 20-7 record heading into the Sun Belt Conference Tournament at Birmingham, Alabama. After a 57-46 win over South Florida, we faced regular-season champion and host UAB, who we had beaten twice already that season. Despite 18 points and eight rebounds from Ray, the third time was not a charm, as UAB defeated us, 57-45, to win the tourney title and get the automatic bid into the NCAA's.

On Selection Sunday we were one of four teams from the Sun Belt—UAB, Old Dominion and Jacksonville were the other three —to receive a bid into the field of 64. We were set to play Nebraska in a first-round Southeast Region game in Charlotte, North Carolina. The winner would face none other than Kentucky. We then proceeded to knock off the Cornhuskers, 67-59, to finally set up the long-awaited confrontation with the Wildcats.

I think I had a personal grudge against Kentucky. When my Minnesota team played them in the 1997 Final Four, I had gotten over the bitterness towards Kentucky. I had put it behind me. But in 1986, believe me, it was still burning in my belly.

I wanted to beat Kentucky because I never got the chance to play against them in my college days and also never had the opportunity to coach against them. They would never play us at Western Kentucky; they thought they were too good to play us. So it was a personal thing with me. No one thought we'd ever be able to beat Kentucky.

After we beat Nebraska, Jim Richards brought Dr. Kern Alexander, the new president at Western, by the locker room to say a few words to the team. We were all fired up after beating Nebraska, and then President Alexander gave us this speech about how glad he was that we won the game, but that we had no chance against Kentucky and that we had a good year anyway.

Basically that's what he said and I was so pissed off. I was so irritated that he had no idea about what it meant to me, what it meant to the players and what it meant to Western Kentucky University to play against Kentucky. And we had a chance to win that game.

That was one of the most negative speeches I've ever heard. From that point on, I've always been very careful, very selective about bringing presidents in my locker room because most of them have no clue what it takes to get a team ready. I can understand why coaches are great motivational speakers, because we know how to get in the trenches and get people ready to perform.

It was a great game against fourth-ranked Kentucky, but we lost 71-64 in front of a sellout crowd. Kenny Walker had a phenomenal night for them, hitting a perfect 11-of-11 shots from the field. He played all 40 minutes of the game and also nailed 10-of-13 free throws to finish with 32 points on the night. For good measure he hauled down eight rebounds. We thought we were doing a good job of guarding him, but he took shots over the top of us.

Kannard had 20 points and Billy added 14 for us. The thing that a lot of people forget is that we lost our starting point guard, James McNary, in the first half of the ballgame with a badly sprained ankle. So James couldn't play in the second half and we still played them that close.

We were down by 12 points at the half, 36-24, and Kentucky increased their lead to 16 midway through the second half. But then we went on a run and cut the deficit to four points, 63-59, and I thought we had them on the ropes. But we just couldn't stop Walker.

The most irritating thing is that Kentucky outscored us at the free throw line, 23-10. In fact, we didn't shoot a single free throw in the first half. It doesn't take a rocket scientist to figure it out. When your opponent has 30 free throw attempts to your 15 in the game, you know it's going to be an uphill battle the whole way. I never said anything about it. I never complained about it after the game. I took it in stride.

In my heart, I knew who won that basketball game. But then that's the way I look at life. I know that when I prepare my team as well as I can, I could care less what anybody else thinks. We had 27 field goals and they only had 24. But we got outscored by 13 points at the free throw line. Go figure that one out.

It was a tough way to end a great, great season. The 23 victories were the most by a Western team in 15 years. The success we enjoyed that season was a real tribute to a group of young men and a coaching staff who hung in there through three very frustrating years.

Our thoughts immediately turned to next season. Billy would be the only senior lost to graduation, and with a strong recruiting class on the way, the sky was the limit in 1986-87.

Deep down, I knew I had the makings of a team that could compete not only for a Sun Belt Conference championship, but one that had all the ingredients in place to make a serious run for the national title.

WHAT HAVE I DONE?

CHAPTER EIGHTEEN

I could hardly wait for the 1986-87 season to start. The pieces of the puzzle were finally in place. Now it was just a matter of working out some of the formalities with President Alexander on a new five-year contract. John wasn't really involved in the process that much since he was retiring as athletics director that Spring.

Prior to the start of the NCAA Tournament I had received a call from Dr. Frank B. Wilderson, the vice president for student affairs at the University of Minnesota, to see if I was interested in becoming the Golden Gophers' new head coach. Clinton Hewitt, an associate vice president at the U of M who has become a close friend of mine, was the chair of the search committee and the person who initially suggested they talk to me about the job. I immediately told Frank no, that I had no interest in ever leaving the state of Kentucky. That was my home.

We were getting ready for our first-round NCAA game against Nebraska, so I told Frank to call me back next week and I'd give him a few names of some possible candidates for the job.

The week after we lost to Kentucky in the second round of the NCAA tourney, Frank called me back and I gave him a few names for them to check out, as I had promised. He asked me if I had changed my mind about the job and I told him no again.

A day or so later I set up a meeting with President Alexander to talk about a new contract. The minute I started talking about a five-year deal, he gave me the cold shoulder. They would only give me a three-year contract and that was it. I was making $41,000 per year my last season at Western. The new deal we proposed was for a modest raise to like $45,000 or $46,000 per year.

Money was not the issue at all. It was more about a commitment to me that I felt I deserved. I felt as though I had earned the right to a five-year contract after leading the Hilltoppers to a 23-win season and the Round of 32 of the NCAA Tournament.

It was one of the most embarrassing things I've ever gone through in my life. I really felt like he was saying that they didn't appreciate me and that I could leave if I wanted. It really hurt me.

I was getting ready to leave Bowling Green to attend the Kentucky state tournament in Lexington when I got another call from Minnesota. They asked me once again if I was interested in their job and I told them that if they wanted to talk to me they had to fly down to Lexington.

So Paul Giel, the athletics director at Minnesota, and the whole search committee flew to Lexington and we met at the Hyatt Regency hotel on a Friday afternoon. I basically interviewed them. You have to understand that I did not want the job. I wanted to stay at Western and honestly thought that we would resolve the issue of the five-year contract when all was said and done.

I talked to the committee for about three or four hours. It was well-documented from coast to coast that the Minnesota program was in rough shape. Its image was severely tarnished earlier that season when three players were charged with sexual assault after an incident in a hotel room following a game at Wisconsin. They were later acquitted, but the damage had already been done.

University of Minnesota President Kenneth Keller forfeited the team's next game. There was talk swirling around that the program might receive the "death penalty." In other words, there was discussion that the program might be disbanded.

Minnesota's head coach, Jim Dutcher, resigned shortly thereafter. That was unfortunate. Not only did he win almost 63 percent of his games at the "U" in 11 seasons, but he also brought the school a Big Ten title in 1982. He was a very good coach and is a fine person as well.

After we finished the interview, I told the committee that I'd be at the Final Four in Dallas the following week. I was still thinking deep down that everything would end up working out at Western.

A week passed and no progress was made on my contract situation at Western. President Alexander wanted nothing to do with the five-year deal. He didn't even want to talk about it.

First I had to fly to Dallas for some coaches meetings Wednesday and Thursday, and then I went back to Lexington Friday to watch Clemette play in the Women's Final Four. I flew back to Dallas, and on the Sunday before the national championship game, I met with President Keller and Frank Wilderson for a couple of hours. I agreed that on Tuesday, the day following the national championship game, Yevette and I would come through the Twin Cities before returning to Western.

We arrived in the Twin Cities and met with the search committee once again. The job was mine if I wanted it. They were offering a five-year deal with a base salary of $80,000 per year.

Yevette and I took some time to think it over. I asked her what she thought and she said, "It's up to you. If you want to do this, I'll support you every step of the way." So I agreed to take the job.

What happened next is a true story. We were in Paul's car heading back to the airport when I said, "You know, I haven't been to the gym yet." Thank God I did not see Williams Arena before I gave my word that I would take the job.

I couldn't believe what I saw when we got inside. There were rats running across the floor and the place still wasn't cleaned up from the last game of the season. It was a complete mess. It smelled awful and it looked awful. The court was raised up, almost like a stage. The lights were just starting to come on and I could hardly see a thing.

It was like someone had stuck a pin in my side and let all the air out of me. I thought to myself, "Oh my God, what have I done?" I walked around wondering how I could ever recruit anyone to play in this dump. I was down and both Paul and Frank saw it.

When we got back into the car and headed toward the airport, I didn't say a word for about five minutes. I was saying to myself, "I don't want this. I don't need this." Then all of a sudden Paul looked back and started into a sales pitch about how "it's a great place when it's full. We fill it up every game."

The money wasn't the most important thing in my decision to accept the job at Minnesota. I have never worried about material things. All I want to do is to try to provide my family with the things they need. Given how bad the situation was at Minnesota, I probably could have asked for and gotten a whole heck of a lot more money. They needed me to turn the program around at Minnesota.

Western didn't have good leadership in place at the time. I never would have left the school if they would have given me a five-year contract. Any man in his right mind would've given me a five-year deal. That's what a strong leader would have done. He would have built for the future.

After all I had done for Western both as a player and coach, it was absolutely devastating to know the leadership in place at my school didn't appreciate me. I thought they had forsaken me. So I realized it was time to leave.

It was hard for me to leave Western. It was tough as a coach to say goodbye so suddenly to an outstanding group of young men to whom I had become so attached. Kannard, Tellis, Ray, Clarence, Bryan—all the guys. I really, really felt bad about leaving my players behind.

When I got back to Bowling Green after accepting the job at Minnesota, one of the hardest things I've ever done in my life was having to walk into our locker room at Diddle Arena and tell the guys that I was leaving. I tried to explain to them that they would get a great coach who would help them continue to grow.

Each and every one of those guys knew that I loved them, that I cared about them and was just a phone call away. In all honesty, I probably spent almost as much time talking to the players at Western that first year as I did with my own guys at Minnesota. I encouraged them to play hard, do the right things and go to class.

It was also tough because I didn't get to see Clemette play at all during her senior season at Western. She could have gone to school anywhere in the country coming out of high school, but she decided to stay at home and play for the Hilltoppers so that her family could see her play.

She thought about transferring to Minnesota. If they would've had a quality program at the time, she might have sat out a year as a transfer and then played her senior year for the Golden Gophers. She had helped lead Western to two straight Final Fours, really loved the place and decided it was best to stay and finish what she had started.

Of course Yevette tried to get back to Bowling Green as often as possible to see her play during her senior year. The phone bill was outrageous that year. We're really close as a family so it was tough to leave her behind.

After we tied up all of our loose ends in Bowling Green, I hit the ground running at Minnesota. When I got there I think I only had one eligible player. I also had to hit the recruiting trail and put my staff together. Those first two years there was just so much to do. I didn't have time to say, "My God, what have I gotten myself into?"

I was worried about trying to put a team together that could at least be competitive. I never once stopped to think what I had to do, how hard I was working and the stress it put on me. I really think that I aged about 10 years in those first two seasons. Quite honestly, I don't think I ever fully realized how bad the situation was at Minnesota, what kind of shape the program was in.

In addition to dealing with the fallout from the sexual assault incident, there was the Luther Darville trial and subsequent NCAA investigation that I also had to go through. Darville, an administrator in the Office of Minority and Special Student Affairs (OMSSA) at the time, was on trial for stealing nearly $200,000 in university money.

Darville said that he was merely acting as a middleman for the athletics department, funneling most of the money to minority student-athletes. He was ultimately found guilty in November of 1989 and spent some time in prison.

It started with football and then carried over into basketball. There were accusations about me, the basketball program and the football program. I will never forget the people in the courtroom during the trial who sat there and lied. God knows I can never forget that. I never want to go through something like that ever again.

They were accusing me of things that I knew nothing about. They said that I talked to Darville about giving me some money to help "buy" some players so that they would come to Minnesota. I never even talked to Luther Darville. Never talked to him.

That's the thing that just eats at me. I would never, ever want to go through that again because it's not worth it. It was beyond belief to me that some people could walk into the courtroom, put their hand on the Bible and lie. Now I know that people will do that. That's why it's so hard to prove who's innocent and who's guilty. Some people lie. Until it happened to me, I didn't think people would flat out lie under oath.

Those are the things that I went through my first couple of years at Minnesota that I wouldn't want to go through again. That investigation started with football and should never have carried over into basketball. It filtrated over into basketball because they were trying to take the pressure off some other people and put it on me.

That's the thing that I will never be able to forgive the administration in place at the University of Minnesota at that time for. Because the University of Minnesota did not come forward and support Clem Haskins. I knew nothing about those things. It cost me $57,500 out of my own pocket for legal fees to clear my name and my reputation for something I had absolutely nothing to do with.

No one has ever come forward to talk about reimbursing me for those costs. But I think my doing that helped save the image of both the University and the program. It's the principle of the matter and one of those things that I'm still very bitter about to this day.

My attorney, Ron Zamansky, really saved Clem Haskins' career when the University of Minnesota administration turned its back on me during the investigation. He brought direction to what was going on and I also think he saved the "U" a lot of money as well.

I was very disgruntled and upset. But Ron stood by me and I never would have made it without his help and support. He's not only a good attorney, but also a dear friend and also a very caring individual.

No matter how much money they would pay me, it would never be enough to pay me back for what I went through back then. Would I do it again? If it was just coaching basketball and dealing with the kids, I'd have no problem with it. It's the other bullshit, like the investigation and dealing with the fallout from the rape incident, that I would not want to go through again.

It was tough to leave the Western Kentucky job, not only because it's my alma mater and I genuinely care about the school, but also because I was at the time the only black head men's Division I basketball coach in the history of the state. I felt a tremendous amount of responsibility to help continue to break down barriers of that nature, not only in my home state of Kentucky, but throughout the South.

Taking the job at Minnesota, however, allowed me to break down some more barriers. By accepting the challenge, I became the first permanent black head coach ever at the school.

Those first few years, especially at Minnesota I dealt with a lot of threatening phone calls and hate mail. Some of them were just downright bad; the same kind of stuff that I had to deal with back in the '60s in high school. Just different voices, different names, a different location. My past experiences in Kentucky, however, had prepared me to deal with it better at Minnesota.

There wasn't a lot left in the cupboard when I took over as coach. The program was about as down as it could get at the Division I level, much less at a Big Ten school.

The returning players from the 1985-86 season were Terence Woods, a six-foot-five senior forward from Houston, Texas; Tim Hanson, a six-foot-six junior forward/guard from Prior Lake Minnesota; David Holmgren, a seven-foot junior center also from Prior Lake; Kelvin Smith, a six-foot-seven sophomore forward from Conroe, Texas; Ray Gaffney, a six-foot-two sophomore guard from Dayton, Ohio; and Jon Retzlaff, a six-foot-two walk-on guard from Apple Valley, Minnesota. We also signed Kim Zurcher, a six-foot-two guard out of Kilgore Community College in Texas.

Willie Burton, Richard Coffey, Mario Green, Connell Lewis, Melvin Newbern, Terence Williams and Jim Shikenjanski comprised my freshman class that first year. Jim Dutcher's staff had already signed Willie, "Shik" and Melvin before I got the job, but we had to work our tail ends off after all the problems to keep them in the fold.

Quite honestly, Willie was the only one out of the group who was highly recruited. This group would take its share of lumps early-on, but they would go on to make history by the end of their careers.

Willie was out of DePorres High School in Detroit where he averaged 22 points and 12 rebounds per game as a senior. A two-time all-state selection, his ability was raw, but he had all the makings of becoming a big-time player for us down the road.

Richard came in as a 21-year-old freshman straight out of the Airborne unit of the U.S. Army, where he was a paratrooper. We signed him exactly three days before the start of fall semester. He was a well-chiseled six-foot-six, 212 pounds who was initially short on offensive skills, but long on determination and intestinal fortitude. He developed into one of the finest rebounders I've ever coached.

A native of the Bahamas, Mario was a six-foot-two guard with some natural scoring ability. Connell was a six-foot-one guard from

Cass Tech High School in Detroit with limited offensive skills. He had a huge heart, however, and he ended up being a fine defensive player for us.

"Shik" was a six-foot-nine, 230-pound center out of Hononegah High School in Roscoe, Illinois. He wasn't blessed with great athletic talent, but by the end of his career, I think I can say that he got as much out of his ability as any player I've ever coached.

Melvin was a talented six-foot-four guard who could play at the point or at shooting guard. A Prop 48 student, he would not be eligible to play until the 1987-88 season. Terence, a six-foot-one guard from Ecorse, Michigan, stayed in the program for three seasons and played sparingly.

Don Evans made the move from Western with me and was an assistant on my first staff at Minnesota. Milton Barnes, Ray Jones and Jay Williams were the other assistants, while Dan Kosmoski was my graduate assistant coach.

Don is like a brother to me, so it was great to have him by my side once again at Minnesota. A hard-working, loyal individual, he is now an assistant coach at Bellarmine College in Louisville where his wife, Donna, works for WDRB-TV. I trust my life with Don and he deserves a lot of credit for helping me through some tough times both at Western and at Minnesota.

Milt, who is now the head coach at Eastern Michigan, spent a number of hours just putting out all sorts of fires those first two seasons. It seemed as though he had very little time to actually be on the floor coaching back then.

After two seasons with us, Milt left to become the athletics director and basketball coach at Albion High School in Michigan. He then rejoined us in 1991-92 for five seasons, before taking the job at Eastern Michigan prior to the start of the 1996-97 season. He won 22 games as a rookie coach, including a big win at Syracuse. Blessed with a great wife in Lynn, he's the guy that I'd like to see replace me someday at Minnesota.

Dan, or "Koz" as we call him, was a graduate assistant coach on Jim Dutcher's staff and I kept him on my staff my first year. In addition to providing a lot of stability during tough times, "Koz" is a good X's and O's coach. A native Minnesotan who still runs my basketball camps, I owe him a lot because he did a lot to help promote our program to the high school coaches in the state. He is now the head coach at St. Olaf College in Northfield, Minnesota. Yevette and I really value the friendship of "Koz" and his wife, Ellen.

Behind 24 points from Kelvin Smith, we defeated North Dakota State, 70-53, in my first game as coach at Minnesota in front of 11,324 at Williams Arena on November 30, 1986. After all we had been through, I shed a few tears after that one.

Three weeks later we lost, 73-64, to Austin Peay at home and the guys saw another side of me. The game had ended at about 9 p.m., and about an hour or so later, we were back up on the court for a 75-minute practice.

I think we surprised a lot of people, myself included, when we finished the non-conference season with a 7-3 overall record. We opened the Big Ten season against Wisconsin at Williams Arena. With the score tied 67-67 and the clock winding down, Kim hit a 15-foot jumper with three seconds remaining to give us a 69-67 victory. We followed that up with a 60-53 win over Northwestern at "The Barn" two days later and suddenly we were tied with second-ranked Iowa atop the conference standings at 2-0.

Then reality hit us. The Hawkeyes came into Williams Arena and absolutely blew us out of our own building, 78-57. After the 2-0 start, we ending up losing our last 16 games of the season to finish 9-19 overall and 2-16 and tied for last in the conference. In fact, 13 of the 16 losses were by 10 or more points. Don't get me wrong, these guys never quit and gave it all they had. We were just overmatched, plain and simple.

After registering a 6-4 non-conference record to start the 1987-88 season, the brick wall hit us again once we entered the rugged Big Ten schedule. We lost our first five conference games to make it 21 straight losses in the league over two seasons.

"The streak" ended when Willie scored 20 points and Melvin added 16 of his own in a 59-56 win at Michigan State on January 27. It was a big win for that group of guys because they had been plugging away for so long and finally got rewarded for their efforts.

I remember that in the locker room after the game, our sports information director, Bob Peterson, had a Cuban cigar for me to smoke in celebration. I guess "BP" had been carrying it around for the past two seasons just waiting for us to end the streak. I don't smoke at all—it took me about 10 minutes to light the darn thing—and I think I turned a number of shades of green after a few puffs. That was a win to really savor.

Kevin Lynch and Walter Bond were freshmen on my second team at Minnesota and both would end up playing big roles in the resurgence of our program. Kevin was a six-foot-five guard from

Jefferson High School in Bloomington, Minnesota. He collected all-state honors as a senior after leading the school to back-to-back state titles. Walter was a six-foot-five forward out of Collins High School in Chicago where he was a great all-around athlete.

Just when the fans at Williams Arena were getting used to me tossing off my sportcoat during games, the 1987-88 season marked the debut of my now ever-present stool which I use to sit on during games up on the raised floor.

I tried going up and down the stairs for a few games that first season and then I gave kneeling on a towel up on the floor a shot. My knees just couldn't handle it. It's funny because a lot of other coaches around the Big Ten started doing the same thing before long.

Longtime Michigan State coach, Jud Heathcote, openly talked about his dislike for the floor. The season he retired we gave him his own little stool, painted half in Michigan State's green and white colors, and half in Minnesota's maroon and gold.

We finished my second season at Minnesota with a 10-18 overall record and a 4-14 Big Ten mark which placed us ninth in the conference for the second straight season. The last game that season was a 93-66 drubbing at Purdue.

I took the losses hard, but deep down I realized that we just weren't good enough. As long as we were competitive and played as hard as we could, in my heart I felt like we had won the basketball game. That's what I professed to my team and to our fans.

The key word was hope. If they stayed with us, I promised the fans that we would be good someday. I never promised we'd win the Big Ten championship or that we'd ever win 20 games in a season. I promised them we'd play hard and that we'd do it with kids in our program that have character and class. That's all I ever promised from day one.

TURNING THE CORNER

CHAPTER NINETEEN

When you take over a program like Minnesota's that was so far down, you need to have people in your camp who will support you through thick and thin. We had two tough, lean years in 1986-87 and 1987-88, and yet a very special person befriended me and his support has always been instrumental to the success of our program.

Governor Arne Carlson was the state auditor when I first became the coach at Minnesota. He used to come over and watch us practice whenever his work schedule would permit it, or take me to lunch and tell me to "hang in there." Even in the toughest of times, he always had an encouraging word or two to give me. I'll never forget that. It meant a lot.

I can't even begin to tell you how much Arne's friendship means to me. It makes me mad when some people just assume that we became friends after he took over as governor. That couldn't be further from the truth. I think that the state has been better off to have a governor like Arne Carlson. I wish that more states around the country had governors like Arne who support their athletics teams and are more vocal about the right things.

My executive secretary, Carolyn Allen, and our team trainer, Roger Schipper, have also been with me since day one. Carolyn, who celebrated her 25th year at the University of Minnesota in June of 1997, runs our office and takes care of my busy schedule. She does a tremendous job for us year after year. Carolyn and her husband Dan, the director of the department of recreational sports at the U of M, have always been so loyal and committed to our program.

Roger has been a loyal worker to the "U," to our program and to Clem Haskins. He's a very caring person, and all of our players who have come through the program have placed a great deal of trust in him and he's always delivered. He's not only dependable, but he's very fair as well.

Right before the tipoff of every game, I walk over to Roger, he gives me a piece of gum and then usually tells me a joke to loosen me up. He's had some good ones through the years.

Roger and Carolyn were with me long before we saw any light at the end of the tunnel. They both deserve a lot of credit for our success by keeping the ship sailing straight through some crazy times.

I remember walking off Purdue's Mackey Arena Court after the Boilermakers drubbed us, 93-66, in the 1987-88 season finale and thinking to myself that I hope the rest of the league has enjoyed their opportunity to beat up on us the past two seasons. Now it was time to turn the corner.

I made two key additions to our coaching staff in the offseason. Al Brown and Silas McKinnie joined my staff as assistant coaches and they proved to be wonderful additions at a crucial stage in our program. In fact, Al is now an assistant women's coach under Pat Summit at Tennessee. The Volunteers won back-to-back national championships in 1996 and 1997.

The bumps and bruises we had suffered through together the first two seasons started to reap dividends in 1988-89. This group had grown up together and we went into the Iowa game at Williams Arena on January 14 with an 8-4 overall record and an 0-2 mark in the conference.

If I had to point to the one game that helped our program turn the corner, it would be our 80-78 win over Iowa that year. "Shik" tipped one in with one second to go to win that game. It was his only field goal of the game, but an awful big one. The Hawkeyes called timeout and then Roy Marble hit a shot at the other end that was just after the buzzer to set off a wild celebration in Williams Arena.

That was a great Hawkeye team. They came into the contest 13-1 overall and ranked fifth in the nation. The week before they played us they had gone into North Carolina and beat the Tar Heels and Coach Dean Smith on their home court. They had a collection of great players: Marble, B.J. Armstrong, Ed Horton and Les Jepsen.

Willie led the way for us with 28 points. Melvin and Ray also had great games for us with 27 and 18 points, respectively. Our sixth man, the Williams Arena crowd, was into the game, all 15,491 of them. "The Barn" was hopping.

When I accepted the job at Minnesota, I looked at "The Barn" as an eyesore. Now I was realizing how special the place could be when we were able to give our fans something to cheer about. A few years back a national magazine ranked it the third best college basketball arena in the entire country.

A massive renovation project was completed just prior to the 1993-94 season which will keep the storied arena among the nation's finest for many years to come. It's one of the loudest arenas I've ever been in and the atmosphere is tremendous.

That win over Iowa gave our players great confidence and I think we gained a lot of respect around the country as well. It showed that we had come a long way and now we were good enough to play with anybody on any given night, especially on our home court.

I think it also helped us gain the respect of the officials too. They are human beings, and I've always felt that they referee a given game based on who is the best team. It's still like that today. The good teams and the nationally renowned programs still get the close calls. A lot of people don't like to hear that, but it's a fact of life.

I'm a good enough coach that we'll beat our opponents when we're better than or as good as they are. I have to be as good or better than they are in order to win. It's really tough when we're an underdog. It's just the way it is. It's sad to say that.

I cried after the win over the Hawkeyes. I was so happy for this program and for our kids. I had worked them so hard and had pushed them to the limit. I have never pushed a team any harder than that one. At one time or another during their careers, I took their car keys away.

"Shik" had a nice car with personalized licence plates on the back and I took his keys away when he was a freshman. Believe it or not, I still have a set of those keys today. I took Willie's keys from him when he was a junior. In the end they respected me for that, because we not only wanted to win, but I also wanted them to do what was right.

I prepared them to get into the position to win their last two years. I built for the future. I wasn't worried about the first two seasons. All I wanted was for our fans to stay with us and then I really believed in my heart that we'd be good enough to win.

And they did. I was so proud of my players after that game. I was so happy for them. They had gone through so much and finally they had won a big game against a nationally ranked team. They were very deserving of it because of the time, effort and work that they had put in.

It was also a big win for our fans because they had stuck with us through the tough times. Those tears of joy were also for them. I wanted to let them know how much we appreciated their support, win or lose. I think that hands down we have the very best fans in all of college basketball.

That win got us over the hump, gave us great confidence and then things really started to snowball after that. The very next game we defeated Purdue, 76-66, after trailing by eight points with just under seven minutes to play.

We had great balance with four great players in double figures; Willie had 15 points, Melvin 14, and Kevin and Ray had 12 apiece. Richard controlled the boards once again with a game-high 10 rebounds. It also marked the first time in six games that I had beaten my good friend, Gene Keady.

We beat top-ranked Illinois, 69-62, at Williams Arena behind 20 points and 13 rebounds from Willie. Coach Lou Henson had a great team, led by Kendall Gill (who was injured and didn't play in that game), Nick Anderson and Kenny Battle. They came into Williams Arena 17-0 and they eventually made it to the Final Four that season.

Later in the season, 10th-ranked Michigan came into Williams Arena on February 11. Rumeal Robinson, Glen Rice, Terry Mills, Loy Vaught and company would go on to win the NCAA title over Seton Hall at the Kingdome in Seattle a little over a month later. Willie and Ray paced us with 27 and 24 points, respectively, as we came away with an 88-80 upset of the Wolverines.

It was no secret that Willie had become our go-to guy. He and Rice, who led all scorers in the game with 29 points, went toe-to-toe in this one and it was a sight to behold. In addition to scoring 27 points, Willie also had 11 rebounds in the game. Richard hauled down 10 rebounds of his own as we finished with a commanding

41-21 edge on the boards. That was the difference in the game right there.

In addition, Ray came off the bench to provide us with a big spark. He hit eight-of-nine from the field, including a perfect three-for-three from three-point range.

The rest of the nation was standing up and taking notice of what was happening at the University of Minnesota. Williams Arena was fast becoming the place to be for sports fans in the Twin Cities and Gopher tickets were in short supply.

After a four-game losing streak where we also lost Richard with a severe knee injury during a 38-point loss at Iowa, we bounced back to defeat Northwestern, 78-59, and then Michigan State, 77-61. When Richard went down with the injury, Walter stepped up down the stretch and gave us some quality minutes as a starter.

We knew what was on the line when we went into our season finale at Ohio State on March 11 with a 16-11 overall record and an 8-9 mark in the Big Ten. If we beat the Buckeyes we were in the NCAA Tournament.

If there was ever any doubt about whether or not this team had come of age and belonged in the NCAA Tournament, those thoughts were put to rest with a 78-70 win over the Buckeyes at St. John Arena.

The game showed how much grit and determination this group really had. Willie and Melvin scored 17 points apiece to lead us, but that doesn't even begin to tell the story of this game.

Willie broke his nose with 6:17 left in the game. I'll never forget when he came to the sidelines after breaking it. His nose was bleeding and it was sitting off to one side. I was looking at him and he was saying to me, "Coach, I'm ready to go. I'm ready to go back in."

Our trainer, Roger Schipper, was stuffing cotton up his nose to try to stop the bleeding and I felt so bad for Willie. But I also knew that we needed to have him out there for us to have any chance to win the game. After just 53 seconds had ticked off the clock, I put Willie back into the game and he stayed on the floor the rest of the way.

It showed the heart of an individual and was a test of character for our ballclub. That's why I can point to so many instances where that team and that group of individuals rose to the occasion and did whatever it took to get the job done. That's why they're so special as players and as young men.

We had to play the waiting game to see if the NCAA would select us as an at-large team for the field of 64. There was no question in my mind that we belonged in the tourney. We were on a roll after finishing the season with three straight victories. On top of that, we had defeated four top-20 teams during the season, including No. 1 Illinois.

We watched the Selection Sunday show together as a team the next day and I can't even put into words how satisfying it was when Minnesota went up on the board as the 11th seed in the East Region. It marked the first time since 1982 and only the third time in school history that the program would be in the NCAA Tournament. Just a little over a year after ending a 21-game Big Ten losing streak, we were in the "Big Dance."

Our first-round opponent was sixth-seeded Kansas State out of the Big Eight Conference at the Greensboro (N.C.) Coliseum. We had already beaten Coach Lon Kruger's Wildcats, 72-67, at Williams Arena back in early January. They were a fine team with a great outside shooter in Steve Henson. A year earlier they had advanced to the "Elite Eight" of the NCAA tourney.

Despite the broken nose, Willie played in the game wearing a specially designed mask that Roger had gotten for him. Replicas of the mask ended up becoming the rage throughout the Twin Cities during the tournament.

Kevin's baseline jumper just over two minutes into the game gave us a 5-4 lead and we never trailed after that as we came away with an 86-75 win over the Wildcats. Willie had 29 points and 13 rebounds, while Kevin came up big as well with 18 points.

We did a great job of shutting down Henson. Although he scored 25 points, he shot just 8-of-23 from the field, including 5-of-15 on three-pointers. I knew it was our day when sophomore reserve forward Rob Metcalf actually banked in a key free throw down the stretch to help preserve the win.

We caught a break when 14th-seed Siena upset third-seeded Stanford in the first round. Two days later behind 19 points and 11 rebounds from Willie, we beat Siena, 80-67, to advance to the "Sweet 16." "Shik" and Melvin had 17 points apiece, while Kevin gave us four players in double figures with 14 points. We put the icing on the cake when Bob Martin, a seven-foot freshman center from Apple Valley, Minnesota, took a perfect lob pass from Melvin with less than two minutes in the game and slammed it through for a 78-63 lead.

It hardly seemed possible, but we were one of 16 teams left in the country. It didn't matter that powerful Duke, led by an All-American in Danny Ferry, was our next opponent.

The East Regional semifinal was held at the Meadowlands Arena in New Jersey. Richard had recovered enough from the knee injury to play in the game and I hoped that his return would provide us with a boost. In reality, however, the Blue Devils were just too good for us. They opened the game by taking a 20-7 lead in the first six-plus minutes, and we never got closer than 11 points after that in an 87-70 loss that ended our season at 19-12 overall.

Willie was sensational once again. He led all scorers with 26 points, while Kevin finished with 14. Phil Henderson and Robert Brickey paced Duke with 21 points, while Ferry added 18. The Blue Devils shot 64 percent from the field in the first half and that was basically the ballgame right there.

That was a team that was picked by many of the so-called experts at the beginning of the season to finish ninth or 10th in the Big Ten. They went out and proved to themselves and the rest of the country that the University of Minnesota not only belonged in the NCAA Tournament, but also that we were a program that was going to have to be reckoned with in the future.

THE STAGE IS SET

CHAPTER TWENTY

Our late season run in 1988-89 gave our team a taste of success. Now they wanted more, much more. That set the stage for a special season in 1989-90.

We went to Australia and New Zealand on our foreign trip in August. I really think that trip helped prepare us for our great run that season. We had the chance to practice and be together for about a month.

It was a great opportunity for me to spread the minutes around and give some of our reserves quality playing time. Mario, Connell, Bob and Rob played quite a bit on that trip and I knew that would really pay off once we got into the heart of our Big Ten schedule.

We were a perfect 7-0 on that trip. Every other school that had gone on that same trip up until that time had either gone to the Final Four or Elite Eight of the NCAA Tournament the following season. However, we were the first ones to ever go undefeated on the trip. It's a tough trip, but we were able to pull it off.

I knew going into the foreign trip that we were going to be a good team. Afterward I realized that we had the chance to have a great ballclub. I felt that we were ready to compete for not only the Big Ten title, but that we also had a shot of really doing well in the NCAA Tournament.

With all five starters coming back from our "Sweet 16" squad from the previous year, we were ranked No. 20 in the preseason Associated Press national poll. Optimism was at an all-time high in the Twin Cities heading into the season.

Our first game was at Cincinnati on November 25. It was the first game in their new Shoemaker Arena. I had put that game on our schedule because of my relationship with Tony Yates, the head coach at Cincinnati prior to Bob Huggins. Tony ended up getting fired the previous year. The deal was made for Tony and we still had to fulfill the terms of the agreement after the coaching change was made.

It was a hard-fought game and we led by a point, 64-63, with eight-tenths of a second left and they had the ball out of bounds underneath their basket. We played great defense and they had to pass it to Steve Sanders, a Bearcat football player who had never scored a point, or even taken a shot, in a college game. He shot it and nailed the three at the buzzer to give them a two-point win.

Looking back, it was probably a blessing in disguise for us to get beat. I think we were a little bit too cocky, a little bit too complacent, heading into the season. Everybody was telling us how good we were going to be and it was all based on what we had done at the end of the previous season.

The loss caused us to get refocused and I think made the guys look back at why we were so successful down the stretch and in the tournament. It was because we worked hard and did all the little things right within our game plan. Once they took a step back after that season-opening loss, they regrouped, got their heads together and came back and had a tremendous year.

Then we reeled off nine straight wins, including a 69-68 win at Kansas State in a rematch of our NCAA Tournament game, to head into Big Ten play with a 9-1 overall record. The game at Kansas State was a scary one for a couple of reasons: first it went right down to the wire and I had visions of a replay of the Cincinnati game dancing in my head; second I almost collapsed walking off the court after the game. I guess it was tension. The blood rushed to my head and I blacked out.

Illinois came into Williams Arena on January 6 for the Big Ten opener. Fresh from a Final Four appearance the previous season, Lou Henson's ballclub was unbeaten on the year at 11-0 and ranked fourth in the country. The atmosphere was absolutely electric with 16,545 fans jammed into "The Barn" like sardines.

The spotlight on that night belonged to Kevin and Melvin who completely outplayed the Fighting Illini's highly touted backcourt of Kendall Gill and Steve Bardo to propel us to a convincing 91-74 victory. Melvin scored 27 points and Kevin had 17 as they outscored Gill and Bardo 44-17 in the game. That just might have been Melvin's finest game. He did it all that night for us, including dishing out eight assists.

There were a lot of stars in a game that we completely dominated. Willie had 21 points and seven rebounds, while Richard grabbed 12 rebounds. That was probably the biggest win of the year for us and one of the most exciting games I've been involved during my career at Minnesota.

We brought a 13-4 overall record and a 4-3 Big Ten mark into an ABC national TV showdown with Indiana on Super Bowl Sunday in front of 16,636 at Williams Arena. Willie scored 22 points in the game to lead a total of six players in double figures as we throttled Bob Knight's Hoosiers 108-89.

Kevin and Walter with 17 points apiece, "Shik" with 16, and Richard and Melvin with 14 each, joined Willie in double digits. Connell, or "Corn" as I like to call him, just missed it with eight points. The win snapped a 15-game losing streak to the Hoosiers and the 108 points were the most ever against a Knight-coached Indiana team.

More importantly, for the five seniors—Willie, Richard, "Shik," "Corn" and Melvin—the win held special meaning since Indiana was the only team that they had never beaten during their collegiate careers at Minnesota.

It was just as sweet when we beat the Hoosiers, 75-70, in the rematch at Assembly Hall in Bloomington on March 1 to run our record to 20-6 overall and 11-5 in the Big Ten. It was really special to share the victory with my good friend George Suleon, who had followed my career and supported me since we were in high school. He lived in Louisville and always made the trip to Assembly Hall to see us play the Hoosiers. That was my first win ever there.

Two years removed from a forgettable 21-game conference losing streak, it was an incredible feeling to get that 20th win that night. Only four teams in school history had ever accomplished that feat.

Senior Night came on March 3 against Michigan State. Those are always tough for me to go through, knowing that it's time to let go of young men who have become so much a part of your life for the past four or five years.

That particular evening was the most difficult one I've ever experienced because of what that group and I had gone through together to rebuild a basketball program. They meant so much to me and they always will. Willie, Richard, "Corn," Melvin and "Shik" were introduced one last time along with their parents to the 16,732 fans at Williams Arena. They received a thunderous standing ovation that went on and on and on.

Looking back, I think that our emotions got away from us. We were jacked up a bit too high, and we paid the price for it. We missed our first seven shots of the game and played catch-up the rest of the way. Trailing 62-57, Willie drained a three-pointer with 46 seconds left and then a jumper with five seconds left to tie it up and send the game into overtime.

With the game tied at 73-all, the Spartans' Steve Smith, a fantastic player who had 39 points in the game, hit a bucket with 29 seconds left to give the eventual Big Ten champions the win. Despite the loss, I sent the five seniors back up on the floor to take one final lap around the Williams Arena floor and the crowd loved it. Win or lose, those guys deserved that.

We closed out the regular season at 20-8 overall and 11-7 in the Big Ten after losing, 93-83, at Ohio State in the regular season finale on March 10. We had tied for fourth in the Big Ten with Illinois.

This time around we knew that we had an NCAA berth in the bag. The questions of who, when and where were all that remained. On Selection Sunday we learned that we were the sixth seed in the Southeast Regional and that we would play 11th-seeded UTEP in the first round at Richmond, Virginia.

The game against UTEP was ugly. Just plain old ugly. We were badly outshot and outrebounded, but we hung in there somehow and came away with a 64-62 win in overtime. UTEP was a very solid team and Don Haskins is one of the all-time winningest coaches in college basketball history.

They had some great players in Greg Foster, who is still playing in the NBA today, and Marlon Maxey, who also wound up playing some pro ball. We were all familiar with Marlon who signed to play with us as a freshman in 1987-88, but then transferred after his first season.

The most important thing in postseason play is to win and advance. You don't get any style points for how you do it. You just win and advance. Lose and you go home. Kevin led us with 18 points, while Richard had 11 rebounds.

It was a similar situation as the year before when a 14th seed knocked off a third seed. This time Northern Iowa knocked off Missouri, a team that had been rated No. 1 earlier in the season, by a score of 74-71. Northern Iowa coach Eldon Miller always had his teams well prepared. They also had a big center named Jason Reese who could really play.

We came out of the gate quickly, shooting 61 percent from the field in the first half to take a 46-40 lead at the break. Reese killed us inside all afternoon. He scored 29 points and had 10 rebounds. We tried a lot of different defensive looks, but we could never find the right formula to contain him.

Once again, we got on Willie Burton's shoulders and he took us for a ride, and what a ride it was. He scored 36 points and had 12 rebounds in the game. Melvin did a wonderful job of getting him the ball within our offense. He finished with nine assists. Kevin and Walter joined Willie in double figures with 12 points each.

Even though our "Sweet 16" game against powerful Syracuse wasn't until Friday night, we left for New Orleans a day early. We checked into our hotel on Tuesday and I gave them one night to experience Bourbon Street.

I've always tried to make sure that the kids have a good time during postseason play. I want them to enjoy the experience. A lot of times coaches get so wrapped up in winning that we forget to make sure that the kids get an opportunity to fully soak up the experience as well. I think that if you have the right young men in your program you can trust them. You know that they'll do the right thing.

So we did go in early. It was the first time that we had been to New Orleans. We had heard so much about it and it is a great city. So I wanted them to go out and enjoy Bourbon Street. We had a mature group of seniors and I gave them no curfew that first night.

I knew in my heart that they would be back at the hotel at a reasonable time, but I didn't expect them to be back by 11 o'clock. Those guys had one thing on their minds and that was to advance to the Final Four. They didn't want to do anything to hurt their chances of accomplishing that goal. They were on a mission.

No one gave us a chance to beat Syracuse. On paper, there was no way that we were supposed to beat them. Their three big guys up front—Derrick Coleman, Billy Owens and LeRon Ellis—all ended up being first-round draft picks in the NBA. In fact, Coleman was the first pick overall in 1990 and Owens ended up being a lottery pick in 1991. On top of that, one of their guards, Dave Johnson, was a first-round pick in 1992.

We trailed 39-35 at the half, but shot 79 percent from the floor in the second half and came away with an 82-75 upset that shocked a lot of people around the country. It didn't faze us though. We used a variety of defensive looks and combinations to try to confuse Syracuse on the other end of the floor. They shot just 37 percent in the last half.

Melvin, with 20 points, four assists and four steals, and Kevin, with 18 points, including 16 in the second half, were great in the backcourt. We had some foul problems up front, but Bob Martin came off the bench and played exceptionally well. He hit four-of-five field goal attempts, was two-of-two from the line and had three rebounds in 16 minutes. I would have to say that it was without a doubt the finest game of his college career, especially when you consider the circumstances.

Everything clicked. You go into every ballgame with a game plan, but for whatever reason, it doesn't always work out the way you want it to. On that particular night, things went according to the agenda and it was one of the most satisfying wins in my career.

Two days later we met Georgia Tech for the right to go to the Final Four in Denver. Coach Bobby Cremins' team had three great players in Kenny Anderson, Dennis Scott and Brian Oliver. In fact, they called them "Lethal Weapon III" after the popular movie. They were three talented players who could really hurt you with the three-pointer.

Georgia Tech, from the Atlantic Coast Conference (ACC), had advanced to the regional final with an emotional 81-80 overtime win over Michigan State. With the Spartans leading by two and the clock winding down, Anderson hit a shot at the end of the game that had sparked a lot of controversy.

It was debated whether he had got the shot off before the buzzer and whether or not it was a three-pointer. At first the referees called it a three-pointer and Tech celebrated. Then they huddled up and said that his foot was on the line and that it should have only been two points. Television replays afterwards indicated that he actually had taken the shot after the clock had expired.

Of course, we didn't care who we had to play because they were the final roadblock on our mission to get to the Final Four. It would have been great for the Big Ten Conference, however, to have us and Michigan State play for the right to move on to Denver. Steve Smith is a real special player and Jud Heathcote is a good friend so it was hard to see him lose a tough one like that.

It was the first and only time I've ever coached against Bobby. It's funny how things go. We ended up becoming good friends when we were assistant coaches under Lenny Wilkens at the '96 Atlanta Olympic Games.

The Georgia Tech game was a phenomenal game. It seemed like it was the Final Four. We had a pair of 12-point leads in the first half, 42-30 and 44-32, but we couldn't hold onto that and we were ahead by just two points, 49-47, at the half. The game went back and forth the whole second half; there were 11 lead changes in the final 20 minutes. Willie was just amazing for us. Every time we needed a big bucket he came through.

Melvin hit a 16-foot jumper to put us ahead for the last time, 83-82, with 4:10 remaining. Georgia Tech then went ahead for good when Oliver made a pair of free throws. Down 93-91 with six seconds to go, Anderson missed the front end of a one-and-one and Mario brought the ball up the court where he found Kevin on the right side. Kevin dribbled the ball into the right corner and he had to hurry to launch an off-balance three-pointer that didn't connect as the buzzer sounded.

Anderson, Scott and Oliver ended up combining to score an amazing 89 of Georgia Tech's 93 points in the game. Scott hit 7-of-12 threes that afternoon and ended up with a whopping 40 points. He hit some from so far out that he probably had a tough time even seeing the basket.

Willie was equally sensational for us. He scored 35 points and shot 5-of-10 on three-pointers. He also had seven rebounds. Melvin had 17 points, six assists, five rebounds and three steals.

It just wasn't in the cards for us I guess. But I was proud of my guys for the way they played. Georgia Tech had a huge 35-11 advantage in free-throw attempts during the game. I still don't understand how they could have ACC officials work that game. That made no sense to me and that makes it tough. As if trying to contain "Lethal Weapon III" wasn't enough, it was just one more thing for us to overcome.

When you look at the boxscore, we never really got a fair chance to win that game. It's a shame to say that, but those are the facts of life. At that stage of the game, with that much riding on the outcome, those things should never happen in postseason play. To think that we got outscored 27-5 at the free throw line, and only lost by two points with a shot to win it at the end, that's why I was so proud of that team. It was a great game, a great effort.

"Corn" and "Shik" may have played their finest games as Go-phers and that went unnoticed because we got beat. They were just outstanding. This may sound crazy, but even though Anderson scored 30 points, "Corn" did a tremendous job on defense. "Shik" scored 19 points and had five rebounds to close out his career.

It was tough in the locker room after the game. It was very emotional because we knew that it was the last time that we'd be together as a team. I remembered how hard it was for me to take my jersey off for the last time in college. I knew how they felt. They had been through a lot together. All the hard practices and ass-chewing. But in the end it was worth it because we went to the "Elite Eight."

Richard Coffey, Willie Burton, Connell Lewis, Melvin Newbern, Jim Shikenjanski; those were the seniors who had started out with me four years ago. I was so attached to them as young men, as people. Forget about basketball. To know in my heart that it had finally come to the end was tough, real tough. It was hard to say goodbye.

When we got back that night from New Orleans, the scene at the airport was something to behold. An estimated 2,000 fans turned out to greet us once we got off the plane. It reminded me a lot of that great reception we had received when I was a junior at West-ern Kentucky and we came back to Bowling Green after beating Chicago Loyola in the NCAA Tournament. It had that same kind of impact.

It was a tremendous tribute to those guys. So many people came out just to say, "Thank you. We love you, we care about you and we support you." That's what Golden Gopher fans are all about. Win or lose, they've always been there with us.

Not only for the players, but it was also uplifting for me as a coach. You have to understand that coaches also need some things to go on, to feed off of, to keep us going. In the end, win or lose, it's great to know that people respect you and appreciate what you do.

There was a love affair and a great deal of respect between the state of Minnesota and that team, that group of young men. The fans respected those guys so much because, no matter what the outcome, they always worked hard. They knew that every night out, they were going to give them an honest effort. It wasn't always pretty and they didn't always win. But they knew that when they paid their hard-earned money to watch us play, they'd get a group of young men who would lay it on the line for them.

That's the team that will always, always, be the closest team to me ever. They were part of my first ballclub at Minnesota in 1986-87. They went through so much. They lost so many games together those first two seasons, 37 to be exact. They turned it around to win 42 games their last two years.

That's the team that I will always be the most fond of because they went through so much abuse those first two seasons. They hung in there and never quit. Then their last two years, the same group of guys for the most part ended up advancing to the "Sweet 16" and "Elite Eight" of the NCAA Tournament.

Those guys are the backbone of our program today. They are special as players and as young men. They lost a lot of games their first two years and they became close because of that. Whenever one of those guys gets married or there's a sickness or death in the family, they will all end up going and supporting their former teammate. They still care that much about one another.

We had accomplished so much together. They came to a program that was down in the dumps and rebuilt it from the ashes back to respectability. They proved it could be done at Minnesota by working hard, staying committed and doing it the right way.

They put the honor, pride and dignity back into the basketball program at the University of Minnesota. Because of that special group of young men, Golden Gopher basketball was back on the map in a big way.

THE BIG APPLE

C H A P T E R   T W E N T Y - O N E

I made up my mind after the 1989-90 season that this was it for me. Four years earlier I had wondered what I was doing taking this job. Now I had decided that this was the last stop for me. I wanted to retire from coaching at the University of Minnesota.

I really feel that the people here at Minnesota genuinely care about the program. They will support us win or lose if we continue to play hard and have quality young men with character in the program. Those are the types of things that you can't find every place. Other places talk that talk but don't walk that walk, but Minnesota is the real deal. I love the people here and want to do whatever I can to try to bring them a national championship.

In no way am I trying to say that our program has been perfect. When I recruit young men, I promise their parents that I will do my very best to try to show them the right way both on and off the basketball court.

I'm proud of the quality of young men my programs have produced through the years. There are so many success stories that few people ever hear about. Rob Metcalf is now a lawyer in the Twin Cities, Kim Zurcher works with Honeywell in Dallas, "Corn" is now an ordained minister in the Twin Cities, and the list goes on and on.

It hurts me deeply when one of my players gets into trouble. In my heart, these kids are like my own family. This is a societal problem, not just a problem that athletes, entertainers or politicians have. It just gets magnified more in those cases. It's getting tougher and tougher for kids in today's society. There are more temptations and problems out there than ever before.

That makes the job of a coach in today's world that much more complex. One thing I won't do is turn my back on one of my players when he gets into trouble. Depending on the severity of the problem, he will pay the price in a big way no matter how good he is on the court and how much he can help us win games. My track record speaks for itself in this area.

It seemed like every time I turned around somebody was asking me if I was going to take this or that NBA job. Following the 1997 Final Four, some Kentucky alumni contacted me about replacing Rick Pitino after he went to the Boston Celtics. I have not and never will actively pursue another coaching job. But you always owe it to your family to check out those opportunities when you are contacted. Anyone in their right mind would do that.

All that talk takes its toll on recruiting. I wanted the world to know that this is it. The 1989-90 season showed me that we had turned the corner and I realized that this was where I wanted to be.

My initial contract when I came to Minnesota was a five-year deal. I signed a new five-year contract following the 1987-88 season and then made the ultimate commitment when I signed a 10-year deal on February 11, 1994, that was retroactive to the 1992-93 season. That will be the final contract of my coaching career, and it takes me through the 2001-2002 season.

Looking back, I've worked for six different athletics directors at Minnesota. Paul Giel was the first, followed by Holger Christiansen who was the interim director after Paul left, Rick Bay, then Dan Meinert as interim director after Rick left, Mac Boston and now Mark Dienhart.

I've also worked with four presidents at Minnesota. Kenneth Keller was the first, followed by Richard Sauer who was the interim president after Keller left, then Nils Hasselmo and now Mark Yudof. I've managed to survive them all, as well as three different football coaches in John Gutekunst, Jim Wacker and now Glen Mason.

The support and leadership that you get from your president and AD are very important to the success of a Division I college basketball coach. I've always had good working relationships with the presidents and athletic directors here at Minnesota and I can't stress how important that has been.

A good friend of mine, Mac Boston is now the vice president for student development and athletics at the U of M. I have a lot of respect for my athletic director here now, Mark Dienhart. I had a good relationship with Nils Hasselmo, who retired in the summer of 1997, and I'm looking forward to working more with our new president Mark Yudof. He will be the key to how long I decide to stay at Minnesota.

We went through two frustrating seasons after our glorious NCAA Tournament run in 1990. Kevin, Walter, Bob, Mario and Nate Tubbs, a six-foot-four forward from Fort Wayne, Indiana, were all back from our "Elite Eight" team and provided a solid foundation to build upon the previous season's success. Our program was in a transitional phase. We had lost all those great seniors who had meant so much to our program.

The "next generation" was a solid group I was really excited about: Randy Carter, a six-foot-eight forward from Memphis; Chad Kolander, a six-foot-nine forward/center from Owatonna, Minnesota; Arriel McDonald, a six-foot-two guard from Raleigh, North Carolina; Ernest Nzigamasabo, a six-foot-nine forward/center from Bujumbura, Burundi, by way of Mound, Minnesota, where he spent his senior year in high school; and Townsend Orr, a six-foot-one guard from Dolton, Illinois. We also added sophomore Dana Jackson, a six-foot-eight forward who transferred from San Diego State.

We got an indication of things to come when Walter fractured his right foot in our first game of the 1990-91 season, a 74-61 win over Robert Morris at Williams Arena. He had scored 31 and 19 points in our first two exhibitions games that season and was ready to have a great senior season before the injury.

Walter, a multi-talented player who ending up playing in the NBA, rejoined us for our last non-conference game of the season, a 95-77 win at Youngstown State. He was just starting to get back into the swing of things when he reinjured the foot and was lost for the remainder of the season in a loss at Ohio State on February 23. He had scored 13 first-half points and was five-of-five from the field in the game before suffering the injury.

That's the game where afterwards I called referees—Ted Hillary, London Bradley and Steve Welmer—"three jackasses" for calls that cost us a chance to upset the second-ranked Buckeyes on their home court. If I had to do all over again, I wouldn't use those exact words, but I truly believe that they had taken the game away from a bunch of young kids who had absolutely played their hearts out.

The calls had gone against us most of the game, but the clincher was a five-second call made on Arriel as he was dribbling the ball out front with 46 seconds left. We had a 62-61 lead, their guy had just backed off Arriel and then they made a call like that. It was a disgrace, and my comments did earn a reprimand from the Big Ten, but I didn't care at the time. Ohio State then hit the game-winning shot.

We finished the season 12-16 overall and ninth in the Big Ten with a 5-13 league record. The bottom line was that the conference at that time was as tough from top to bottom as I can ever remember and we just did not have the talent level to be able to compete.

With Walter sidelined, Kevin was joined in the starting lineup by three freshmen, Arriel, Randy and Ernest, and a sophomore in Dana. I've always said that there's no substitute for experience. This was a talented group, but they needed to get a few more games under their belts to compete with the heavyweights in the Big Ten.

We added another talented freshmen class heading into the 1991-92 season, highlighted by Voshon Lenard, a six-foot-four guard out of Detroit, and Jayson Walton, a six-foot-six forward from Dallas. They were both big-time recruits who could step in and play right away. We also added David Grim, six-foot-seven forward from Massillon, Ohio, and Ryan Wolf, a six-foot-four guard from Martinsville, Indiana.

David, by the way, went on to become the first player in school history to ever be named Academic All-Big Ten four straight years. That's a real credit to him, as well as to Alonzo Newby, our program's outstanding academic counselor who joined us prior to the 1992-93 season.

Once again, the key word here was patience. We were re-stocking the talent level, but this was still a young team. We had only one senior, Bob, and two juniors, Dana and Nate, on the team. You also have to remember that in 1992 the Big Ten had not one, but two teams in Indiana and Michigan that played in the Final Four. It was the second straight Final Four appearance for Michigan's fabled "Fab Five."

Two games certainly stand out from the season and I'll always remember them. We had opened the Big Ten season with a 96-50 loss at Indiana on January 9—the 46-point defeat was the worst in school history. Two days later at Williams Arena we came back to upset Michigan's "Fab Five," 73-64, behind Voshon's 25 points.

The other game was our rematch on February 12 with fourth-ranked Indiana in front of 16,212 fans at "The Barn." I had circled that date on my calendar ever since they routed us at their place back in the league opener. I really felt that Bob Knight ran the score up on us in that game and I wanted this one bad...real bad. Arriel scored 18 points and Voshon had 16 to lead us to a very satisfying 71-67 win over the Hoosiers.

Despite battling injuries all year long, we finished the season with a 16-16 overall record. We were sixth in the Big Ten with an 8-10 mark and lost at Washington State, 72-70, in the first round of the NIT. I got thrown out of that game in the first half for arguing a call and actually watched the whole second half back in the media workroom.

Much like that first group that came in with me in 1986-87, this one certainly left their stamp on the program as well during their careers. Randy, Arriel and Ernest ended their careers in 1993-94 when they helped lead us to a 21-12 overall record and a 10-8 Big Ten mark good for fourth in the league.

During the season we had a 106-56 thrashing of Indiana in front of a national television audience on February 27. Voshon had 35 points in that game and Arriel dished out 10 assists. It was the largest margin of victory ever for a Minnesota team over a Big Ten opponent.

We wrapped up an NCAA Tournament spot with a thrilling 107-96 victory over Iowa in three overtimes at Williams Arena on March 5. Voshon had 39 points and played 51 minutes, Randy had 19 points and 12 rebounds and Arriel had 22 points and 13 assists.

The season was capped off by a trip to the NCAA Tournament where we were seeded sixth in the West Regional at Sacramento, California. We beat 11th-seeded Southern Illinois, 74-60, in the first round, and then lost to third-seeded Louisville, 60-55, after leading 34-22 at the half.

That was such a disappointment. People tend to forget, however, that Jayson didn't play in the game because of a severe ankle sprain. So we didn't have all our guns.

We had dominated the game, but we let it get away from us the last five minutes. Louisville's Dwayne Morton was a perfect seven-of-seven from the field in the game, including five-of-five on three-pointers. We concentrated on shutting down their star center, Clifford Rozier, and we did that by holding him to just two points. You have to give Louisville a lot of credit for making the adjustments and getting the job done.

I wanted to beat Denny Crum and, personally, I wanted to beat the University of Louisville. So from that standpoint I probably took it a little more personally. I was devastated at the time because I thought we were the better team, especially if Jayson could have played.

I really felt bad for my three seniors. We had been through the wars together for four or five years. Arriel scored 1,273 points in his career and is also the all-time school career leader with 547 assists. Randy, a warhorse who battled through injuries throughout his career, scored 1,186 points in his career and is ranked in the school's all-time top 10 with 736 rebounds. Ernest was a solid player for us who was the all-time school career leader for games played with 124 when he finished his career. It was tough to say goodbye to those three.

During that offseason, Voshon was the first guy to test the waters of the new NCAA rule that allowed you to enter the NBA draft and then return to school if it didn't work out. The team that drafted you as an underclassmen still retained your rights. I voted against the rule and spoke out about it because it screwed up kids' minds. Without the rule, I don't think Voshon would have ever come out early.

Voshon was drafted by the Milwaukee Bucks in the second round, went to their summer mini-camp and then decided to return to school that fall to play his senior season. When Voshon came back for the 1994-95 season, the 100th year of basketball at the University of Minnesota, I think the whole attitude of our team changed and his attitude changed. Voshon, who is now having a great pro career with the NBA's Miami Heat, is a fantastic young man. But I think that move hurt him personally as well as our team. The whole chemistry and camaraderie of our team was altered.

Two key recruits for us heading into the season were Eric Harris, a six-foot-three point guard out of the Bronx, and Sam Jacobson, a six-foot-five guard/forward out of Cottage Grove, Minnesota. He was probably the most sought-after Minnesota prep player ever.

We did get off to a great start that season by beating Arizona, Brigham Young and Villanova to win the Great Alaska Shootout. Three more victories brought us to 6-0, before we lost back-to-back games to Cincinnati, 91-88, in overtime at home, and then California, 82-75, on the road.

The high point of the season came when we beat Indiana, 64-54, in Bloomington to bring our Big Ten record to 7-3 on the season. Injuries were really beginning to take their toll. Chad played with two bad ankles and a hip pointer the whole season. Jayson's knees were bad the whole year so we really had to keep track of his playing time. He couldn't go full out in practice most of the time.

We limped down the homestretch and into the NCAA Tournament by going 3-5 in our last eight games. On Selection Sunday we learned that we were seeded eighth in the East Regional and would play St. Louis University in Baltimore, Maryland.

It would be an understatement to say that it was an ugly game against St. Louis. We didn't score a point until almost five minutes into the game and didn't hit a field goal in the first 10 minutes of the first half. I think we missed five layups in a row at one point.

That was the worst NCAA Tournament game I've ever been a part of. We just couldn't get anything going and St. Louis wasn't much better on that day. We fought back from an early 19-3 deficit and tied the game on Chad's layup with 12 seconds to go to send it into overtime.

In the overtime, St. Louis was up, 64-61, and we had the ball with the clock winding down. We must have had four or five good looks to tie the game, but nothing would fall.

It was a tough way to go out for my five seniors, Voshon, Chad, Townsend, Jayson and Ryan. It marked the first time in the history of the program that five guys on the same team played in more than 100 games during their careers.

Voshon finished his career as the all-time school career leader with 2,103 points in 127 games. He holds virtually all of the school three point shooting records, and is also in the top five with 322 career assists and 173 career steals.

Townsend set a new school record with 128 career games played. He also surpassed the 1,000 point mark with 1,069 career points and is ranked second in career assists with 401 and tied with Voshon with 173 career steals. Jayson played in 120 career games and scored 1,112 points. Chad saw action in 123 career games and Ryan 102. They became the first Golden Gophers to qualify for postseason play four straight years.

It still bothers me when people talk about that group, along with the 1994 seniors, Randy, Arriel and Ernest, and say that they never really reached their full potential. That group of young men battled through all sorts of adversity and were champions in their own right.

The legacy of that group will burn brightly mainly because they led the University of Minnesota to an unforgettable NIT Tournament run in March of 1993. Exactly 17 days after watching in disbelief when we were not included in the NCAA Tournament's field of 64, we held the NIT championship trophy up high for all to see in New York's Madison Square Garden after defeating Georgetown, 62-61, in the championship game.

Due to injuries, I was forced to go with eight different starting lineups during the season. Our regular starting lineup—Randy and Jayson at the forwards, Chad at center, Arriel and Voshon at the guard—started together as a full group in just 13 of our 32 games. And yet, those guys finished with a 22-10 overall record and 9-9 in the BigTen, tied for fifth-place with Purdue in the final league standings.

We were getting healthy and jelling as a team at the right time. When it came time for Selection Sunday, however, we sat as a team in front of the television for the call that never came.

We had defeated Purdue and Glenn Robinson by 21 points at home in January and lost by just six points to them on the road in February. The win over the Boilermakers at home was a special one because it was my 200th career victory.

Freshman walk-on Hosea Crittenden, a five-foot-nine guard from Rosemount, Minnesota, who was a real crowd favorite, put the icing on the cake with a basket at the buzzer. A student assistant coach on our 1997 Final Four team, the crowd in "The Barn" used to chant "Play Ho-Zay-A" late in games throughout his career if we were ahead.

The bottom line is that I think both Purdue and Minnesota deserved to go to the NCAA Tournament, but if there was any question, I truly believe that we should have gotten the nod over them.

Purdue got in instead of us because Glenn was a marquee player and that's good TV. We didn't have a "star" player and I'm convinced that's why they got in and we didn't. It's all about respect, something I've been fighting for ever since I came to Minnesota. I think the committee sold out to TV, plain and simple.

Don't get me wrong, I think we both deserved to be in the field of 64. But once they took Purdue, they should have taken Minnesota. That's what I don't understand. That's what I fight for every day, to make sure that the University of Minnesota basketball program and its players are treated fairly.

I will fight for what's right. I always have and I always will. When something isn't right, I'm going to speak my mind and let people know about it. Once the brackets were announced, I felt an emptiness inside of me. I felt left out. I felt cheated. I was bitter.

Once we got over the disappointment, we shifted our focus to the NIT. There was never any doubt whether or not we would play in it. My assistant coaches—Milt, "Koz" and Dave Thorson, a fine basketball mind who is now head coach at De La Salle High School in Minneapolis—and I immediately went to work to prepare for Florida, our first-round opponent. We were in it for one reason and that was to win the whole thing.

In the end it turned out to be a great thing for our players and fans. We played five games in two weeks and every single one of the games was on national TV on ESPN. That's more national TV games than we had the entire season. We also beat five quality teams from four different big-time conferences.

Due to the renovation of Williams Arena we couldn't play any NIT home games there. We beat Florida, 74-66, from the Southeastern Conference in our first game in front of 11,944 at Target Center in Minneapolis. Voshon led the way with 15 points.

Next we beat Oklahoma out of the then-Big Eight Conference, 86-72, before a near-capacity crowd of 18,254 at Target Center behind 17 points from Voshon and eight rebounds from Jayson.

As I said earlier, we have the greatest fans in all of college basketball and they really got behind us and supported us on the road to the NIT crown. Our guys were down initially after the NCAA Tournament snub, but I think our fans picked them back up and got us on the right track. We fed off their support. It was a fun ride because the state of Minnesota fell in love with that team and got pretty attached to them because of all they had been through.

Since the Timberwolves were playing at Target Center, our quarterfinal game against USC from the Pac 10 Conference was played at the Met Center in Bloomington. A standing-room-only crowd of 15,393 watched us beat Coach George Raveling's Trojans, 76-58. Voshon scored 25 points, while Randy and Jayson cleaned up the boards with seven rebounds apiece.

It was a crazy atmosphere after the game. The crowd was great. After the game, the guys took a lap around the arena to a standing ovation. That was a special night. Next stop was New York's Madison Square Garden. There was a personal satisfaction in advancing to the NIT semifinals in New York. I'll never forget when I played in the NIT as a college sophomore in 1965. It was a big thing to go to New York City and we were so excited about being there. I think that there is so much to learn through travel and New York City is a place everyone should try to visit at least once in their lifetime. It's an education in itself.

I remember when we pulled up to the Marriott Marquis hotel the day before we played Providence in the semifinals and there was a bum on the street corner. A bunch of the players in the back of the bus were laughing and making jokes at the homeless man and I stood up and told my players that in many ways, "the only difference between you and him is that you can shoot a jump shot."

The bus grew silent immediately. I wanted them to realize that when they see people out on the street, they're out there for a reason. Maybe they had no father or mother and there was no place left for them to go; you never know. Even so, they can still make something of their lives rather than taking to the streets.

I wanted them to realize that because God had blessed each of them with some athletic ability, they had the chance to get an education. I also don't want my players to ever get false hope. Playing the sport of basketball will come to an end sooner or later, so they should work hard now so that they don't end up out on the streets. I wanted them to realize that they could take their jump shot and get a good education.

I'm always trying to give the players in my program lessons in life. The game itself is easy, but sometimes the lessons they learn from the game are hard. I try to let them know every day that they have this wonderful opportunity to go to college, play basketball and travel around the country and the world. They should take advantage of it.

Sometimes I think kids take it for granted that they have the right to play this great game. God's given them the ability to play and I think it's a privilege, so they shouldn't waste the opportunity.

Down by 11 points to Providence from the Big East Conference in the semifinals with just over 13 minutes remaining, this gutty group refused to quit, battled back, and came away with a 76-

70 victory. None other than Voshon led the way once again with 25 points. Jayson had 16 points and Randy added 10.

Georgetown, another Big East Conference foe, was our opponent in the finals. We led 62-51 after Arriel hit a short jumper with 4:27 remaining in the game. Everything was going our way and it looked to the average fan like the title was as good as ours.

John Thompson is a good friend of mine and a great coach who has done a fantastic job at Georgetown. When you play one of his teams, you can't celebrate until the final horn sounds. They will battle you every step of the way until there's no time left on the clock.

Little did we know, however, that Arriel's bucket would be our last points of the game. The Hoyas scored the final 10 points in the game and had the ball with a chance to win it at the end, but the shot wouldn't fall and they got the ball out of bounds underneath the basket with four-tenths of a second left.

All I could think of was that Cincinnati game we lost in the 1989-90 season opener where they scored on an out-of-bounds play with eight tenths of a second on the clock. I knew all they could do was try to lob it towards the basket and tip it in. You couldn't catch it and shoot it with that little time left. They threw it inbounds, Voshon intercepted it and the clock expired to set off a wild celebration.

Arriel, who was named to the all-tournament team, led us in the championship game with 20 points, while Voshon added 17. Randy contributed seven big rebounds for us. Voshon was named MVP of the tournament, and deservedly so after scoring 99 points in the five tournament games.

It was a great thrill, a great honor for me. It made up for not getting selected for the NCAA's and I think it brought our program instant respect from around the country. At that stage in my coaching career, winning the NIT title was my finest hour. It was a storybook finish for a group of young people who had hung tough all season long.

The players and coaching staff of the 1993 NIT champions will forever be the answer to the trivia question of who was the first University of Minnesota basketball team ever to win a postseason championship. We made history and no one will ever be able to take that away from us.

RED, WHITE AND BLUE

CHAPTER TWENTY-TWO

I'm an American through and through, and in my opinion, there's no greater thing you can do in life than represent your country. I considered it to be one of the greatest honors of my coaching career when my good friend and 1996 USA Olympic Team Coach Lenny Wilkens called and asked me to be one of his assistant coaches on the U.S. team that competed in Atlanta.

Heading into the 1997-98 season, Lenny is still the only coach in NBA history to ever win more than 1,000 games. That says it all right there. Red Auerbach won a lot of NBA championships, but he never won 1,000 games. It was great to be able to work alongside Lenny, a Hall of Famer whom I had played against during my career. He's someone I respect and admire so much.

Utah Jazz coach Jerry Sloan, my good friend and former teammate with the Bulls, along with Georgia Tech coach Bobby Cremins, were the other two assistant coaches. It was a real treat to be able to work alongside those two guys as well.

It was something else to be able to coach 12 of the very finest basketball players in the game today: Charles Barkley, Penny Hardaway, Grant Hill, Karl Malone, Reggie Miller, Hakeem Olajuwon, Shaquille O'Neal, Gary Payton, Scottie Pippen, Mitch Richmond, David Robinson and John Stockton.

The red white and blue means a lot to me. I've been all over the world and there's no place better than the United States. I went into it with one thing in mind and that was to help America win the gold medal.

I've been involved with USA Basketball quite a bit during my career. Executive Director Warren Brown, Assistant Executive Director Craig Miller and the whole staff there do a wonderful job.

It's hard work for a coach and the involvement is usually in the summer months when you'd normally like to relax a bit, but I think it's important. We all need to continue to work hard to make sure that the game continues to grow and develop in this country. The rest of the world is getting better, and believe me, we can't afford to sit back and rest on our laurels.

I take a lot of pride in the fact that I have never, ever lost a game in three coaching stints with USA Basketball. The first time I was the head coach of the North team that won the gold medal with a perfect 4-0 record at the 1991 U.S. Olympic Festival in Los Angeles.

Glenn Robinson had just finished his senior season at Roosevelt High School in Gary, Indiana, and was on his way to Purdue to play for Gene. Alan Henderson of Carmel, Indiana, was also heading into his first season at Indiana. The remaining 10 players on my team had just finished their first year in college.

In fact, eight of my players were from Big Ten schools. In addition to Glenn, Alan and one of my own in Randy Carter, there was also Linc Darner of Purdue, Kevin Smith of Iowa, Patrick Baldwin and Kevin Rankin of Northwestern, and Anthony Miller of Michigan State. Eric Piatkowski of Nebraska, Sean Robbins of Emporia State, Richard Scott of Kansas and Jevon Crudup of Missouri were also key members of the team.

It was a great group of guys who came together in a short period of time, worked their tail ends off and won the gold. A lot of the credit for the success of that team goes to my two assistant coaches: Jim Burson and Dan Bush. You only have a couple of practices to get things in order, and Jim and Dan did a wonderful job.

Glenn scored 18 points and had 11 rebounds to lead us to an 84-79 win over the East in the gold medal game. He was named MVP after averaging 17.0 points and 9.3 rebounds per game in four tournament games. Eric, who averaged 11.8 points per game, joined him on the all-tournament team.

There were so many great players in that tournament. The East team that we beat for the gold featured Donyell Marshall of Reading (Pennsylvania) High School. He went on to have a great career at Connecticut. The West roster included two more prep standouts in Damon Stoudamire of Arizona and Juwan Howard of Michigan, while the South had Auburn's Wesley Person.

My second USA Basketball coaching assignment came in 1994 when I served as the head coach of the USA Junior National Team that competed in the COPABA (Confederation of Pan American Basketball Association) World Junior Qualifying Championships in Argentina. Clint Bryant of Augusta College and Mike Montgomery of Stanford were my two assistant coaches.

To be eligible to participate, players had to be 18 years old or younger. We conducted our initial practice sessions at Williams Arena and then cut our roster down to the mandatory 12 players for the trip overseas.

The list included five high school seniors and seven college freshmen: Shareef Abdur-Rahim of Wheeler High School in Marietta, Georgia; Isiah Epps from Kingstree (South Carolina) High School; Tremaine Fowlkes from the University of California; Eric Harris, who was headed to the University of Minnesota to play for me; Trajan Langdon, Richard Price and Steve Wojciechowski of Duke; Mike Maddox of Georgia Tech; Stephon Marbury of Lincoln High School in Brooklyn; Robert Traylor of Wright High School in Detroit; Albert White of Inkster (Michigan) High School; and Tim Young of Stanford.

When we were over the ocean on our flight to Argentina, I told the guys that there was a lot of water down there and if we didn't win the gold, they were going to have to swim all the way back. I reminded them of that during a couple of our games when it was close.

I can't even begin to tell you how proud I was of that group. They laid it on the line for me every game. We went 8-0 in the tournament and had an average margin of victory of just over 40 points per game. Our defense was the key; only one opponent shot better than 44 percent against us and we forced almost 21 turnovers a game. We averaged 106 points per game and shot over 53 percent from the field, while limiting our opponents to 66 points a game on just 36 percent shooting.

In front of a partisan sellout crowd that went absolutely bananas the whole game, our young guys showed a lot of composure as we beat host Argentina, 77-72, for the gold medal. Believe me, the atmosphere over there at a game—especially when they're playing the Americans—is like nothing you'll ever see in the states.

The game was tied, 30-30 at the half, but we put together a 9-0 run five minutes into the second half to take command of the game. Stephon and Shareef led us to the win with 21 points apiece.

We had five high school seniors who were all recruitable—Stephon, Shareef, Issiah, Robert and Albert. Nevertheless, I coached the only way I know how. I worked them hard and demanded perfection. In reality, that probably hurt me when I tried to recruit those guys later that year to Minnesota. But I didn't go into the coaching assignment with that idea in mind. I went over there for one reason, and one reason only, and that was to win the gold.

I'll never forget the first two practices when I told Stephon that he was a better defensive player than offensive player and that he should give the ball up and play defense. It really hurt his feelings. I don't think anybody ever talked to him like that before. I think he thought I was crazy at first.

But I was looking down the road. The international players can all shoot the three, and in order to beat those guys, I knew that we had to apply great pressure in the backcourt. From the first day of practice I was trying to get Stephon to understand that he must guard people. I was planting the seed three weeks before we got to the championship game.

Our best backcourt over there was Stephon and Eric. They just turned people inside out with their great defense. Those two guys really buckled down and got after it. After we beat Argentina to win the gold medal, Stephon came over, hugged me, cried and said, "Thank you."

Stephon went on to play his freshman season in 1995-96 for Bobby at Georgia Tech and then was a lottery pick in the 1996 NBA draft. He was the runner-up for the NBA's Rookie of the Year in 1996-97 after a great first season with the Minnesota Timberwolves.

It's neat to have Stephon in town playing for the T'Wolves. He and Eric are good friends going back to when they grew up together in New York City. I really think that Stephon has had a tremendous impact on Eric's development as a player since coming to the Twin Cities. They work out together, they talk, and they share thoughts and ideas about the game.

I really admire Stephon as a young man because he has a good heart and he does the right things both on and off the court. He's a tremendous person who is also really, really close to my wife Yevette. I don't think he knew what to make of it when I got on him those first few days in practice, but he respects me and we've become very close.

I graduated from college in 1967 so I missed having the opportunity to play in the 1968 Olympics in Mexico City by one year. The 1992 Games in Barcelona marked the first time that NBA players were allowed to play in the Olympics.

I can remember the opening ceremonies in Atlanta just like they were yesterday. Since we were the host country, we were the last ones to enter the Olympic Stadium. We were in a holding area behind the stadium for about two hours. I remember sitting there and watching the television monitors as the athletes from the other countries entered the stadium. I got goosepimples and couldn't wait for our turn to come.

It was an exciting experience to be there with the finest athletes from around the world, representing the United States of America. It was something that I had always dreamed of since I was a little boy.

Then our turn to enter the stadium finally came. We had to walk up and over a ramp. The thing I worried about more than anything was my bad knees. Due to the wear and tear of so many years of playing the game, I've had a number of surgeries on both knees, with the most recent one in the summer of 1995. I remember saying to myself, "Please God, don't let me fall."

Going up the ramp was tough, but going down was even harder because I knew that if I started falling I wouldn't be able to stop. I tried to get close to the side where there was a railing that would help me keep my balance. It's kind of funny. There I was walking into Olympic Stadium, with the whole world watching, and all I could think of was trying not to trip and fall!

When I finally had successfully negotiated the ramp and got down to the track level, I looked up and said, "Wow, this is something." The home crowd was giving us a standing ovation. It was incredible. A fantastic feeling.

The opening ceremonies were something else, but the highlight was seeing Muhammad Ali light the Olympic flame. That was a real thrill. You have to remember that he's from Louisville. I remember growing up and hearing about a Golden Gloves boxing champion named Cassius Clay, his name before he changed it because of his Muslim faith.

It was exciting to see, but I have to admit that my heart nearly stopped before he lit the torch. The Parkinson's disease has caused him to shake quite a bit and I was hoping that he wouldn't burn himself. I think everyone around the world held their breath for a moment when he had the torch, but like the true champion that he is, he got the job done.

That was a moment that I'll cherish for the rest of my life. He came to our team hotel one day and it was almost like God was walking into the room. It was something to see how the "Dream Teamers" reacted to Ali. We were all in awe of the man, to tell you the truth.

Desmond Tutu also came to practice one day. He's real short —only about five-foot-four or five-foot-five—but this guy is obviously a giant in the world. He spoke to the team about the need for them to be positive role models for young kids, particularly young black males. Once again here were all these superstars just captivated by the aura of this man. It was like we were all in Sunday school. Everybody sat down on the basketball floor, crossed their legs and just soaked up what the man had to say.

Afterwards he took the time to embrace every one of us and wish us good luck. We all took individual photos with him, but there was one team shot that will always stand out in my mind: we are all standing around the man flashing the peace sign. That said it all right there.

The Olympic Games are all about bringing the world together. That peace was shattered in the early-morning hours of Saturday, July 27, when a bomb that was planted exploded in Centennial Olympic Park. We had just returned to our team's headquarters in Atlanta, The Omni Hotel, following a one-sided 133-70 win over China at the Georgia Dome.

I knew that my sister, Nora, and two of my children, Brent and Lori, had planned to take a walk through Olympic Park at around 1 a.m. There was always something going on there. It was a neat place to hang out. I can't even begin to tell you how relieved I was when I found out that they had gone to the Olympic Park, but then decided against walking through it because it was so crowded.

The Olympic Games are wonderful and it's awful to even think that someone or some group would be responsible for a cowardly act like that. I don't get it.

Security had already been airtight since we arrived in Atlanta and for good reason. It took a little more time to go somewhere or do something, but we all appreciated it, believe me. The Omni was close to Olympic Park, so we took a team vote to decide whether to change hotels or not, but everyone agreed to stay. Karl did decide to send his family home early, but that was about it.

We were awesome on the basketball court. We stormed through the competition with a perfect 8-0 record and had an average margin of victory of 31.7 points per game. We scored a whopping 102 points per game and shot 56 percent from the field, while limiting our opponents to 70.3 points and 42 percent shooting.

We were just as dominating on the glass, as we outrebounded the opposition by 13 rebounds per game. That team played great defense as well and forced an average of almost 22 turnovers per game.

Four players averaged in double figures for us during the tournament and nine averaged 8.4 points per game or more. Charles led the way at 12.4 points per game, while David, a three-time Olympian, averaged 12.0 points a game. Charles was also the leader with 6.6 rebounds per game, while Shaquille was next at 5.3.

After trailing by as many as seven points in the first half, we came back and routed Yugoslavia, 95-69, in the gold medal game. David scored 28 points in the game and Reggie had 20. The better teams in the tournament usually played us pretty close in the first half, but then our size, strength and depth always wore them down in the second half.

No doubt about it, that was the greatest collection of talent I have ever been associated with. I played against better players—'erry West, Oscar Robertson, Elgin Baylor, Wilt Chamberlain and Bill Russell come to mind—but the "Dream Team" had great talent. If Michael Jordan had chosen to play, it would have been the very best players in the game today assembled on one team.

Barkley is a total package as a player. He can do so many things at both ends of the court. He scores, he rebounds, plays great defense, blocks shots, he does it all. I came to respect and appreciate his game even more.

I didn't like his bullshit, however, and I told him that one day. I told him that I had a hard time tolerating it, but that he really played the game hard once he stepped on the basketball court. That young man, when he steps on the basketball court, he's all business and can really play.

I have strong feelings on what's right and wrong. I think women should wear earrings and men should not. That's just my philosophy. But you can't make a man do anything he doesn't want to do. You must earn his respect. If he respects you as a coach, he will take his earrings off before he steps on the basketball court.

When we went on the court each day, Charles would always walk over to me and give me his earrings. He didn't do it because I made him do it. That was out of respect. I earned that respect not only from Charles, but also from the rest of the team.

Malone and John Stockton are real classy guys, 24 hours a day. It was a real pleasure to see them lead Utah, with Jerry as their head coach, to the 1997 NBA Finals and have Karl be named league MVP. I liked the way they carried themselves on and off the court.

David had a bad back, but he's such a great player that he played right through the pain and still finished second on the team in scoring. He's a real class guy too. Shaquille is a big, strong, powerful youngster. Wow, what physical tools! He just destroys people in the post.

I also realized that Gary could really play. He was without a doubt our best defender on the team. He put pressure on the other team's guards and that really made things happen for us.

Penny did a great job, but I don't think he played his best basketball. He is a tremendous player with loads of athletic ability. I remember he gave us fits in college when Memphis State played us at Williams Arena on New Year's Eve during the 1992-93 season. We beat them, 70-55, but Penny still scored 30 points in the game. Mitch is a tremendously talented player. That was easy to see based on the things he could do for us on the court.

Reggie is a tremendous shooter, but I have to be honest and say that I never was a Reggie Miller fan until I worked with him at the Olympics. Now I have so much respect for him because of how hard he practices and plays. I found out that he's not only a great shooter, but a real competitor who leaves it all on the court. I was really impressed with his approach to the game.

Scottie Pippen was just a joy to work with every day. He's a guy who comes to play and work hard. He and I used to go at each other in shooting contests, usually playing a game called 7-Up where you get points for making shots at various spots on the floor.

I can't run and jump with those guys like I used to be able to, but I can still shoot the ball. The thing is, I used to let him win the games. That's the honest to God's truth. It was a challenge for him to beat me. I didn't want to put on a display. I had nothing to prove. I did it to make him work and stay hungry. I'd win one game and he'd win two.

After a while, Hakeem wanted to shoot with me. I'd beat him once and then I'd let him win two in a row. But Hakeem can really shoot the ball for a big man. I'm talking 17, 18 feet from the basket. I was really impressed with his shooting touch.

Grant is a bright, young, up-and-coming guy. I really think that he will be the next Michael Jordan-type superstar in the league. He won't be on the same level as Michael, but I think Grant has earned a tremendous amount of respect already from the other players around the league. He has the total package as well and will be a star in the league for a long, long time.

Grant is also a very gifted young man. We always used to sit around at night in the hotel lobby listening to him play the piano. We had a fantastic relationship with the USA women's team and a number of them used to hang out with us and sing while Grant played.

I could listen to Ruthie Bolton and Nikki McCray sing all night long. I loved to hear their voices. They'd sing gospel music and that's my first love, along with country music. I really enjoyed that, those were fun times away from the basketball court.

Lenny did a great job as the head coach. His impact and influence on the success of that team should never be overlooked. Just because you have the best talent doesn't guarantee that you'll win. You still have to play as a team. He brought that group together, gave them direction and made them understand that they had to play together as a team.

Coaches don't get medals at the Olympics, but it was great to watch our young men go up on the podium and receive their gold medals. I got goosebumps all over again when they played the national anthem. It was fantastic to know that the USA was still the best in the whole world. We are now 101-2 overall in Olympic basketball competition and have won 11 out of a possible 13 gold medals.

But I have to say this. If we don't continue to shoot the ball —I mean really work at shooting better—we're going to have our hands full in the 2004 or 2008 Olympics, even with the pros. A lot of folks might think I've gone off my rocker for saying that, but we can't sit back and rest on our laurels. That's because other countries have caught up with us and have actually surpassed us as far as shooting the ball. Athletic ability still wins outright now, but someday soon when we start going up against comparable athletes with that great shooting touch, we could be in for a world of trouble.

A YEAR TO REMEMBER

CHAPTER TWENTY-THREE

A new era in Golden Gopher basketball was ushered in during the 1995-96 season. After the 1995 NCAA Tournament loss to St. Louis, we were faced with the tough task of replacing five seniors—Voshon, Townsend, Jayson, Chad and Ryan—who had meant so much to our program.

David and Hosea were our only two seniors on the 1995-96 team. A pair of big juniors from the state of Minnesota—six-foot-nine John Thomas from Minneapolis and Trevor Winter, a seven-footer from Slayton—handled things in the middle for us. Eric and Sam were now sophomores.

But there were a lot of new names and faces for our fans to get used to as we started the season, including a pair of junior college standouts. Bobby Jackson, a six-foot-one guard from Salisbury, North Carolina, joined us after two outstanding seasons at Western Nebraska Community College. Mark Jones, a six-foot-six guard from Milwaukee, came to us from Anderson Junior College in Anderson, South Carolina.

We also added four key freshmen to the team. Courtney James, a six-foot-eight power forward, joined us after leading Ben Davis High School in Indianapolis, to the 1995 Indiana state title. A six-foot-seven guard/forward out of Parkview High School in Little Rock, Quincy Lewis had been named the Gatorade Player of the Year in Arkansas as a senior.

Charles Thomas, a six-foot-four guard, was honored as "Mr. Basketball" in the state of Kentucky as a senior at Harlan High School. A six-foot-eight forward from Oakland, California, Miles Tarver had fought through early-season back problems to lead Maine Central Prep Institute in Pittsfield, Maine, to the championship game of the New England Prep School Tournament.

The season started out on a sour note right away when Bobby fractured his left foot in our very first practice of the year. It was already a tough enough task to try to fit all the new pieces of the puzzle together and then that happened.

Bobby missed the first seven games of the season before making his debut in a 70-67 loss to California in front of 25,614 fans at the Metrodome. He scored 10 points and had eight rebounds in 21 minutes, but he was still not in shape after missing two full months. We were still trying to find ourselves as a team when we entered the Big Ten schedule after registering an 8-4 record in non-conference play.

We reached the halfway point of the Big Ten season with a 3-6 league mark after an 81-66 loss to Indiana at Williams Arena. It took that long, almost two months, for Bobby to get in shape and understand our system.

Once he did, we may have been the best team in the conference the second half of the season when we won seven of our last nine ballgames to finish 18-12 overall and 10-8 in the Big Ten. The final game of the regular season was an impressive 67-66 win at Illinois on March 9 in Lou Henson's final game as coach of the Fighting Illini.

History was on our side on Selection Sunday the next day. No Big Ten team with a winning league record had ever been denied a berth in the NCAA Tournament's field of 64. The criteria for selection also supposedly puts an emphasis on how well you're playing at the end of the season. Overcoming injuries to key players is also supposed to be a factor in the selection process. All of that was in our favor.

It seemed like 1993 all over again when the field of 64 was announced and Minnesota's name wasn't included. I felt like we got ripped off back then. This time I thought it was highway robbery. I'll have a sore spot in my heart about both of those snubs forever.

It's just not right. In other words, all the standards and criteria that they have in place were just thrown out the window twice when it came to Minnesota. I think we've been screwed big-time by the NCAA selection committee twice and it teed me off. They blew it. That's why I raised so much hell both times. It was wrong, no doubt about it.

Our record and our play down the stretch spoke for itself. Michigan was 10-8 in the Big Ten just like us and they got in. It all goes back to the marquee players and the marquee schools. Michigan has more clout and more recognition than Minnesota. I'm not complaining. That was wrong and I've always fought my entire life for what I believe in my heart is right.

We went on to beat St. Louis, 68-52, in the first round of the NIT behind 17 points from Bobby and 15 from David. With Courtney on the sidelines with a foot injury, Tulane came into "The Barn" and ended our season by defeating us, 84-65, in the second round.

A lot of people afterward said that the one-sided loss to Tulane proved that we didn't belong in the NCAA Tournament. That's hogwash. Tulane was a big, powerful team up front and we needed to have Courtney in the lineup to have any chance. He was the one player whom we could ill-afford to lose against a team like that.

Not to take anything away from Perry Clark's team, because they were a fine ballclub who also should have been in the NCAA Tournament, but I really believed we would have won that game if Courtney had been able to play.

The disappointment of not getting selected to the NCAA Tournament motivated our team throughout the offseason. I don't know if I've ever been associated with a team that worked as hard as this group did to get ready for the 1996-97 season. They were dedicated to having a great year.

The mind is a powerful thing. In order to be a great player, you need to get your head on straight. In addition to working on every facet of their games, our players became tougher and stronger, both mentally and physically, from that last game in the NIT against Tulane to the first practice of the season on October 15.

Going into the 1996-97 season, I think a lot of people were surprised when I publicly said that we had four goals as a team heading into the year: win at least 20 games, win the Big Ten title, get into the NCAA Tournament and win the national title. We met the first three of those four goals and just missed the national championship by 40 minutes.

It was out of character for me to make predictions like that, but I wanted to make a statement to the media, our fans and the NCAA selection committee that we were for real. I wanted to plant the seed right away.

A lot of folks thought that my comments may have put too much pressure on the team, but I didn't think we had anything to lose. We had lost David and Hosea to graduation and Mark had transferred in the offseason, but we had everybody else returning.

We also added Russ Archambault, a hard-nosed, six-foot-one guard from Sartell, Minnesota, and a pair of big men—six-foot-ten forward/center Kevin Loge from Morris, Minnesota and six-foot-eleven center/forward Kyle Sanden from Thief River Falls, Minnesota—who we decided to redshirt since we already had John and Trevor in the middle.

I set the goals and made them public because we had a great ballclub coming back. I wanted to bring some attention to our team, let them know that I had great confidence in them.

I knew the temperament of my players. Setting lofty goals like that was the right thing to do for this particular team. My three seniors—John, Trevor and Bobby—had the ability to take it all in stride. They were the keys. They never got too high or too low. They're even-keel guys. So I realized that I could say those things without affecting my team and their approach to the game. They were a very mature team and I knew that they could deal with it.

I really took a lot of great things away from my Olympic experience and I think it provided a great boost for me personally and as a coach. I have always taken a lot of satisfaction out of squeezing every last ounce of ability out of my players and teams through the years, and I think our 1996-97 team reached its full potential. That's what it's all about.

When I watched Gary Payton, or "The Glove" as he's called because of his great defensive pressure, play for the Olympic Team, I realized that if Bobby Jackson could do some of the same things for us, we'd have a chance to compete for the national championship.

At the wing spot, if Sam Jacobson and Quincy Lewis could give us the same type of production that Penny Hardaway or Reggie Miller did for the Olympic Team, we would have a chance to have a great season.

Eric Harris needed to provide the same type of leadership at the point for us, much like John Stockton did in our run to the gold medal at the Olympics. We had to have strong inside play from John Thomas like Shaquille O'Neal had done for the Olympic Team. A guy like Trevor Winter needed to come off the bench and give us some quality minutes like Hakeem Olajuwon and David Robinson had done in the Olympics.

I made those comparisons, translated what we had done with the Olympic Team over into my own team at Minnesota. Obviously, our 1996-97 team didn't have anywhere near the quality of players that the Olympic Team had, but I wanted to approach the game the same way we had played in Atlanta.

We played 10-to-12 guys on the Olympic Team and I came back to Minnesota fully committed to using nine or 10 guys each and every game. From the first game, I knew the importance of developing our bench. I understood that it wouldn't always be pretty, but I knew that most of the time we could use our depth to wear our opponents down.

Ranked No. 23 in the nation, we opened the season with an easy 101-55 win over Stephen F. Austin at Williams Arena, followed by a 76-61 victory over West Virginia from the Big East Conference at Target Center. We trailed at one time by 10 points to the Mountaineers, but our depth eventually wore them down and we won the game going away.

Up next was the San Juan Shootout in Puerto Rico over the Thanksgiving holiday break. After routing host Puerto Rico-Mayaguez, 104-62, in the opener, we beat Creighton, 64-63, in the semifinals the next night. Looking back, that was one of those wins that often gets overlooked, but one that was critical to our success the rest of the way.

Creighton had come back from an 11-point second-half deficit to take the lead and we were in serious danger of losing the game. Then Eric stepped up and hit the game-winning jumper with just seconds remaining to lift us to the victory. He ended up being named tournament MVP.

That was a great confidence-booster, not only for our team, but also for Eric who had battled through two tough years and faced his share of criticism from the media as a result. He had averaged only 2.3 points and shot 36 percent from the field as a freshman in 1994-95, and 4.7 points and 39 percent from the floor as a sophomore in 1995-96.

I had said from day one that Eric was the most improved shooter on our team. A lot of people laughed at me at the time and said I was crazy. He had worked so hard in the offseason to improve his shot and I knew that. To make that last-second shot in the fourth game of the season that led to a big win for us, was a big confidence-booster for Eric.

The win over Creighton set up a meeting with 10th-ranked Clemson in the championship game. Little did we know that we would meet up with them later in March in the "Sweet 16" of the NCAA Tournament.

Coach Rick Barnes' squad was the most physical team we have ever played against during my coaching career at Minnesota. They were a big, powerful club. We held Clemson to just 20 first-half points, and led by as many as 18 points in the second-half, en route to a big 75-65 victory. After we beat them, that's when I knew that we could play with anybody in the country. I knew that we were the real deal.

In 1994-95 we had won the Alaska Shootout after big wins over Arizona, Villanova and Brigham Young. That ended up being the highlight of that season. I told the team after we won the San Juan Shootout that this was not the time to celebrate. This was just the start. We still had 25 regular season games to go. I told them that we had the ability to win 25 in a row, but we could also lose 25 straight if we didn't keep our heads on straight and stay focused.

We moved up to No. 16 in the national rankings with a perfect 5-0 record after winning the San Juan shootout title. We got back home from Puerto Rico late on Monday, December 2, and then had to turn around and get on a plane Wednesday and play at Alabama Thursday. We were tired and still suffering from some jet lag.

It was a hard-fought, physical game the whole way. Trailing by three points, Bobby got fouled on a three-point attempt with 15 seconds remaining. He calmly stepped up to the free throw line and made all three attempts to tie the game.

Then Eric Washington, Alabama's big gun who had struggled all game long, nailed a three-pointer with five seconds left to push the Crimson Tide's lead back up to three. Sam had a great look to tie it back up, but the shot wouldn't fall and we lost our first game of the season.

I think the defeat really caused us to get refocused. We turned around and won our last six non-conference games to head into the Big Ten schedule ranked No. 15 in the nation with an 11-1 record. Along the way, we absolutely destroyed St. John's from the Big East Conference, 77-39, at Williams Arena, and then away from home also beat Rhode Island from the Atlantic 10 Conference, 82-72, and Nebraska from the Big 12, 70-56.

In the past I've been teased a lot about the quality of our non-conference schedules. Some of our opponents in the past were called "cupcakes" by the media and I went along with that. That's not fair to those schools to be called that when they're trying the best they can to build a basketball program.

Sometimes we say some corny things that embarrass other people. I've gone along with the media in calling other schools "cupcakes" in the past and I'd just like to apologize to anyone that I've offended over the years for that.

In 1996-97 we deliberately tried to make our non-conference schedule stronger. Alabama is a tough team to play, especially on the road. But I wanted to play them because they're always a big, strong, very athletic team. Playing at Rhode Island and Nebraska were also big challenges for our ballclub. It's no secret that our tough non-conference schedule really helped prepare us for Big Ten play.

Behind 20 points from Bobby and 14 from Eric, we opened the Big Ten schedule on January 2 with a 65-48 victory over Wisconsin at Williams Arena. Two days later, we went into Michigan State's Jack Breslin Center and came away with a relatively easy 68-43 win. Once again, our defense and depth wore down our opponent. We had an 18-point run in the final eight minutes or so, while at the same time we held the Spartans virtually scoreless during that critical time of the game.

We took a 14-1 overall record, 3-0 league mark and a No. 11 national ranking into Indiana's Assembly Hall on January 8. This was another game that really showed the heart and character of this team. Things didn't look real promising for us when we trailed, 79-72, with 58 seconds left in the game. Our guys didn't push the panic button. They were so focused and committed to winning all season long, that I don't think the thought of losing ever entered their minds. It didn't matter how much time was on the clock, they always thought they were going to win.

A key point in the game came with four-and-a-half minutes remaining when everyone in the building thought that Sam had gotten whistled for his fifth foul. I knew that it was going to be awfully tough to pull it out with one of our big guns on the sidelines.

A couple of minutes passed when my son, Brent, and our basketball sports information director, Bill Crumley, communicated with each other and cleared up the mess. The foul was actually called on Bobby, so Sam only had four fouls. Once Brent and Bill confirmed it, Brent, who fills so many roles as a program aide on our staff and is going to be a fine coach someday, immediately alerted me to the situation and I checked Sam back into the ballgame. That was a real heads-up job by those two guys.

We turned up the defensive pressure, forced some Indiana turnovers, and got big three-pointers from Sam, Bobby and Eric to tie the game with 33 seconds remaining. Both teams had chances to win it in regulation play, but neither could convert and the game went into overtime.

Sam, Bobby and Quincy all hit big shots in the extra session and we won the game, 96-91. This team had a great understanding of who was supposed to shoot the ball for us in key situations and how we could get the ball to them. It's tough to win on the road in the Big Ten, so that was a big victory for us. We were able to capitalize on some critical Indiana turnovers.

The win at Indiana was a big one for us psychologically and made us realize that we could make it through the Big Ten schedule undefeated. But the guys never looked ahead all season long; they just took it one game at a time. They knew that if they went out there and executed our game plan that we could beat anyone on our schedule. They never strayed from that philosophy all season long.

We came back home and beat Michigan, 70-64, behind 20 points and 11 rebounds from Bobby, to run our record to 15-1 overall and a perfect 4-0 in the Big Ten. We moved up to No. 7 in the national polls. Up next was an ESPN national TV game at Illinois on January 14.

Led by an outstanding guard in Kiwane Garris, Illinois was the type of team that I knew could give us problems. They neutralized our size and strength up front by turning the game into a track meet. If they hit their three-pointers, I knew we'd be in for a long night.

The game went back and forth all night long, but turned for the worse when Eric was called for his fifth foul with about five minutes remaining. We had a lot of stupid fouls in the game and Coach Lon Kruger's team capitalized to the fullest. The Fighting Illini hit 33 of 40 shots from the charity stripe as we saw our 10-game winning streak snapped in a 96-90 defeat. Garris and backcourt mate Kevin Turner did us in with 24 points apiece.

After a 73-67 win at Ohio State, it was a showdown for first-place in the Big Ten on January 23 when Coach Tom Davis' Iowa Hawkeyes came into Williams Arena for an ESPN nationally televised game. The entire nation got the chance to see Sam at his very best. He scored a career-high 29 points to lead us to a 66-51 win over the Hawks.

The game also marked the first time that Bobby and Iowa's Andre Woolridge—the two names mentioned most prominently for the Big Ten Player of the Year award—went head to head. Bobby played his usual great all-around game with 15 points, nine rebounds, six assists and five steals.

Hounded by Eric all night long, Andre missed 10 of his first 11 shots and didn't make a field goal until almost two minutes had elapsed in the second half. He shot 3-of-14 from the floor in the game and finished with just 12 points. Andre's a great scorer and shutting him down was the key to our victory, which gave us sole possession of first-place in the conference. There was no looking back.

We then beat defending Big Ten champion Purdue, 91-68, at Williams Arena, which snapped a seven-game losing skid to Gene Keady's Boilermakers. A 75-56 win at Northwestern and an 85-70 victory at home over Penn State followed as we raised our record to 20-2 overall and 9-1 in the Big Ten.

Then we took a No. 3 national ranking into crucial back-to-back road games at Purdue and Iowa. Gene had once again done a marvelous job with his Boilermakers and they were in second-place in the conference standings and breathing down our necks heading into the game at Mackey Arena.

I had never won a game at Purdue. In fact, the last Minnesota win ever at Mackey Arena came in 1982. By the way, that was also the last time the Golden Gophers had won the Big Ten title. John scored 12 points and had seven rebounds, and along with Courtney, did a great job on the inside to lead us to a big 70-67 win over the Boilermakers that gave us a three-game lead in the Big Ten standings.

I think that there were still a lot of doubters out there. This was Minnesota and this was Clem Haskins. I told our kids many times that the Big Ten championship goes through West Lafayette and Bloomington, Indiana. That's the way it's always been in my 11 years at Minnesota. If we hadn't beaten Purdue they would have been right there knocking on the door to win another Big Ten title.

The victory meant a lot to me personally since it was my first one ever at Mackey Arena. I also think so much of Gene Keady. I have always had the utmost respect both for him and his program. When we walked off the floor with the win, I think our kids realized that we were capable of winning the Big Ten title.

Despite 24 points from Woolridge, three days later we went into Carver Hawkeye Arena and came away with a thrilling 68-66 win over Iowa. We had the game under control, but let a 15-point lead get away from us in the last seven minutes. Andre had a shot to win the game at the end, but his jumper wouldn't fall. The win closed out a big two-game road sweep that left us 22-2 overall and 11-1 in the Big Ten with a three-game lead over Michigan with six games remaining.

Over the years, my teams and I have always taken a lot of heat for not being able to win on the road. I think that has been unfair. It's always been tough for anyone to win on the road in this conference. The back-to-back wins at Purdue and Iowa shut a lot of people up and made them realize that this team was capable of winning on the road as well as at home. We won seven of nine Big Ten road games during the season, a great accomplishment for a coach and a team that supposedly never could win away from Williams Arena. Not many teams ever go 7-2 on the road in this league.

After a 60-48 win over Ohio State at Williams Arena, we took a 23-2 overall record, a 12-1 Big Ten mark and a No. 2 national ranking, the best in school history, into the rematch with Illinois at Williams Arena on February 22. It was obvious what was on the line in this game: win and we clinched at least a tie for the school's first Big Ten championship in 15 years.

The speed and athleticism of Illinois presented a lot of problems for us in our first game in Champaign and the rematch was no different. Sam was battling the flu and scored just four points in the game. Bobby had another great game with 18 points, six rebounds and four assists, before fouling out. Charles came up with some quality minutes for us, especially when Bobby went to the sideline.

The afternoon's heroics belonged to my big senior center, John Thomas, who finished the game with 12 points and seven rebounds. Trailing by one point with the clock ticking down, "Big John" made two free throws with 4.7 seconds left to give us a one-point lead. Illinois had a chance to win the game at the other end, but turned the ball over before taking a shot. We had clinched the title with the 67-66 win and the 14,554 fans in "The Barn" went crazy.

I can't put into words what it meant to me personally, our players and our program to clinch a tie for the Big Ten title. When I was heading off the court after the game, one of my assistant coaches, Bill Brown, looked at me and said, "Coach, you need to go back out there."

When I went back on the court, I didn't know what to do at first. But then I started blowing kisses to the crowd, to try and say "thank you" to them for all their support through the years and let them know that they were a big part of this accomplishment.

Once I got to the locker room I tried to hold my emotions in. I told the team that I was happy but that it wasn't time to celebrate. We had too much work left to do yet. We had not won the title outright yet and that would be the time to celebrate.

We journeyed to Ann Arbor to take on Coach Steve Fisher's Michigan Wolverines on February 26. Minnesota had only won one game ever over the Wolverines in Crisler Arena. It was the only remaining place in the Big Ten where I had never come away with a victory.

With the score tied at 54-all, Michigan had the ball and was getting set to take the last shot. Then there was a wild scramble, a loose ball and next thing I knew, Eric was diving through the air to bat the ball to Bobby who was streaking to the other end of the court. Bobby got the ball, went in for a layup and was fouled with 2.9 seconds left. He made one free throw to give us a 55-54 lead and then Courtney intercepted the inbounds pass to seal the win and the outright Big Ten title. Let the celebration begin!

It was such a joyous moment. It was extra special to have two of my former assistant coaches, Milt Barnes and Silas McKinnie, along with Willie Burton, there to share it with us. People forget that 11 years ago the basketball program was an embarrassment to the University and the entire state.

But those three guys, as well as all of my former players and coaches were a part of this championship season. Jim Shikenjanski, Melvin Newbern, Richard Coffey, Connell Lewis, Tim Hanson, Dave Holmgren, Kim Zurcher, Terence Williams, Walter Bond, Kevin Lynch, Mario Green, Randy Carter, Arriel McDonald, Townsend Orr, Voshon Lenard, Jayson Walton, the list goes on and on. There are so many people responsible for helping to lay the foundation that this program is standing on now.

I did not want to cut down the nets after the game. I thought that it would be rude for us to go into someone else's building and cut their nets down. But in a real classy move on their part, they told us that it would be okay for us to do it.

They brought out a ladder and each one of my players, assistant coaches and Roger, our trainer, had the opportunity to cut down a piece of the net. I cut down the final strands. A small piece of the net went into my billfold where I will carry it for the rest of my life.

When we got back into our locker room, the kids were hootin' and hollering. Now I can't dance a lick, but I hopped up on one of the benches and did my own little dance. I was so excited. I twisted my hips a little bit, really got into it. I'm normally pretty conservative, so the guys just had a ball with it. I wanted to let them know that I was human, that I could let my hair down a bit. It was a special occasion, one that I will cherish for the rest of my life.

We returned home to Williams Arena where three days later we beat Indiana, 75-72, behind 14 points and 10 rebounds from Courtney. We led by 15 points at the half, but struggled to hold on to the win in the second half. It marked the first time since 1966 that the program had swept Indiana and Purdue in the same season.

After the game, Big Ten Conference commissioner Jim Delany presented the championship trophy to the team and then an incredible celebration followed. I don't think anyone in the season-high crowd of 14,625 left the arena. They all wanted to share in this special moment.

It was a thing of beauty. There was so much excitement and satisfaction over what we had accomplished. Did I ever think 11 years ago when I took the job that we would arrive at this point? I don't know. But that was my dream, my goal. I had tears in my eyes and joy in my heart when I held that championship trophy up in front of our great fans.

We were 27-2 overall, 16-1 in the Big Ten and No. 2 in the country when we entertained Michigan State at "The Barn" on March 6 in the home finale. Senior Night is always tough on me and this one was no exception. It marked the final home game for my four seniors: Bobby, John, Trevor and Aaron Stauber, a six-foot walk-on guard from Sheboygan, Wisconsin, who had transferred to our program from Michigan Tech.

Before the game, the four seniors were introduced to the crowd along with their parents. Then all four of them pulled a cord underneath one of the baskets to unfurl the 1997 Big Ten championship banner that hung in the rafters.

We started slow in the first half, but Sam scored 18 points and Courtney scored 15 points and had nine rebounds, to lead us to an 81-74 win over the Spartans. That set off another great post-game celebration and put the finishing touches on the program's first undefeated home season at 15-0 since 1949. That was a great way for my seniors to go out.

Wisconsin beat us, 66-65, in the regular season finale at the Wisconsin Fieldhouse on March 8. The win secured an NCAA bid for Coach Dick Bennett's Badgers. After Sam had drained a three-pointer to give us a 65-64 lead, Wisconsin's Ty Calderwood hit two pressure-packed free throws to help the Badgers retake the lead with 11 seconds left. We set up a play to have either Sam or Bobby take the last shot. The ball was stolen from Sam before he could get a shot off, however, and that sent us into the NCAA Tournament with a 27-3 overall record.

I want to win every game. We competed hard and had an opportunity to win that game, probably should have won the game to be honest. Wisconsin was a good ballclub and Dick's done a great job since taking over as coach.

But it was probably a blessing in disguise for us to get beat. We had won 12 games in a row up to that point. I was disappointed that we lost, but if we were going to lose one, that was the time to do it. It showed our guys that we weren't invincible. So from that standpoint it was a very good loss in that it forced us to get refocused heading into the NCAA Tournament.

A lot of the credit for our championship season in 1996-97 should go to my great coaching staff. Larry Davis is an outstanding coach who worked his fanny off for me for three years. He is a workaholic and a super recruiter. Shortly after the NCAA Tournament, he became the head coach at Furman.

My other two assistants, Bill Brown and Charles Cunningham, have great basketball minds. After Milt took the head job at Eastern Michigan prior to the start of the season, Charles stepped in and did a fantastic job. Bill is a young guy who is going to make a wonderful head coach someday.

My son, Brent, was also an important member of our staff, along with Hosea Crittenden, who after finishing his playing days in 1995-96, became a student assistant coach for us. I think those two both have fine careers ahead of them in the coaching profession. Kudos should also go out to our strength coach, Bob Rohde.

A lot of credit for keeping everything running smoothly in our office should go to Carolyn Allen and principal secretary Kimberly DeKam. They did a wonderful job during a very exciting, but hectic time. I must also extend a heartfelt "thanks" to Ty Knoff who never missed a roadtrip during the season. He and his wife, Nancy, are tremendous people, and their friendship and support mean so much to Yevette and me.

It would be an understatement to say that I was more relaxed as we gathered together as a team to watch Selection Sunday. We had received an automatic bid as the Big Ten champions. The only suspense was whether or not we would be a No. 1 seed.

There was a lot of joy, a lot of personal satisfaction when Minnesota went up on the board as the No. 1 seed in the Midwest Regional. Our first-round opponent would be Southwest Texas State, the No. 16 seed out of the Southland Conference. I was so proud for our University, the state and for all the people who had supported us through the tough times.

I was asked a lot of questions about whether or not I felt vindicated after being snubbed by the NCAA Selection Committee twice before. To be quite honest, I didn't even think about that. That was in the past. This was a new year and we had a job ahead of us. I expected to be a number-one seed and didn't feel any extra pressure going into the NCAA Tournament because of it. We had gone 27-3 overall and 16-2 in the Big Ten. We deserved it.

I will never forget when we came out on the court just before our first-round game with Southwest Texas State at Kemper Arena in Kansas City. I thought I was back at Williams Arena for just a second. Well over half of the crowd were Gopher fans and they followed us every step of the way through the tournament. Their support was a key ingredient in how well we played.

A No. 16 seed has never beaten a No. 1 seed in the history of the NCAA Tournament and we made sure to do our part in keeping that streak intact by bolting out to a 13-0 lead in the first four minutes of the game. We had a 46-17 lead at the half and the final score was 78-46. It was the most lopsided NCAA Tournament victory in school history.

Bobby, Eric, Sam, John and Charles all scored in double figures as we once again displayed the depth that had carried us all season long. The only scare we had in the game came in the second half when Bobby fell to the floor and hurt his right knee, the same one that he had injured in junior college a few years earlier. It ended up just being a bruise and we sailed into a second-round matchup with Temple and Coach John Chaney's matchup zone.

Before the game everyone was saying that we couldn't handle the matchup zone. Nobody gave us any credit. It was almost like we were the underdog. That was kind of funny to tell you the truth. I mean we had only won 28 games and played against just about every style of play that you could have imagined.

I love John. I've always respected him a great deal. Temple is always a hard team to play against because they're always a well-coached and disciplined team. But I had no fear whatsoever of going up against his team's matchup zone. I don't care what offense or defense you throw at me. I feel I can stop it, or master it, if I have enough time to prepare the game plan.

We had a great game plan against Temple and our guys really executed it. The question was whether or not we could knock down our shots once we got them out of our offensive set. You can't control that part of the game as a coach. You can set up the game plan to get good looks, but then it's up to the guys to put the ball in the hole.

A lot of people stepped up big-time for us and we came away with a convincing 76-57 win over the Owls. We hit a season-high 10 three-pointers in the game. Sam shot the eyes out of the basket for us. He hit four three-pointers and scored 13 points. Charles led us with 14 points and really took some big shots. Eric did a great job of quarterbacking the club. Bobby was phenomenal and John and Trevor did a nice job on the boards.

In addition to sending us into a "Sweet 16" showdown with Clemson at the Alamodome in San Antonio, Texas, the following week, the win over Temple had some extra special meaning to this old coach. It was my 300th career victory and it couldn't have come at a better time.

The game with Clemson was one of the finest I've ever had the privilege to be involved in both as a player and coach. We led by 15 points in the first half, but they closed the gap to six points at 41-35 by the intermission and we knew that we were in for a fight the whole way. Bobby and Sam were almost exclusively carrying the load for us on the offensive end of the floor.

We lost Eric with a right shoulder injury with just over seven minutes remaining in regulation. That was obviously a big blow, but we still had a chance to put the game on ice with 8.2 seconds remaining. We had a 72-70 lead and Quincy had two free throws. He missed them both and then Clemson's Tony Christie tied the game up at the buzzer with a beautiful twisting jumper in the lane.

Things didn't look so good when we fell behind by six points two minutes into the first overtime, but then we scored six straight points to force a second overtime. Bobby had four of those and Quincy bounced right back from the disappointment of missing the free throws to hit the other bucket. The second overtime was all ours and we came away with a physically and mentally emotional 90-84 double overtime win.

That was the most physical game that I've ever been involved in during my coaching career. Believe me, Clemson pounded us. Sam was on fire, especially in the first half, and matched his career-best with 29 points. Bobby was just unbelievable the entire game and finished with a career-high 36 points.

Clemson was an outstanding team and for us to win that game after being down by six points in the first overtime was truly a testament to the heart and the desire of that team. In the face of adversity, they showed the will to win. That's something that you can't put a stamp on. You must have the right players, the right ingredients, the right chemistry. That team felt that as long as there was a tick left on the clock, we still had a chance to win. That's the attitude that I tried to instill in them.

We were well aware of what we were up against in the Midwest Regional final two days later when we met UCLA, a school that has won more national championships (11), than any other in the country. The task was that much harder without a healthy Eric Harris in our lineup. He couldn't practice the day before the regional final and had to go through treatment and get a couple of shots before the game just to kill the pain.

Down by 10 points in the second half, we took over the game with a crucial 16-4 run. Unlike the Clemson game where Bobby and Sam took over most of the scoring load, we got back to what had brought us this far in the first place: team depth. Charles and Quincy scored 14 of those 16 points in that run.

Bobby led the way with 18 points in the game and hit some clutch free throws down the stretch to seal the 80-72 win over the Bruins that sent us to Indianapolis and the Final Four. Bobby, who was a second-team All-America choice, was named Midwest Regional MVP to go along with his Big Ten MVP honors that he had already collected.

We wore UCLA down, especially when their starting center, Jelani McCoy, was injured and went to the sidelines. Because of our depth and commitment to playing nine or 10 guys all season long, we could overcome the injury to Eric and have someone else step up to fill the gap. Like so many other games that season, we won that game because of our depth.

We couldn't have made it to the Final Four without Quincy, Charles, Trevor, Miles and Russ doing a great job coming off the bench for us. I knew that going into the season and that's why I played them. I took some abuse for it, but that's why they pay me to coach.

I have to take my hat off to Eric for going through what he did to get himself ready to play. Physically he wasn't ready, but mentally he got himself prepared and he gave us 23 minutes. Without those 23 minutes from him, we wouldn't have won the game.

It was another great performance, another gut check, from a group of young men who refused to lose. When the buzzer sounded and we started to celebrate, I kept thinking to myself, "My God, is this for real? Are we really going to the Final Four?"

I remember after I cut down the final strands of the net, taking a small piece of it over to Ray Christensen, a class guy who has served as our radio play-by-play announcer on WCCO radio for many, many years. He had suffered through so many tough times with us and I wanted him to know that he was an important part of the celebration.

Afterwards in the locker room, I told the team to celebrate and enjoy the victory, but to remember that we had to play Kentucky in the Final Four. That we still had 80 minutes to go to win the national championship.

The scene when we flew back home to the Twin Cities was something that I will never ever forget. A welcome home party was held for the team back in Williams Arena. I was told that the fans started lining up outside Williams Arena at 4:30 p.m. The doors were opened at 9 p.m. and the place was jam-packed almost immediately with 15,000 loyal fans. They turned thousands more away. I keep saying it, but it's true: the college basketball fans at Minnesota are the very best in the country.

They had a big screen in Williams Arena so that the fans could follow our progress from the airport to the gym. Every television station in the Twin Cities carried it live. We landed at about 10:45 p.m. and they showed us getting off the plane and then a helicopter with a camera aboard followed us every step of the way to the arena. I guess every time they showed the bus on the screen, the place just went nuts.

The reception at the airport in 1990 was great, but this one was absolutely incredible. This really did remind me of my junior year at Western Kentucky in 1966 when we returned to Diddle Arena after upsetting Chicago Loyola in the NCAA Tournament.

You had to be in Williams Arena that night to feel the excitement, the electricity in the air. When we were introduced and went up on the court, you couldn't even hear yourself think.

It's a moment that I will cherish for the rest of my life. I want to get the tape out 20 or 30 years down the road when I'm in a wheelchair and watch it all over again. I'm sure I'll cry and get goosepimples from the joy and excitement.

Even though our semifinal game against Kentucky at the RCA Dome wasn't until Saturday, I decided to take the team down to Indianapolis on Tuesday. It was crazy back in the Twin Cities. Bobby went to the Mall of America to pick up some things he needed one day and he got mobbed. John went to the Timberwolves game the day after we beat UCLA and there was a line all the way up the lower level aisle and out in the concourse to get his autograph.

I wanted to get the team out of town so that they could get their minds back on the game. On top of that, I've always tried to take my teams in early during the NCAA Tournament. I think that's important. The main objective is to go in and win the game, of course, but it's also a once-in-a-lifetime opportunity for your players, especially the seniors. This is the last shot for them.

I wanted to get there and let them go down to the Fan Jam at the arena, walk in the city, go to a movie, things like that. Just have some fun and enjoy the experience. Every coach has to do what they feel works best and that approach has always worked for me.

The Final Four is very hectic. The media requests that you have to fulfill are unbearable. I don't think you can ever prepare for something like that. I was also fortunate to receive several coach of the year awards and I had a number of banquets and awards ceremonies to attend. As a matter of fact, Yevette had to accept some of the awards on my behalf because it was physically impossible for me to do so. With everything going on, I honestly don't know if I was ever able to get refocused as a coach.

A lot was said in the media about my personal feelings toward Kentucky. When my Western Kentucky team played them in the second round of the 1986 NCAA Tournament, I really took it personally. That was a different thing altogether. I had a lot of animosity in my heart toward the University of Kentucky at that time.

No matter what anyone else says, I did not feel any of that animosity going into our 1997 Final Four matchup. Believe me, I had put all of that behind me. I was driven to beat Kentucky because I wanted to win the national championship. They were the next roadblock on our way to the national title.

I thought we were well-prepared for the Kentucky game, but we just didn't do a very good job of handling the basketball against their pressure. We uncharacteristically turned the ball over 26 times in the game and that was the difference as Coach Rick Pitino's defending national champions beat us, 78-69.

We did not play one of our better basketball games, but I think you have to give Kentucky a lot of credit for that. We were a team that prided itself on taking care of the basketball. A team that didn't beat itself with mistakes.

It definitely hurt once again to not have a healthy Eric Harris in the lineup. He gutted it out and played 29 minutes, but the shoulder injury definitely limited his effectiveness.

Kentucky jumped out to a 14-5 lead, and as badly as we had played, we trailed by only five points, 36-31, at the half. Trailing 47-43 with 14:31 remaining in the game, Bobby broke their press and delivered a great pass to Courtney who dunked it over Kentucky center Jamaal Magloire.

The whistle blew and right away I was thinking that we had the deficit cut to two points and Courtney was going to the line with a chance to cut it to one. But the referee called Courtney for charging; a terrible, terrible call. I couldn't believe it. Magloire was standing right underneath the basket when it happened. TV replays confirmed my worst nightmares.

I wasn't a happy camper and I let the referees know it. A strong official probably could have thrown me out of the game, but I think that they were so embarrassed with the call that they let me get away with more than they should have.

The technical, however, really brought us to life. Trailing 51-43, we scored nine straight points, seven of those by Bobby, to take a 52-51 lead with 10:45 left in the game. I really believed that the game was ours.

Tied at 54-all, Kentucky went on a 12-3 run to take control of the game. In addition to the high number of turnovers, we just didn't get the production from our bench that had been our trademark all season long. Bobby had 23 points, but Kentucky's bench outscored ours 28-18. We shot only 42 percent for the game, including just 3-of-16 on three-pointers. We were 4-of-10 from the free throw line in the second half.

After the loss to Kentucky, we stayed in Indianapolis to let the guys soak up every last ounce of the Final Four experience. I don't know if anyone had ever done that before. I think that most times the semifinal losers take the first plane out of town. The experience is about more than just winning and losing. The entire team attended the championship game together.

The day after Arizona beat Kentucky for the national title, we flew back home and were honored on the field before the Twins' season opener against the Detroit Tigers at the Metrodome. We were honored in a similar fashion after the loss to Georgia Tech in the 1990 Southeast Regional final. When I threw out the first pitch then, my son Brent was so embarrassed because it took about 10 bounces before it crossed the plate. This time I threw a "perfect" strike to Twins catcher and former Golden Gopher Terry Steinbach.

Once I got over the initial disappointment of falling 40 minutes short of our national championship dream, I realized what kind of year this team had put together. We set a new school record with 31 victories against just four defeats, we won the school's first Big Ten title in 15 years and we were the first to ever go to the Final Four. There may be other Golden Gopher teams that come along to match or surpass those accomplishments, but the 1996-97 team will *always* be the first.

S TATE OF THE GAME

CHAPTER TWENTY-FOUR

C ollege basketball is the greatest game in the world. Young people can grow and mature in so many ways by playing the game. Discipline, a strong work ethic and teamwork are just a few of the important lessons that the game delivers back to those who play it. I really believe that college basketball and college athletics as a whole provide a positive supplement to a young person's academic pursuits in the classroom.

However, the direction the game is heading and the young people who play the game today concern me. The game has become a very individualistic, "me-first" pursuit, and that troubles me.

Because of that I'm probably going to be forced out of coaching in a few years. Some people tell me that I'm from the old school. I guess I am a throwback of sorts, but I believe strongly in certain things and I'm a man of principle.

When I was on the rules committee a few years ago, I was responsible for having a rule passed that required jerseys to be tucked in at all times. A lot of people call it "The Clem Haskins Rule." I think you should look the part when you're out on the basketball court. To me, how you dress has a lot to do with how you carry yourself.

I don't like the tattoos, the earrings, the gold chains, the shorts hanging down past the knees, the caps worn backwards. No doubt about it, I just don't think that there's any place for those things in the game of basketball.

Men shouldn't wear earrings, women should. That's just my philosophy. Tattoos are a fad and everyone's a copycat. The times have changed and coaches are as guilty as anyone for selling out and giving in. We need to confront people with what's right and wrong.

Does the fact that I speak out against this sort of garbage hurt me in recruiting? To a certain extent it probably does with some of the blue-chip recruits who already have visions of making a million dollars in the NBA dancing in their head.

But I also think that there are a lot of young men and parents out there who buy into my philosophy. I want to recruit the guys who will work hard, are coachable and believe in what we're trying to do here at Minnesota. That still leaves a lot of good kids out there.

The recruiting game is an interesting business. You win some and you lose some. I've lost my share of great players over the years. You work hard to sell yourself, the program and the school, but if you end up number two on his list you might as well have been number 202 when all is said and done.

Recruiting is like shaving; you have to do it every day. If you do a good job and work hard at it every day, you wind up getting the student-athletes that you deserve.

There's the seedy side of the recruiting business too. Some kids are driving brand new cars, getting free plane tickets, receiving cash. I wish that there was some way to clean it up, but as long as we keep score and the stakes are so high, cheating will be a part of the game.

Through the years there have been a number of extremely talented kids we didn't even begin to recruit because they told us right away that a scholarship wouldn't be enough. They wanted this or that on top of the scholarship. Some of the things that you see out there from other schools are just outrageous and it makes it tough for the programs like ours that play by the rules.

I'm all about preparing young men for life. When a young man comes to the University of Minnesota to play for Clem Haskins, I give him more than a jump shot. I try to prepare him for life, give him survival skills, try to teach him how to be a good husband down the road, a good father to his kids and a positive role model.

Those are very important things that we talk about every day. I've always done that. I try to set an example for my players by the way I lead my own life, what I say and do, and how I treat my family and the people around me.

When I recruit a young man, I tell his mom and dad from the start that I can't guarantee I'll turn their son into an All-America basketball player. But I do guarantee them that he'll be a better person if he plays four years for me. I promise moms and dads that I will work with their son each and every day, and explain to him what life is about and how to become a better person, a better citizen.

We have a family atmosphere in my program. My players become a part of my own family and I treat them like that. They mean that much to me. Anyone who has ever played for me will tell you that I'm hard on the basketball court, but that I'm fair. I run a disciplined program. People can't do and say what they want here. We have only one rule and that is *do right*.

It's a lot tougher for kids today in our society. The peer pressure is unbelievable. The pressure is there to drink, smoke dope, hang out with the wrong crowd, all sorts of roadblocks are in place to take them off course. I think one of the reasons for the problems kids have today is that in most homes both parents have to work in order to make a living. As a result, the parents are not at home and don't have the opportunity to spend quality time with their kids. The discipline is not there. The kids come and go as they please.

There's also an ever-increasing number of one-parent homes. I see that more and more today, and it's sad. The percentage of marriages that end up in divorce today is alarming. In that situation, of course, the parent who stays with the children usually must work to provide for the family and then you run into the same problem I just talked about.

A young man needs a father figure growing up. It's tough on him when there's no father figure at home. I've met so many incredible women in my life who have raised families on their own and my hat goes off to every one of them. God bless them! But young men miss that father figure, that strong male role model. That's a fact.

That's what's missing in many homes today and it hurts. When I recruit players into my program who have come from one-parent homes where there was no father figure, it's a tough adjustment for them to make when they get here because I come across pretty strong.

But after they're here for awhile, they realize that this was the way it was supposed to be all along if they would've had a dad at home. They realize how much they've missed it because they want that discipline, they want that strong male role model in their life. That's what Clem Haskins is all about.

The young men in our program are like sons to me. When one of your own kids gets in trouble with the law or in trouble in school, you discipline him and get after him. I can't tell you how much it hurts me when that happens.

I take it personally, because I work so hard to mold them from boys into young men and I hate to see them make mistakes. Particularly after we've talked to them repeatedly about certain things, and they still go out and do something wrong, go against what you've been preaching to them all along. It affects me quite a bit.

I try to realize that all young men experience growing pains and that I have to accept that they will make mistakes from time to time. It's the same thing as a parent when one of your own kids makes a mistake. You try to deal with those mistakes and work through them so that they learn from the experience and become a better person because of it.

When a player in my program makes a mistake, believe me, he pays the price. It's hard, but I like to call it tough love. It may be that he has to get up every morning for a month straight at five o'clock and run a mile or maybe five miles. He may need to get some help through counseling. Or I may decide that both he and our program would be better served if he moved on. The level of acceptance and the punishment that I dish out depends upon the severity of the mistake.

The Big Ten will have its first postseason conference tournament ever in 1998 at the United Center in Chicago. I've been totally against it all along. I think the regular season schedule is enough right now. On top of that, we're asking our kids to miss even more school than they already do. Aren't we supposed to be about education? There's a big-time contradiction in there somewhere.

The bottom line is money. It's come to the point in college athletics where that is the bottom line. We're prostituting our kids for the sake of making more money.

We need to look at what more we can do for the kids. Basketball student-athletes should receive a stipend. I'd also like to see a rule put in place where their parents could receive plane tickets and a hotel room to come and watch them play during the postseason.

We ask these kids to play games from coast-to-coast on any given day and time. It usually depends on television. Other student-athletes aren't asked to do that. In football, virtually all of the games are on Saturdays and they generally only play 11 or 12 regular season games. We played 35 basketball games at Minnesota in 1996-97!

They deserve something not only because of the stress, the strain and the pressure we put on our players at this level, but also because of the revenue that these kids help generate for their schools.

I've always felt that the coaches should have more power to implement rule changes and legislation at the NCAA level. We're the ones in the trenches every day. The majority of college presidents are white, with middle-to-upper middle class backgrounds. They've never been in the trenches.

I just don't understand some of the decisions they make. For example, a few years back they decided to reduce scholarships for men's Division I basketball programs from 15 to 13. Division I women's basketball programs are still allowed 15 full scholarships. During the 1993-94 season the NCAA refused to reinstate a 14th scholarship. I was and still am furious about the decision.

As a member of the Black Coaches Association (BCA), I was heavily involved in talks about a possible coaches boycott across the country. A large percentage of coaches across the country, both black and white, were real close to walking out. We decided against doing it, but the issue remains.

This is not a black and white thing. We as coaches care about education. I feel that my job is just as important as a professor. When you take opportunities away from young people there is something seriously wrong with that.

Most college presidents don't know what it's like to be a black growing up in the South. Most of them don't know what it's like to be poor. They have no clue what it's like to not know where your next meal's going to come from. They don't understand that kids don't always steal just to steal. They steal to survive. That a young man may have actually stolen some food to feed his belly, to feed his mother and his brothers and sisters.

The people calling the shots today in collegiate athletics have no clue what young people go through. We need to have more people in there making the decisions who have been there and that includes hiring more minority presidents, athletics directors, coaches and administrative staff members at universities around the country.

I'm going to be fighting the fight until the day I die, because I'm for what's right. I hate it when people say, "You've got a certain amount of white players and a certain amount of black players on your team." That really pisses me off. I don't care if they're white, black, yellow, green or whatever. I try to put the best team out on the floor every game, regardless of color.

There is a stereotype out there that when a white player is good, he's a "smart" or "intelligent" player, while a good black player is "a great athlete." When a white coach wins it's usually because he's a good "X's & O's" coach. Black coaches are usually considered to be "great recruiters."

That's the mentality that we have in our society and it's not fair to blacks or whites. Larry Bird was a fantastic athlete, as well as a smart player. Magic Johnson was not only a great athlete, but also an incredibly intelligent player. Both those guys had the total package.

Quincy Lewis, who helped lead us to the 1997 Big Ten title and the Final Four as a sophomore, can't jump very well and he isn't very quick. But he's a smart basketball player and that's why he's so productive. He does all the little things so well for us.

I think a lot of people don't give me credit for being a good X's & O's coach. I've never recruited a McDonald's high school All-America player at Minnesota—not a one. That's a regular thing at North Carolina, Duke and Kentucky.

But we've been successful at Minnesota because we've recruited good players who work hard and believe in our system, and then we've coached the hell out of them. I must be one heck of a coach if I can lead a team with no superstars to the Final Four.

I used to get all bent out of shape and I fought hard to get the recognition and respect that I thought I deserved as a coach. Now, I could care less. I'm a guy that believes in hard work, strong fundamentals and execution. I take a lot of pride in having my team be as well-prepared as they can be once they take the court.

For anyone who's ever been to a game and seen me on the sidelines, they know that I'm a pretty emotional coach. It's kind of ironic, because during my playing days, I can't say that I ever played for a coach quite like me. I guess it's just my personality, my makeup. I bring a lot of intensity to the game and I think that rubs off on my players.

I pride myself in being able to motivate and get the maximum effort and potential out of my players. I don't think you can do that with a laid-back style. I think you have to be aggressive as a coach. When we take the court, I want us to be so focused and so intense that we're ready for anything that our opponent may throw at us.

It's no secret that media coverage of college basketball is at an all-time high and it's given the sport a tremendous boost as a result. On just about any given night during the season, you can turn on the television and watch games from coast-to-coast.

Newspaper and radio coverage also continues to grow and that has had a positive effect in most instances too. The growth and popularity of the NCAA Tournament can be directly related to the media coverage that the event receives. It wasn't like that at all when I was growing up. I rarely got to see or hear about the great players in college and the NBA back then.

There's two sides to the coin however. Sometimes I think reporters have a tendency to look for garbage, the stuff that will sell papers. There are so many positive stories out there in our great game, but at times it seems like they are more interested in the dirt.

I also think there needs to be some restrictions on talk radio. I'm not saying that I have the answers, but there's something wrong when some of these people swear and use God's name in vain and basically say anything they want to on the air.

Sometimes they can get very personal. They'll talk about you as a man, your family, what you say, how you talk and so on. The funny thing is it's usually someone who doesn't even know you or has never even met you in his life.

It seems to me that the more they swear, lie and talk about people, the higher ratings they get. That's why I don't listen to talk radio shows. I enjoy listening to gospel and country western music. Country western music usually tells a story about life and I enjoy that.

A few seasons ago we were struggling as a team at about the halfway point of the Big Ten season. We just weren't playing well at all. To take some of the pressure off the team, I said some things about talk radio, and the people who listen to talk radio, and then the focus shifted immediately from our struggling team to me for about three weeks. That's exactly what I wanted to happen.

There are some great television commentators out there to-day, but there are others who can be very cruel; they're the ones who get on a coach if he doesn't call a timeout when they think he should, or don't shift to a zone defense from a man-to-man when they say so.

I've always found that interesting. Here's someone who has spent very little time studying a team's strengths and weaknesses, trying to tell a coach who has been with his team day-in and day-out what to do. I understand it's show business, but I still don't get it.

Looking back, I had very little media coverage when I was the coach at Western Kentucky, compared to what I have today at Minnesota. Sometimes I wish I could go back to those times, when all I had to worry about was handling the coaching end of my job.

It's tough because there are so many good members of the media out there that do a great job. They do an honest and fair job of covering your team. But when you have one or two bad apples, it has a tendency to spoil the whole basket ,which I know shouldn't be the case.

I really feel that overall I have had a good working relation-ship with the media both at Minnesota and around the country. We have an outstanding television partnership at Minnesota with Mid-west Sports Channel and WCCO-TV, a great radio deal with WCCO-AM, and the largest Twin Cities newspapers—the Minneapolis *Star Tribune* and the St. Paul *Pioneer Press*—cover us on a daily basis.

Through the Big Ten Conference, our regional and television packages are with ESPN and CBS. Our media coverage is as good as any school's in the country. It has certainly had a dramatic impact on the exposure of our basketball program, not only in our own state of Minnesota, but throughout the entire country and around the world as well.

When I first took the job at Minnesota, I was well aware of the state's outstanding reputation for churning out great talent in the sport of ice hockey. My dream was to someday see the sport of basketball in the state reach the same level of proficiency.

We worked hard from day one to sell basketball throughout the state to both boys and girls. By reaching out to state high school, junior high school and local youth programs, and through our an-nual summer basketball camps, I think that we have made a big impact in the quality of play in this state. I think that our success on the court has also gone hand-in-hand with the growth of the sport at both the NCAA and NBA levels.

I would say that the quality of play has improved 100 percent since my first year in Minnesota back in 1986. It's only going to continue to get better and better, too. Just watch. I've heard that the boy's and girl's youth basketball programs are growing so much throughout the state that some communities don't have enough gym space to accommodate all the kids and teams.

That's a great "problem" to have. If you had told someone a few years back in the basketball hotbeds of Indiana, Kentucky or New York City that the Golden Gophers would play in the Final Four one day with six players on their roster from the state of Minnesota, two of which were starters, they would have asked if you were crazy. Could it happen one day that we might be in the Final Four with five starters from Minnesota? Who knows? That would certainly be exciting!

If I had the opportunity to change one thing in the college game, I would probably outlaw dunking. There's so much emphasis put on dunking the ball that I think that a lot of players don't take the time to fully develop the other phases of their game.

Dunking is a show, more of a crowd pleaser than anything else. I like the old-fashioned way of making shots, executing on both ends of the floor and great all-around team play. I think that has been lost in the mix somewhere. The game wasn't invented to include the dunk or the three-point shot.

I realize that since the fans love the dunk and the three-pointer, there's probably going to be no turning back to the way it was. But I don't know if those are changes that are good for the game. Young players today don't want to work on jump shots, layups and their individual skills. They're more worried about dunking and shooting threes.

What has happened is that it has taken away the game between eight and 16 feet of the basket. Nobody shoots anymore from 10, 12 or 14 feet away from the hoop. It's made for a more exciting game for the fans, but I really think that the dunk and three-point shot have hindered the development of good players and teams.

Basketball has changed a lot since I started playing the game in the fields of Kentucky and I'm sure that it will continue to change long after I'm gone. I hope that in some small way I've left my mark on the players I've coached and the game I love so much.

BEST OF THE BEST

CHAPTER TWENTY-FIVE ■

I never imagined how tough it would be to pick the best players, teams and coaches looking back over my career. I've really been fortunate to be surrounded by so many talented and classy people through the years.

It's extremely hard to pick out the best team that I ever played on in my career. We had a couple of great teams my first two years in high school at Campbellsville Durham under Coach John Whiting. I played alongside a number of good friends and players: J.W. Allen, William "Peaches" Robinson, Donald K. Smith, John Henry Anderson, Charles Johnson, Donnie Johnson, and Jimmy Scott.

We had a 62-7 overall record in my two years under our coaches Billy B. Smith and Fred Waddle at Taylor County High School. Going to the "Sweet 16" my senior year was something incredibly special. Not only because it was the first time in school history that Taylor County had ever advanced to the state tournament, but also because my brother Paul, who was just a freshman, was a big part of it along with me.

As a junior at Western Kentucky, we registered a 25-3 overall record after falling to Michigan on the controversial call in the NCAA Tournament. Then I was a member of that great Washington Bullets team that lost in the 1975 NBA Finals after tying the Boston Celtics for the best regular-season record in the league at 60-22.

The 1966-67 Western Kentucky team when I was a senior was awfully good. That may have been the finest team that I ever played on. Dwight Smith, Greg Smith, Wayne Chapman, Butch Kaufman and I formed the "Fabulous Five."

We won 21 games in a row that season and had a legitimate shot to win the national title until I broke my wrist. We lost in overtime by two points to Dayton in the NCAA Tournament, with me playing basically left-handed. Dayton went on to lose to Lew Alcindor and UCLA in the national championship game.

Dwight Smith was the best teammate I ever had—that includes high school, college and the pros. He could just flat-out play. It was a crying shame that he was killed in the car accident shortly after our senior year at Western Kentucky. He had just been drafted in the first round by the NBA's Los Angeles Lakers.

Dwight never had the opportunity to show his great ability at the professional level. I'm convinced that he would have ended up playing at least 15 years of pro ball. He was the best defender I have ever seen. I have a young man named Eric Harris at Minnesota who is an outstanding defensive player and Dwight was better than him.

It didn't matter if the opposing player was five-foot-five or seven-foot-five, he could guard the ball better than anybody I've ever seen. He is without a doubt the finest player at all levels that I ever played with.

I can't pick out just one team that would be the best I've ever coached. I won't consider the 1996 "Dream Team" in any of my Best of the Best lists because that just wouldn't be fair.

My last team at Western Kentucky in 1985-86 went 23-8 overall and advanced to the second round of the NCAA Tournament. We only lost one key senior off that team, so I actually left my best squad talent-wise behind at Western Kentucky. The deck was stacked and I thought we had a shot to win the national championship. They went 29-9 the following year and lost to Syracuse on their home court at the Carrier Dome in the NCAA Tournament. The Orangemen advanced all the way to the championship game where they lost to Indiana on Keith Smart's last-second shot.

My 1989-90 ballclub at Minnesota is one that I'll be always be personally attached to more than any other team. Those guys came from out of nowhere their first couple of years to the "Elite Eight" of the NCAA Tournament as seniors.

Our 1993 NIT championship team at Minnesota will always be special. Those guys rebounded from the disappointment of not getting selected for the NCAA Tournament to go all the way in the NIT. That will always rank right up there in my heart because it was the first postseason championship that the Golden Gopher basketball program had ever won.

My 1996-97 Minnesota team went to the Final Four for the first time in school history. That group, which captured the Golden Gophers' first Big Ten title in 15 seasons and set a new school record with 31 victories, really came together as a team.

You see, it just can't be one team. Those four teams really stand out and will always be special, each in its own right.

Following the 1996-97 season, in addition to getting the Big Ten Coach of the Year award, I also received the following national coach of the year awards: AP; John and Nellie Wooden; Henry Iba; CBS/Chevrolet; Black Coaches Association; NABC; Claire Bee; and Basketball America.

People still laugh at me when I say this, but I still believe in my heart that my best job of coaching came during my first two seasons at Minnesota when our combined record was 19-37. I really mean that. I worked as hard at coaching those two teams as I ever have in my career.

I took over a program under difficult circumstances. We were 9-19 in 1986-87 and 10-18 in 1987-88. I had a group of guys from all walks of life that couldn't walk and chew bubble gum at the same time. They weren't great athletes or players right away, but they were good people, good students and hard workers.

That was what coaching was all about. I took that group of young men and developed them into a very good team their last two years. We made it to the "Sweet 16" of the NCAA Tournament in 1989 and then to the "Elite Eight" in 1990, just a jump shot away from the Final Four.

I learned so much from my first coach, John Whiting, at Campbellsville Durham High School. He taught me a lot about life at a young age. He taught me how to shoot properly and to play hard all the time. He has retired as the principal from Seneca High School in Louisville and still is a professor at the University of Louisville. He and his wife, Pat, were at all of our 1997 NCAA Tournament games. John is a tremendous man who knows how to work with young people. I respect him so much and he will always be close to me.

My college coach at Western Kentucky, John Oldham, is a tremendous man who also taught me a lot about life. I never saw him get upset at all, on the sidelines, in a game or in practice. He never raised his voice and he showed me the way in terms of honesty and dignity.

Three of my coaches in the NBA had an impact on my life. Cotton Fitzsimmons with the Phoenix Suns is a guy that I have the utmost respect for. I had the most fun playing for him. Dick Motta played me a lot when he came to the Chicago Bulls during my second year in the NBA and I ended up starting six-and-a-half seasons after that. I really enjoyed playing for Dick. K.C. Jones with the Washington Bullets had the best relationship with his players of any coach I've ever been around. The players really loved to play for him.

I think I have to have a 1A and a 1B for the best backcourt I've ever coached. My 1990 NCAA "Elite Eight" team had a great backcourt in Kevin Lynch and Melvin Newbern. Our 1997 Final Four team had another great backcourt tandem in Eric Harris and Big Ten MVP Bobby Jackson. Kevin and Melvin would have an edge because of their size and strength, while Eric and Bobby would get the nod with their athletic ability and quickness. On top of that, all four players were winners. Those were two phenomenal backcourts, so this one's a tossup.

Without a doubt my best frontcourt would be in 1985-86 at Western Kentucky with Tellis Frank, Kannard Johnson and Clarence Martin. Those guys had it all: size, strength and great athletic ability. They were all back in 1986-87, so you can imagine how tough it was for me to leave them behind.

If I had to pick an all-opponent team that I've coached against in college it would include Patrick Ewing of Georgetown, who we played three straight seasons when I was at Western. We lost to them in overtime during the 1982-83 season.

I would also pick Louisville's Darrell Griffith, who we lost to my last season as an assistant coach at Western in 1979-80. The Cardinals went on to win the NCAA title later that season. Memphis State's Penny Hardaway is also on my list. During the 1992-93 season we beat the Tigers, 70-55, at Williams Arena on New Year's Eve, but Penny was still magnificent. He finished the game with 30 points and 10 rebounds.

A couple of Big Ten players—Michigan's Glen Rice and Ohio State's Jimmy Jackson—round out my top five. Both of these guys had a number of great games against us. Rice led the Wolverines to the 1989 NCAA title, while Jackson paced the Buckeyes to back-to-back Big Ten titles in 1991 and 1992.

The best five guys that I ever played against in my NBA career would be Jerry West and Oscar Robertson at the guards, and then Elgin Baylor, Wilt Chamberlain and Bill Russell up front. Elgin would play the small forward and then Wilt and Bill would split time between the power forward and center positions.

If I was a general manager of an NBA team and could pick any 10 players in the history of the game to play for my team who would they would be? Don't be surprised that there's only one active player out of the 10.

Clem Haskins' 10 best all-time players are: Jerry West, Oscar Robertson, Michael Jordan, Elgin Baylor, Wilt Chamberlain, Bill Russell, Kareem Abdul-Jabbar, John Havlicek, Larry Bird and Magic Johnson.

DOWN ON THE FARM

CHAPTER TWENTY-SIX

A lot of people enjoy going to Hawaii, Hilton Head, the Florida Keys or someplace like that for vacation. Don't get me wrong, all those places are very nice.

But when I get some time off, I get excited about going to my farm in the rolling hills on the east side of Campbellsville, Kentucky. After a long, hard season on the basketball court, nothing energizes me more than a trip "home" to my farm.

There is absolutely no place like it in the world for me. It gives me an opportunity to get back to nature, to get away from it all. I enjoy the serenity of the place. When I go home to the farm, my dogs, cattle and horses don't know if I've won or lost all my games. They're just happy to see me.

My dog, Ike, is a Rottweiler. He's a big, strong dog that weighs between 150 and 160 pounds. I turn him loose around the farm when I'm around and he absolutely loves that. He's also a good watchdog. He doesn't bite people. He just scares strangers away more than anything.

I used to have two border collies, Rex and Topper, that I just loved. Rex died a few years back and Topper just recently passed away at the ripe old age of 20. They were both real good cattle dogs who were great to have around the farm.

I love the sights and the sounds on the farm. I love to get on my tractor and get some work done. There's the creek that runs through the property. When I walk through my woods, I love to hear the birds chirp, see the squirrels hustle about. I also put salt blocks out for the deer on my land. It's sounds kind of crazy, but it kind of seems like all the animals sense when I'm back.

I'm proud of the fact that not only was I born and raised on a farm, but I also own that farm today. In fact, I own about 500 acres in all and I worked every inch of it growing up as a kid. I used to tell everybody that I worked for back then that I was going to come back and buy their land someday.

They all told me that they would sell their land to me one day if I still wanted to buy it. I'm sure they thought that it was kind of cute that a boy would talk like that. I doubt if they ever thought I'd actually follow through with it, especially since I was one of 11 children in a family that didn't have a lot of money.

The land where our small white house sits once belonged to George Wayne, a man whom I worked for as a boy. I used to call him Mr. George. I started milking cattle for him when I was about nine or 10 years old. I'd do it in the morning before I went to school. I did a lot of work for George and his wife, Bessie, when I was growing up.

I remember telling him over and over, "Someday I'm going to buy your farm." This was a nine- or 10-year-old talking. He used to say to me, "If I ever sell it Clem, I'm going to sell it to you."

I helped him build the porch on the house when I was 10. It's built out of cedar wood. George was a great carpenter and I learned how to build things by watching him. We eventually put heat and air conditioning out there, and screened it in. That's where he used to spend most of his time.

One day in 1972, George came to me and asked, "Are you ready to buy this place?" I said, "Yes, give me your price." I bought it from him for $50,000. That included the house, a barn, 50 acres of land, the cattle and all his machinery.

When I first met him, I didn't know the difference between black and white. Even though he was white, he looked at me as a young boy and he respected me. He knew I worked hard and would give him an honest day's work.

George kept his promise to me when he was ready to sell his farm. He knew how much I wanted it and also that I would take good care of that farm and that land that had meant so much to him. After he sold the farm, he retired and then moved into town with Bessie. When Bessie died, he moved to Louisville to live with his son George Jr. Mr. George is a great man, a man of his word. I owe a lot to him.

It's been a dream of mine since I was a boy to come back and buy the land where I grew up. Only in a great nation like America is something like that possible. To be able to accomplish so much is truly remarkable and it gives me great satisfaction to talk about it. I hope it proves a point to young people, black or white; if you work hard and are smart with your money, anything can happen.

There's a total of six houses on my land. I purchased a couple of tracks of land from some neighbors—Leonard Sanders and Mrs. Fannie Smith—but they still live in their houses and can do so for the rest of their lives if they wish.

My Mother lives in the house I grew up in out at the end of Roberts Road. It's located right across the road from the one that Yevette and I live in when we're there. It's probably about 300 or 400 yards from our front door. As I mentioned earlier, my nephew, Hearie, lives with Mother. It's absolutely wonderful to spend time with her, along with my five brothers and sisters who still live in the area, when we get back to the farm.

Mother's in her 80s, but she still takes care of herself. She has great energy, a great work ethic. She still goes to bed early and then gets up every morning at around four-thirty or five o'clock.

My brother, Paul, keeps things in order year-round on the farm, with help from my oldest brother, Willie, and Hearie. My sisters, Lummie, Mable and Betty, all still work at the Fruit of the Loom plant in town.

Family is a big part of why I enjoy coming home. Nearly every year in August we have a big barbeque with my Mother, my brothers and sisters, nephews and nieces, and Yevette's parents, J.C. and Harriet Penick. It's quite the crowd. We usually have over 100 relatives on hand.

There's a lot of work to be done each day on the farm; it keeps me busy. I have about 200 head of cattle all together. I really enjoy working with my cattle. We breed and sell them. I also have seven horses. The last couple of years, however, I haven't been able to ride as much because of my knees.

I have two Arabian horses. A good friend of ours in Minnesota, and a great supporter of the University of Minnesota, Dick Ames, gave me an Arabian mare and told me to take it to the farm in Kentucky because he couldn't get it to foal. I'm an old country boy so I knew how to get that mare to foal. So I took it, bred it and I've had five consecutive foals.

It just blows Dick away that I was able to do that. She's turned out to be a wonderful mare. In fact, she's been in a number of shows. I've also got Tennessee walking horses that I enjoy riding.

Now you ride an Arabian and that's like driving a Chevrolet. You get on a Tennessee Walker and that's like cruising in a Cadillac.

I raise grass and hay on my land, and I used to raise about 200 acres of corn, but I don't anymore. Most of it is pasture land now that my cattle graze and I also cut hay to feed my cattle.

Every day there's something different and challenging to do on the farm. There's never any down time or dead time. That's what I like about it. There are the routine chores to do, of course, but every day brings something different. It's hard work, but I don't mind that. My Dad told me long ago that hard work doesn't kill you. Stress kills you.

I've become a jack-of-all-trades of sorts over the years. That's kind of the way you have to be on the farm to survive. I like to say that I haven't mastered much of anything, but I can do most everything fairly well.

Brent Cox is one of my greatest friends in the whole world, so when I get back to the farm I try to spend as much time with him as I can. I played ball at Taylor County with his brother, Samuel Cox. Brent's about three or four years older than me. Their brother, Jerry, was two years old than me.

Brent, Sam and Jerry all played ball at Taylor County. Jerry was a fierce competitor and the best player of the three. I kid Sam a lot. He couldn't shoot a lick, but when people double-teamed me, I would kick it to him and he could make an open shot occasionally. We had a lot of fun playing together. Brent, a retired teacher and coach who farms full-time now, was a good player as well. He remains one of my dearest friends to this very day.

When I get back to Campbellsville, I also like to get together again with my ex-high school teammate Tommy Brown, who has a construction business in town. A lot of people may not realize that he also got a scholarship to play at Western Kentucky. He ended up transferring back and getting his degree at Campbellsville College.

If I decide to ever build a new home someday in Taylor County, Tommy will be the guy to do it; he's always been a great friend. I also like to stop and spend some time with my high school coach, Billy B. Smith. He's a retired teacher who runs the stockyard in town.

I have a lot of farming buddies who are my good friends too: Lyndon Benningfield, Ester Gray, Henry Ford, Sie Parrish and Willard Farmer. We work hard together and share a lot of laughs too.

I recently purchased another 30 acres of land and I'm always looking for further expansion. There are two more farms around mine that I'd like to buy someday. One is about 90 acres and the other is about 50 acres. All of my land is located within a half-mile radius around me.

It's been exciting to watch the growth and development of not only Campbellsville, but Taylor County as well. It's incredible to think back to when I was a kid and downtown was pretty much just Main Street.

Speaking of that, in 1988 there was a street named after me in my hometown. "Clem Haskins Boulevard" is located in Campbellsville, just around the corner from Baptist Street, where my brother Willie and Yevette's parents used to live, on the western edge of town. It's amazing when I think back to the days when I couldn't sit downstairs in the movie theater, or couldn't eat in a particular restaurant in town because I was black.

Growing up, the thought of having a street named after a black man in the state of Kentucky would have been unheard of. Because of that, it's one of the greatest honors I've ever received in my life.

We really love living in Minnesota. The summers and the falls are beautiful and we really don't mind the winters. I prefer the cold weather over the hot any day to tell you the truth. Our family has always been like that.

When I eventually do retire from coaching, we would probably look at spending our summer months at the farm in Kentucky and the winter months in Minnesota. Some people might think that I'm getting mixed up, that it's the other way around and we'd spend the winters in Kentucky and the summers in Minnesota. But that's the way we'll probably do it.

I remember during my professional career in the NBA when my teammates and I would hear about various trade rumors that were always flying around. It's a crazy business, because you could be playing with a team on the East Coast one day, and then all of a sudden be traded and playing for a team on the West Coast the very next day.

As I said earlier, I was really fortunate in that regard because the two times I was traded during my career were both in the offseason so Yevette and I had the time to get our family adjusted. It was really hard on some players and their families when the trade took place right in the middle of the season.

I remember telling my teammates on several occasions that "they can trade me to another team, but they sure can't trade me from my farm." No matter what, our farm just outside of Campbellsville will always be our "home."

ALL IN THE FAMILY

CHAPTER TWENTY-SEVEN

Sometimes we get so wrapped up in the pressures of our jobs and other aspects of our everyday lives, that we need to step back for a minute and take a look at what's really important in our lives. Next to God, my family is the most important thing in the world to me.

The Lord has really blessed me. I am married to an incredible woman in Yevette and we have three wonderful children: our daughters Clemette and Lori, and our son Brent.

Our first daughter, Clemette, was born on November 28, 1965. I was a junior at Western Kentucky at the time, and Yevette and I had just been married that spring.

I remember that Yevette was about 20 days overdue when she gave birth to Clemette. The weekend before she was born, Coach Oldham let me drive home for the weekend to see Yevette. We had just started basketball practice at Western. Yevette went into false labor late Saturday night, and then I went back to school.

Yevette went into labor for real late the following week. Coach let me go home again, and the morning after I got there, Clemette was born at Taylor County Hospital. Dr. Forest Shelly delivered the baby and Yevette did just fine. I went back to see Yevette and our new daughter the next morning for a few hours, but then I had to return to school at Western Kentucky.

I was only 22 years old at the time and was really excited about having our first child. But I don't think I fully understood the significance of having a baby and the responsibilities that went along with it. I think that most young couples go through that with their first child. Your life changes instantly.

Like any good father, I wanted to have a healthy baby. At the same time, I was worried about the safety of my wife as she went into labor. Those were the two most important things. We actually thought that it was going to be a boy so we were going to call him Clem, Jr. When it was a girl, we chose Clemette—half of my name and half of Yevette's.

As I mentioned earlier, my Mother kept Clemette with her back in Campbellsville for most of the first two years after she was born, until after I graduated from Western. Yevette stayed in Campbellsville with the baby for the first three months after she was born and then joined me in Bowling Green. I was going to school and playing basketball, and Yevette was working on campus full-time making $47 per week.

Whenever we had the opportunity on weekends, Yevette and I would drive back to Campbellsville to see Clemette. It was hard on us not to see her every day, but we knew given the circumstances, that it was the best thing for her.

Clemette has been a wonderful daughter and I wouldn't trade her for the world. She's a fantastic young lady. Since she was a kid, she always loved to play sports. She's always been very competitive.

Throughout my playing career, Clemette always loved to be around the game. I used to take her to practice quite a bit and the guys loved to have her around. She just fell in love with the game at an early age.

When I played for the Chicago Bulls, Dave Newmark and Tom Boerwinkle, a pair of seven-footers, used to take turns putting her up on their shoulders so she could shoot baskets. She was only about four at the time.

We might have an hour-and-a-half to two-hour practice and even at that age she had the discipline to sit and watch practice. She usually guarded the balls. Not too many four-year-olds would have the patience to sit that still for that long. As soon as practice was over, she'd run on the court and want to shoot.

Tom was always her favorite player and he was so good with her; he was probably her first love. As soon as we walked into the arena we had to go and see Tom. He used to wait for her, and when she saw him, she would run and jump into his arms. He usually took her into the locker room and gave her gum before every game too.

Those are some of the special times that you remember when you raise children. I played with some great people during my professional career and Clemette developed some neat relationships with many of them.

We were going through a stack of old mail a few years ago and I came across this wonderful letter from Tom congratulating Clemette after she led Warren Central High School to the Kentucky State championship as a senior. Those are the types of things that mean a lot that you want to put away and save.

I remember when I was playing with the Phoenix Suns and I put a basketball hoop up in our driveway. Since Clemette was so short, I put the basket at about eight feet high. After my brother Charles was killed in the car accident, his son and my nephew Hearie lived with us. He was in the sixth grade at the time and Clemette was in the first grade. They loved to play and Clemette used to beat him all the time.

I used to play her in one-on-one when she was growing up. She was such a fierce little competitor and I didn't make it easy on her. I never let her win and she didn't always like that. But it was a real learning experience for her.

Clemette was born to play basketball. When I was with the Washington Bullets, she used to play against Bob Ferry's son, Danny, all the time and take him to school. Bob was the general manager of the Bullets, and Danny went on to have a great career at Duke University and was a first-round pick in the NBA draft.

She did the same thing to Elvin Hayes' son, Elvin, Jr. Clemette used to beat those guys like a drum. She used to take the ball and just blow by them. When she turned around and played defense, they had a hard time even getting a shot off on her.

When I retired in 1976 we moved back to Campbellsville. That was about the only time I can ever remember having problems with Clemette. As a sixth-grader, she was already good enough to start on the Taylor County High School team, but I asked her coach not to start her.

Instead of starting, she was the third guard on a team that advanced to the state tournament. She couldn't understand why I did what I did. I thought it was too much too soon and I didn't want her to lose her enthusiasm for the game.

We moved to Bowling Green in the summer of 1977, shortly after I took the job at Western Kentucky's Continuing Education Center. Clemette ended up having a great career at Warren Central.

She moved into the starting lineup in the eighth grade, and was named Miss Kentucky Basketball as a senior in 1983. She was also named the Hertz Player of the Year after that season and went to New York to pick up the award from O.J. Simpson.

Clemette went on to become a three-time All-America player at Western Kentucky. She also led the Hilltoppers to two straight Final Fours during her career. The fact that her Dad was a former All-American at Western and had become the head men's coach there never fazed her. For a lot of people that would have been too much pressure to handle, but she took it in stride and just played her game.

In September of 1997, Clemette joined me in the Western Kentucky Hall of Fame. Her induction makes us the first members of the same family to ever enter the Hall.

Clemette had offers to play professionally in Europe or Japan, but she decided to accept a job at the Mona, Meyer & McGrath public relations firm (now called Shandwick) in Minneapolis. I had just finished my first season at the University of Minnesota, so it was great to have her close to the family once again.

When the start of a new basketball season started rolling around, she got the itch once again. The game was still in her blood and she decided to become a volunteer coach for Ted Riverso at the University of St. Thomas in St. Paul. Dave Mona, her boss at the PR firm and who along with Minneapolis *Star Tribune* columnist Sid Hartman does my weekly coaches radio show on WCCO-AM, was kind enough to let her maneuver the coaching schedule around her work schedule.

When she talked about getting into coaching, we sat down and had a long discussion. I wanted to make sure that she saw the big picture, all the potential pitfalls out there in the coaching profession. After a season at St. Thomas, she spent one year as an assistant women's coach at Minnesota under LaRue Fields. From there she was an assistant for four seasons under Joan Bonvicini at the University of Arizona.

Then on Saturday, April 6, 1994, Clemette was named head coach at the University of Dayton. With the announcement, we became the first father and daughter combination to ever serve as head coaches at Division I institutions at the same time.

It was one of the greatest days of my life. I was so proud of her and the way she handled the media interviews and the pressure at the news conference. The spotlight was on her and yet she was so articulate, so professional. It made me feel so good. I was bubbling over with pride and I shed tears of joy. I had to pinch myself and say, "Is that my daughter up there?"

She took over a program that was really down—Dayton had an 8-19 record the year before she accepted the position—and is now in the process of doing a great job of rebuilding it. Yevette and I are her biggest fans.

Our second daughter, Lori, was born on July 4, 1970, when I was playing with the Phoenix Suns. I was working on my graduate degree at the time back at Western Kentucky, so she was actually born in Bowling Green. I remember that we had to induce labor because Yevette was about three weeks overdue.

Lori spent her first four years in Phoenix. I was traded to the Washington Bullets in the summer of 1974 and that's where she started school. From day one, she has always been an excellent student. She's very committed to her studies and I've always been so proud of her for that.

Lori played some basketball and ran a little track, but she has always been more academically inclined. She was always an A student. Most of the time growing up she'd bring a book along with her to basketball games. The game would be going on, she'd be reading her book and when we got home she couldn't tell you the final score of the game, much less any specific details about what happened.

That tickled me to death. Each kid is special in his or her own way. They're not all crazy about sports. She played basketball at Wayzata High School in Minnesota, but she never got too wrapped up in it. She could take it or leave it and that never bothered me at all.

I had four brothers, and my two younger brothers—Paul and Merion—always had to live in my shadow as a player. We put too much emphasis on sports in this country. That's kind of the way it is and sometimes it's not easy. But Lori did a great job of accepting Clemette's success as an All-America player. It didn't affect her childhood or her attitude at all.

Lori had a wonderful childhood. I never tried to force sports on her. I always left it up to my children to decide whether or not they wanted to play, something a lot of parents have trouble doing. A lot of them live their own unfulfilled dreams through their kids, and as a result, the pressure they place on their kids can be too much.

I was the same way with Clemette. I never pushed her. I accepted that she wanted to play. As a matter of fact, she begged me to play; she wore me out.

Lori has a great sense of humor and can laugh at herself. That's one of the keys to a happy life I think. You must be able to laugh at yourself. She's a very mature young lady who knows who she is, what she can do and where she's going.

After high school, Lori earned her bachelor's degree from the University of Minnesota in English, with a minor in African-American studies. She worked as an assistant to the human resources director in the Robbinsdale School District, a Twin Cities suburb.

Lori received her master's degree in English from St. Thomas in the spring of 1997 and now works for Ortho-McNeil in pharmaceutical sales in Chicago. Her plans are to pursue her doctorate in African-American literature sometime in the very near future. Talk about making Mom and Dad proud!

Our son, Brent, was born on August 22, 1973, in Phoenix. He had a happy childhood and is an outstanding young man. I remember that he was a ball boy for us for a couple of seasons when I was the coach at Western Kentucky.

Brent has always been a student of the game; watching, learning, studying and soaking up as much knowledge as he can about the game. He was never a great player himself, but he did play on the varsity at Wayzata High School. He has a big heart and is a good team man. On top of that, he was very coachable.

He wasn't a starter in high school, but he came off the bench and was a hero in a couple of big games. During his senior year he hit the game-winning shot at the buzzer—a three-pointer from way out there—against Hopkins High School, a big crosstown rival of Wayzata's.

Brent is a good-sized kid and after the game his teammates ran out onto the court and I think they were going to pick him up to celebrate the big victory. But suddenly they realized, "Hey, we can't pick Brent up," so they started patting him on the back instead. It was so much fun to be there and see him hit that shot. I will never forget the smile he had on his face that night.

They were also down by 20 points against Edina when he was a senior and he came off the bench and hit about five three-pointers in a row to put them back in that game. He was a great pure shooter.

Brent, who earned his bachelor's degree in sports management from the University of Minnesota, served as a student manager for my teams throughout his undergraduate days. He is now a member of my staff as a program aide and is doing a great job.

It's hard for people sometimes to accept a father-son coaching team. That's probably true in just about any profession when a father hires his son. My son got the job because he earned it. He's a very knowledgeable and very bright young man who really understands the game.

A lot of coaches become cheerleaders or fans and they don't understand how to coach the game. He doesn't let himself get caught up in the emotions of the game. He can really dissect the game and is someone that I really have a lot of confidence in on the bench to give me great information.

Many coaches talk too much or they're too hyper. Brent gives me great information before the game, at halftime, and during the game that helps me as a head coach. I know that he's going to be a great assistant coach for somebody real soon, and down the road he's going to be an excellent head coach someday.

I'm so proud of our three children. They never caused us any problems. It's been a rewarding experience to raise them, and Yevette and I enjoy their company so much.

They were great growing up together. I remember on Halloween when they used to go out trick or treating. They'd come home afterward and it was always so much fun to watch them put all their candy out on the floor and separate it. Then Clemette would begin trading candy. This was when Brent was about four or five years old. She'd trade three so-so pieces of candy to Brent for one real good one, like a candy bar or something. And Brent, only knowing that he got more candy, didn't realize the raw deal he was getting. Lori was three years older than Brent, so she caught on to what Clemette was doing. In the end, Clemette always had the best candy, followed by Lori and then Brent, who had the worst.

I miss those times. Yevette and I are both dealing with our empty nest now, but that's part of life. I keep telling friends of ours who have children to enjoy their kids, because before you know it, they're grown up and gone.

It's funny how the Lord sometimes sends messages to us in different ways. I pride myself on hard work. I'm driven to succeed.

Sometimes that means 16-, 18- or 20-hour work days, one after the other. That goes hand in hand with not always eating right, too. It can be a vicious cycle.

I've had some scares with my health during my career, but nothing quite like what took place on Saturday, July 15, 1995. Yevette and I had just returned home after attending the wedding reception for our basketball trainer Roger Schipper and his lovely wife Kimberly, who is a great supporter of our program.

I had been experiencing pains in my chest for a couple of days and thought it was just indigestion. But they were really bad that evening. I was having a hard time breathing, so I tried to lie down on the couch. That didn't work. So Yevette tried massaging my chest and that didn't help. She suggested calling 911, but I told her no.

Finally we loaded into the car—I had just had major reconstructive surgery on my knee the month before and was on crutches —and decided to go to the health care center near our home. It was closed. Then Yevette drove me, approaching speeds of up to 90 miles per hour, straight to University Hospital.

Dr. Robert Wilson performed angioplasty surgery early Sunday morning. He said that my left anterior descending artery, which feeds blood to the heart, was over 90 percent blocked. If it had become completely closed, I could have suffered a major heart attack.

A couple of weeks after the 1997 Final Four, I had some chest pains on a much smaller scale and spent the night in the hospital just to be safe. I'm not going to take a chance anymore.

Since that summer night in 1995, I've tried to make some distinct changes in my lifestyle. I try to get a good night's rest every night. I've tried as best as I can to eliminate the 18- and 20-hour days. My diet has improved and I've lost weight as a result. I also think that I'm a little calmer on the bench during games than I used to be. Fans at Williams Arena probably have noticed that my sportcoat has come off a lot less during our games the past two seasons.

When I had the angioplasty surgery, I realized that I had to stop and take a strong look at who I am, what direction I'm heading and whether or not I had my priorities in order. It helped me to strengthen my faith in God, as well as my love and concern for my family. I realized that I was spending far too much time on my job and worrying about things that were out of my control.

It really made me stop and count my blessings. It made me realize that I have to be more attentive to the needs of my wife, my children, my Mother and the rest of my family.

A lot of thoughts were running through my head when they had me strapped to that bed and I couldn't move for a couple of hours. It really gave me time to think. I remember thinking that "Wow, this could be it."

Most people don't appreciate their good health. Usually we just take it for granted; we think nothing of it. When I was laying there, however, I thought about how awful it would be if you couldn't run or even walk anymore. I might not be able to walk through the woods anymore and hear the birds chirp and the squirrels talking to each other. Now I appreciate nature and all the little things so much more.

Most of all, I appreciate my family more. I tell my wife and kids that I love them a lot more. I said it from time to time before, but I never said it enough. From here on out, that's not going to be a problem anymore.

M Y BEST FRIEND

CHAPTER TWENTY-EIGHT

The final chapter is reserved for my wife and my best friend —the former Yevette Penick.

Yevette and I first started attending school together in the fourth grade at Campbellsville Durham, the all-black school in town with grades 1-12 in the same building. Her parents, Harriet and J.C. Penick, used to live right next to my brother, Willie, and his family, who moved there when I was a senior in high school. Yevette has a brother James. It's kind of ironic that I also have family on my Dad's side with the last name of Penick.

I have always been really close to both Harriet and J.C. They are great people who have provided so much support to Yevette and me. We've always been able to count on them for anything and we really enjoy it when they come visit us in Minnesota. They love to fish and have found more than a few good "hotspots" in nearby Lake Minnetonka over the years.

James works for United Parcel Service in Louisville. He and his wife, Margaret, are big Golden Gopher fans. They understandably catch some good-natured grief during the season for being bigger followers of Golden Gopher basketball than they are of the Louisville Cardinals. Their son, André, regularly attends my summer basketball camp. He has the ability to be a pretty good basketball player someday.

I used to notice Yevette during our recess breaks at school. She was a tomboy, meaning that she always used to play with the boys. During recess, the boys always used to wrassle with each other. She was this skinny little thing, but I remember how she used to grab the boys and just flip them right over. I was shocked. I'd just stand back and watch her.

I really starting eyeing Yevette in the fifth grade. She was a great athlete and that impressed me too. But I was too shy to talk to her back then. In the seventh grade, she was a basketball cheerleader and I played on the junior varsity team. We used to say hi to each other and stuff like that. At that age back then, if you just looked at a girl it was a big deal.

So that went on for a couple of years. Then when we were freshmen, a big thing for me was to walk Yevette from one end of the hall at school to the other. We might not even say a word to each other, but that was a big deal.

Yevette could really dance and I was absolutely terrible at it. She and a guy named Owen Russell Johnson used to win all the dance contests. I remember telling one of my best friends, John Henry Anderson, that "I've got to learn how to dance with Yevette."

John Henry was a guy like me; neither of us could get a date and neither of us could dance. We figured that just maybe there was a connection there somewhere. If we learned how to dance, maybe we could get dates. We were in the eighth or ninth grade at the time, and we got an old mop and broomstick and tried to learn how to slow dance.

Every afternoon after school we used to go back to his house, which was about a block from school, and he'd try to teach me how to dance. The problem was, he didn't know what he was doing. He would step on my toes, I would step on his toes, and he was attempting to sing a song the whole time we were trying to dance. I was serious about it. I never did get the chance to dance with Yevette, but later on it worked out anyway. I laugh just thinking about the two of us back then.

We started dating when we were sophomores. Every once in a while after school I'd walk her "down the road" to her house. We used to walk along the railroad tracks a lot. I was playing on the varsity team and she was a cheerleader so we saw each other at all the games. We'd also sit by each other on the bus to and from our games.

A big date back then would be going to the Dairy Queen in town. We'd usually get a hot dog and a slush. I'd look at her and she'd look back at me, but we wouldn't say a word. That would last about an hour. On weekends, she might come out to our farm to see me.

That's about the time that Yevette became my favorite rebounder. We had a basketball hoop at our house with no net. I would shoot and she would rebound the ball and throw it back out to me. She was so quick that the ball rarely hit the ground after it went through the cylinder. I'd shoot, she'd rebound and we'd do that over and over for a couple of hours at a time.

One day Yevette and I decided to go fishing. Most of the farms had electric fences. They'd give you a good shock if you ever touched them. Well, I was leading the way as we walked up this hill when I hopped over an electric fence.

Once I got over the fence, which was about three feet high, I kept walking toward the lake. All of a sudden I heard Yevette hollering and screaming behind me. Her legs got caught up when she tried to straddle the fence. She kept yelling, "Get me out, get me out!" The thing is, I couldn't grab her because then I'd get shocked myself. So I finally told her to fall over the wires. She finally did it, but boy did that thing shock her!

I transferred to all-white Taylor County High School as a junior. The move created a big stir and was very difficult in many ways. Yevette understood that it was something that I needed to do. I went to Taylor County because it was the right thing to do. It enabled me to break down barriers that had never been crossed. On top of that, I was a basketball player. My girlfriend would never come between me and basketball.

Yevette was a cheerleader for Durham. You have to remember that it wasn't just a large share of the white folks in town who were mad that I was at Taylor County, a lot of the blacks looked at me as a traitor for leaving Durham. I know she overheard a lot of things that were said about me in school. People criticized her too for dating me. But we were both strong enough to get through that and it just strengthened my love for her even more.

We played Durham three times in my two years at Taylor County and we won all three games. I was never so in love that I couldn't play the game. When I stepped on the basketball court, I was all business.

After graduation, I went to school at Western Kentucky and Yevette attended Kentucky State. We were about 165 miles away from each other. That was hard, real hard.

It's crazy when I think about it now, but on many Friday nights that first year in school I used to hop in my car and drive from Bowling Green to Campbellsville which was about a two-hour drive back then. I'd stop and see Mother and Dad, spend an hour or two, and then drive another hour-and-a-half to two hours to Frankfort to pick up Yevette. Then we'd turn around and drive back to Campbellsville to see her parents.

On Saturday morning, we'd drive all the way to Bowling Green for practice and to watch the Western Kentucky football game. Afterwards, we'd come back to Campbellsville and then on to Frankfort where I'd drop her off. Then I would turn around and go through Campbellsville and all the way back to Bowling Green. All in one weekend!

Now if one of my own kids did that today, I'd tell them they were crazy. If I had a player of mine who was doing that, I'd go crazy. If Coach Diddle at Western knew I was doing that, he probably would have gone absolutely nuts. We also wrote a lot of letters to each other during that year.

We were married on May 22, 1965, by Reverend J.E. Jones in Bowling Green. My teammate, Dwight Smith, was the best man and my sister, Sara, was the maid of honor. Those were the only other people in the church.

Believe it or not, Dwight actually lost the ring. I didn't have any money, so it was like a two-dollar ring that I had bought. So we went back into the house, looked around and found it. That was so funny; Yevette and I both look back and laugh about it now. That was the happiest day of my life. She's the only girl I've ever loved in my life.

We couldn't afford a honeymoon. Yevette was working at the Fruit of the Loom plant in Campbellsville at the time. We were married on a Saturday and she went back to work Monday.

She has sacrificed a lot through the years to make things work for us and our family and I can't thank her enough for that. While I was going to school and playing basketball at Western Kentucky, she worked on campus to make money for us to live on.

When I played professional basketball, my travels took me out of town for extended periods at a time. She was always there to keep things together at home. When our kids were growing up, they knew that I was always there for them whenever they needed me, but sometimes that wasn't physically possible. She was a very hands-on mother. She was *always* there for them.

Yevette kept things together in the family through all the trades and moves; from Campbellsville, to Bowling Green, to Chicago, to Phoenix, to Washington, back to Campbellsville, back to Bowling Green and now to the Twin Cities.

Different houses, new schools for the kids, new friends, all the things that go with pulling up your stakes and moving a family —sometimes all the way across the country— she made sure they went off without a hitch every time.

It's awfully tough to be a coach's wife. I don't think most people realize that. She has to sit in the stands during a game and listen to some fans who criticize her husband for everything he does, or doesn't do, during a game. If it's not the substitution pattern that they yell at me for, it's why didn't I call a timeout at a particular time in the game. Don't get me wrong, 99.9 percent of the fans are great. A very small percentage can really be mean-spirited.

It's awful at times. I can tune all the stuff out once the game starts, but it's hard on my wife and kids when fans are vocally abusive about me or one of our players. I really admire Yevette and my kids so much for what they've gone through. They've heard people say just about everything about me during my playing and coaching career, but they've always shown a lot of self-control and class under some very difficult circumstances.

Yevette has always played a very important role in my basketball program. She's very supportive of our players, almost like a mother figure for them. As I said earlier, a lot of kids today come from one-parent homes and most have been raised by their mother. So I think it's easier and more comfortable for them to adapt to her.

She's a very caring person who has always developed special relationships with our student-athletes. She has helped a lot of them get through some hard times. If they're sick or recovering from surgery, she might invite them out to the house for a good, hot meal. That's not because she feels like she has to do that. It's because she wants to do it. That's just the kind of person she is. Some guys in the past have called her "Mom," but most of them just call her "Mrs. Haskins."

Yevette is a very humble person who wants to get involved in the community to help make it a better place to live in. A lot of people don't realize that in 1983 she ran for a spot on the Warren County School Board and won the election. Talk about breaking barriers. She became the very first female and the first black person to ever be elected to the school board.

She has served on the board for the Courage Center, a rehabilitation center for the physically impaired in Golden Valley, Minnesota, and is a member of the Minnesota Amateur Sports Commission. She is on the board of directors for the ABC (A Better Chance) program in the Twin Cities, which helps provide a better education for less fortunate high school students. She also judges Junior Miss pageants throughout the country and is co-chair of the education committee for the World Figure Skating Championships to be held in the Twin Cities in 1998. On top of that, she serves as the executive director of the Clem Haskins summer basketball camps. She is one busy and talented woman.

Yevette and I do almost everything together. We are like two peas in a pod. Our love has continued to grow and flourish through the years, but I think it's the respect that we've developed for each other that I cherish the most.

I feel that the God has really blessed me. The last thing I do before I go to bed at night, and the first thing I do when I get up in the morning, is give thanks and praise to God.

I have great parents who raised my brothers and sisters right, and instilled in us the proper values at an early age. I have a wonderful wife, three fantastic children and a great job.

When I look back at my life, I can't help but think that I'm the luckiest guy in the whole wide world.